AF811998

New Frontiers in Regional Science: Asian Perspectives

Volume 82

Editor-in-Chief

Yoshiro Higano, University of Tsukuba, Tsukuba, Japan

This series is a constellation of works by scholars in the field of regional science and in related disciplines specifically focusing on dynamism in Asia.

Asia is the most dynamic part of the world. Japan, Korea, Taiwan, and Singapore experienced rapid and miracle economic growth in the 1970s. Malaysia, Indonesia, and Thailand followed in the 1980s. China, India, and Vietnam are now rising countries in Asia and are even leading the world economy. Due to their rapid economic development and growth, Asian countries continue to face a variety of urgent issues including regional and institutional unbalanced growth, environmental problems, poverty amidst prosperity, an ageing society, the collapse of the bubble economy, and deflation, among others.

Asian countries are diversified as they have their own cultural, historical, and geographical as well as political conditions. Due to this fact, scholars specializing in regional science as an inter- and multi-discipline have taken leading roles in providing mitigating policy proposals based on robust interdisciplinary analysis of multifaceted regional issues and subjects in Asia. This series not only will present unique research results from Asia that are unfamiliar in other parts of the world because of language barriers, but also will publish advanced research results from those regions that have focused on regional and urban issues in Asia from different perspectives.

The series aims to expand the frontiers of regional science through diffusion of intrinsically developed and advanced modern regional science methodologies in Asia and other areas of the world. Readers will be inspired to realize that regional and urban issues in the world are so vast that their established methodologies still have space for development and refinement, and to understand the importance of the interdisciplinary and multidisciplinary approach that is inherent in regional science for analyzing and resolving urgent regional and urban issues in Asia.

Topics under consideration in this series include the theory of social cost and benefit analysis and criteria of public investments, socio-economic vulnerability against disasters, food security and policy, agro-food systems in China, industrial clustering in Asia, comprehensive management of water environment and resources in a river basin, the international trade bloc and food security, migration and labor market in Asia, land policy and local property tax, Information and Communication Technology planning, consumer "shop-around" movements, and regeneration of downtowns, among others.

Researchers who are interested in publishing their books in this Series should obtain a proposal form from Yoshiro Higano (Editor in Chief, higano@jsrsai.jp) and return the completed form to him.

Hiroyuki Taguchi
Editor

Sustainability of Economic Growth in East Asia

Toward the Post-COVID-19 Era

Springer

Editor
Hiroyuki Taguchi
Strategic Research Center
Saitama University
Saitama-shi, Saitama, Japan

ISSN 2199-5974 ISSN 2199-5982 (electronic)
New Frontiers in Regional Science: Asian Perspectives
ISBN 978-981-96-3730-0 ISBN 978-981-96-3731-7 (eBook)
https://doi.org/10.1007/978-981-96-3731-7

© The Editor(s) (if applicable) and The Author(s), under exclusive license to Springer Nature Singapore Pte Ltd. 2025

This work is subject to copyright. All rights are solely and exclusively licensed by the Publisher, whether the whole or part of the material is concerned, specifically the rights of translation, reprinting, reuse of illustrations, recitation, broadcasting, reproduction on microfilms or in any other physical way, and transmission or information storage and retrieval, electronic adaptation, computer software, or by similar or dissimilar methodology now known or hereafter developed.
The use of general descriptive names, registered names, trademarks, service marks, etc. in this publication does not imply, even in the absence of a specific statement, that such names are exempt from the relevant protective laws and regulations and therefore free for general use.
The publisher, the authors and the editors are safe to assume that the advice and information in this book are believed to be true and accurate at the date of publication. Neither the publisher nor the authors or the editors give a warranty, expressed or implied, with respect to the material contained herein or for any errors or omissions that may have been made. The publisher remains neutral with regard to jurisdictional claims in published maps and institutional affiliations.

This Springer imprint is published by the registered company Springer Nature Singapore Pte Ltd.
The registered company address is: 152 Beach Road, #21-01/04 Gateway East, Singapore 189721, Singapore

If disposing of this product, please recycle the paper.

Preface

This book discusses the issues on the sustainability of economic growth towards the post-COVID-19 era in East Asian economies. The COVID-19 has brought in structural changes such as the facilitation of digitalization and the slow-down of globalization in their economies. Meanwhile, their economies have adjusted their economic structures to these structural changes and have enhanced the resilience against the shocks beyond the COVID-19 in order to sustain their economic growth. These adjustments have accompanied the transformations of industries (such as servicification), global value chains, and trade and investment patterns. Policy momentums have also been affected by the structural changes caused by the COVID-19 in the areas such as poverty alleviation, environment, and foreign aids. So far, however, there have been only a very limited number of quantitative studies to describe the economic transformations towards the post-COVID-19 era among the vast literature of East Asian studies.

This book applies scientific approaches such as data-oriented and econometric methods. In this manner, the book enriches empirical evidence in academic literature and also contributes to evidence-based policymaking. This study is also based on the research collaboration with Mae Fah Luang University in Thailand, which specializes in border economies in the Greater Mekong Subregion. Thus, the study's outcomes are expected to attract overseas academic researchers and policymakers as target audience.

Chapter 1 (Servicification in Global Value Chains Towards Post-COVID-19 Era in Emerging and Developing Asian Economies) examined the involvement of service industries in Asian global value chains (GVCs) towards the post-COVID-19 era. The Asian GVCs have experienced a structural change from manufacturing-led development to service-led one since the mid-2000s. The change contains the increases in service inputs in manufacturing GVCs as well as the growth in the GVCs of service industries themselves. The COVID-19 has accelerated this trend because information technologies have become a significant input typically due to the expansion of e-commerce trade. These trends provide a policy implication for relaxing and removing service-trade barriers.

Chapter 2 (Economic Impact of Foreign Direct Investment, Gross Capital Formation, and Trade Openness on ASEAN Economies) investigated the impact of foreign direct investment (FDI), gross fixed capital formation (GCF), trade openness (TOP), the COVID-19 pandemic, and the global financial crisis on the economic growth of the ASEAN countries from 2000 to 2023. The study found that in both the short and long run, TOP and GCF significantly and positively impacted economic growth, though the pandemic had a greater detrimental impact on economic growth from 2000 to 2023 than the global financial crisis. The results imply the significance of sustaining open trade structure and capital accumulation towards the post-COVID-19 Era.

Chapter 3 (Effects of Structural Reforms on Labour Productivity of Selected Southeast Asian Countries) examined the effects of various structural reform measures on productivity growth in Southeast Asian countries for 2001–2019, based on the assumption that the severe economic downturn during the COVID-19 has amplified the significance of enhancing resilience through structural reforms. The study revealed that structural reforms such as infrastructure and financial market development positively contributed to labour productivity growth, while macroeconomic instability and the possible deterioration of public sector governance negatively contributed to labour productivity growth.

Chapter 4 (The Progress of the Division of Labour in the Automobile Industry in the ASEAN Region in the Post-COVID-19 Era) clarified the progress in the division of labour in the automobile industry within the ASEAN region. The study confirmed that intra-regional trade of automobile parts and components raised its share of total trades under ASEAN economic integration. Regarding detailed items, key components such as engines are exported from Indonesia and Thailand to ASEAN, whereas other items such as gearbox, axel, and airbag are exported from the Philippines and Vietnam to Indonesia and Thailand. Though the COVID-19 temporarily damaged trade, the intra-regional trade in automobile parts and components has maintained the momentum of its division of labour.

Chapter 5 (Cross-Border Trade Between Thailand and Myanmar in the Post-COVID Era) investigated the border trade between Thailand and Myanmar during and after COVID-19. The study found as follows. The spread of COVID-19 caused a sharp decline in Myanmar's land exports to Thailand but a rapid growth in its sea exports to Thailand in 2020. However, in the following years, this pattern reversed. Such fluctuations in preferred trade routes imply a substitutional relation between land and sea trade. The study also confirmed the robustness of Thai–Myanmar border trade from the commodity flows across the border in the pandemic period. This substitution and robustness of the border trade suggest some resilience against COVID-19.

Chapter 6 (Changes in Thailand's Poverty and Income Inequality Caused by COVID-19) evaluated the effects of countermeasures against COVID-19 on poverty and income inequality in Thailand. Based on descriptive measurements, its poverty and income inequality situations stood at almost the same levels during the pandemic. This study, based on a normative approach with estimated income distribution functions, found that the income share of the lowest income group decreased whereas the income gap between the middle- and high-income classes became more equal. This result implies that countermeasures against COVID-19 pandemic failed in fully alleviating income inequality due to insufficient provision of the measures to the lowest income groups.

Chapter 7 (Future of the South Korean Economy After COVID-19: Focusing on the Semiconductor Industry) investigated the South Korean economy during and after COVID-19 focusing on the semiconductor industry. During COVID-19, the demands for semiconductors have increased sharply due to the spread of remote work, and the country has been able to escape from the recession. However, after the pandemic subsided in 2022, the demands for semiconductors plummeted, and the economy went into recession. The study found that the Korean economy is heavily reliant on semiconductors, particularly, memory, and thus suggests that the South Korea's semiconductor industry should shift its focus from memory semiconductors to logic semiconductors.

Chapter 8 (Air Pollution and its Control Governance in Chinese Provinces in the Post-COVID-19 Era), focusing on air pollution in terms of sulphur, soot, and dust in the industrial and household emissions of different Chinese provinces, investigated how governance shortages for pollution control contribute to provincial pollution levels. The study found that the governance shortage for pollution control accounted for about 50–70% of the province-specific air pollution levels. The results indicate that China still has a significant policy space to mitigate air pollution. In the post-COVID-19 Era, when industrial activities have recovered, pollution-control governance is vital for making China's economic growth sustainable.

Chapter 9 (Economic Functions of Foreign Aid Inflows in Thailand) summarized the research on the effects of foreign aid inflows to Thailand. The main findings are highlighted as follows. First, the impact of foreign aid on economic growth is positively estimated using growth accounting. Second, this impact is caused by investments stimulated by foreign aid including inward foreign direct investments. Finally, foreign aid inflows are considered to reduce fiscal debt without any fungibility nor Dutch disease effects. These results indicate that foreign aid helps to strengthen the Thai economic growth. These fundamental functions of foreign aids are still effective to keep sustainable growth in emerging market economies even after COVID-19 era.

Saitama-shi, Japan Hiroyuki Taguchi

Contents

Contributors

Hidekatsu Asada Graduate School of Humanities and Social Sciences, Saitama University, Saitama, Japan

Yasuhito Asami Department of Global Politics, Faculty of Law, Hosei University, Tokyo, Japan

Chukiat Chaiboonsri Faculty of Economics, Chiang Mai University, Chiang Mai, Thailand

George Randolph Dirth Faculty of Economics, Chiang Mai University, Chiang Mai, Thailand

Akio Egawa Faculty of Economics, Momoyama Gakuin University, Izumi, Osaka, Japan

Takeshi Fujino Graduate School of Science and Engineering, Saitama University, Saitama, Japan

Htwe Ko Faculty of Economics, Chiang Mai University, Chiang Mai, Thailand

Nattapan Kongbuamai Tourism, Hospitality, and Event (TH&E) Research Group, School of Management, Mae Fah Luang University, Chiang Rai, Thailand

Ni Lar Strategic Research Center, Saitama University, Saitama, Japan

Kenji Nozaki Faculty of Economics, Takasaki City University of Economics, Takasaki, Japan

Hiroaki Sakurai Department of International Communication, Gakushuin Women's College, Shinjuku-ku, Tokyo, Japan

Hiroyuki Taguchi Strategic Research Center, Saitama University, Saitama, Japan

Yuichi Takayasu Faculty of Economics, Daito Bunka University, Itabashi-ku, Tokyo, Japan

Chapter 1
Servicification in Global Value Chains Toward Post-COVID-19 Era in Emerging and Developing Asian Economies

Hiroyuki Taguchi and Ni Lar

Abstract Servicification in global value chains (GVCs) has become a trend in emerging and developing Asian economies. However, no scientific studies have elucidated the mechanism of servicification in GVCs. This study investigates the involvement of service sectors in Asian GVCs in terms of the quantitative interactions between service inputs and manufacturing exports and inputs, and also between service inputs and service exports. For this purpose, a panel vector autoregressive model and the Trade in Value Added (TiVA 2023) database of the Organization for Economic Cooperation and Development (OECD) are used for empirical analysis covering 1995–2020. The estimation results show, first, reciprocal interactions between the business services and manufacturing sectors: manufacturing exports induce business service inputs, whereas business service exports cause manufacturing inputs. Second, foreign manufacturing inputs facilitate foreign business service inputs. Third, business service inputs are promoted through business service exports. These trends in the involvement of business services in GVCs have accelerated since the mid-2000s and are expected to expand into the post-COVID-19 era. To enhance the role of services in GVCs, Asian economies should facilitate the removal of explicit restrictions on service trade and address regulatory divergence across countries.

Keywords Servicification · Global value chains · Emerging and developing Asian economies

H. Taguchi (✉) · N. Lar
Strategic Research Center, Saitama University, Saitama, Japan
e-mail: htaguchi@mail.saitama-u.ac.jp

© The Author(s), under exclusive license to Springer Nature Singapore Pte Ltd. 2025

H. Taguchi (ed.), *Sustainability of Economic Growth in East Asia*,
New Frontiers in Regional Science: Asian Perspectives 82,
https://doi.org/10.1007/978-981-96-3731-7_1

1.1 Introduction

Global value chains (GVCs) have become a remarkable trend in international economic activities over the past decades and are a major concern for policymakers and academics. Koopman et al. (2014) initially conceptualized GVCs to trace the value added by countries in global production chains and measure vertical specialization in international trade. Empirical studies have intensified since Koopman et al. (2014) developed an analytical framework for GVCs.

GVCs have experienced two structural changes in recent decades: "slowbalization" and "servicification." Slowbalization refers to the slowdown of GVC activities after the global financial crisis of 2008–2009, resulting in a noticeable deceleration in the pace of globalization, including the trend of GVCs (World Bank 2020; Alvarez et al. 2021). Servicification represents the more intensive involvement of service sectors in GVC processes. The modality of servicification in the GVCs is described by Nano and Stolzenburg (2021) in the following two ways: (1) service sectors support manufacturing as inevitable inputs of manufacturing production and exports (servicification in manufacturing) and (2) service sectors increasingly form their own GVCs as the "production" processes of certain services allow for fragmentation similar to that in manufacturing sectors (GVCs within service sectors).

Multiple studies have found that the share of services in value-added trade is large (significantly larger than in gross trade) and increasing. The increased presence of service sectors in GVCs is due to the inclusion of information and communication technology and professional business services, which has enabled firms to perform better and invest in new business opportunities for better production technologies (Heuser and Mattoo 2017). COVID-19 may have accelerated the involvement of services in GVCs as global e-commerce trade surged during the COVID-19 pandemic (World Trade Organization 2021).

Analyses of GVCs have so far concentrated on the scope within the manufacturing sector (Kimura 2006), and empirical studies of servicification in GVCs have just started by mainly showing the increased presence of service sectors in GVC. There have been no scientific studies to elucidate the mechanism of servicification in GVCs in terms of "servicification of manufacturing" and "GVCs within service sectors" presented by Nano and Stolzenburg (2021). This study aims to fill this research gap in the mechanism of servicification in GVCs.

The purpose of this study is to clarify the service sector involvement in GVCs from the following two perspectives: "servicification of manufacturing" by quantifying the interactions between service inputs and manufacturing exports and inputs, and also "GVCs within service sectors" by quantifying the interactions between service inputs and service exports. This study proposes the following two hypotheses consistent with the two perspectives: (1) Manufacturing exports induce business service inputs to enhance business performance and (2) Business service exports themselves facilitate business service inputs as a result of service sector fragmentation.

For the methodologies, this study considers a panel vector autoregressive (PVAR) model using the Trade in Value Added (TiVA) dataset (2023 version) of the Organization for Economic Cooperation and Development (OECD).[1] It targets emerging and developing Asian economies because the Asian region is a major player in GVCs expansion (Kimura 2006; Taguchi and Thet 2021; Alvarez et al. 2021) and shows progress in servicification in the GVCs (Baldwin et al. 2015). The purpose and hypotheses justify the application of the PVAR model with the TiVA database. This study applies not case studies with specific sectors and countries but comprehensive and data-driven approaches to clarify the mechanism of servicification in GVCs in multiple countries. In addition, the key variables—service and manufacturing exports and inputs—are interdependent. Therefore, single-equation regressions lead to biased and inconsistent estimators due to variables' endogeneity. Instead, a PVAR model allows for endogeneity among the estimated variables and allows the data to determine causality between the targeted variables.

The remainder of this study is organized as follows: Section 1.2 reviews the literature, focusing on theoretical and empirical studies on servicification in GVCs and highlights this study's contributions. Section 1.3 presents the empirical methods, including data on key variables and methodologies for the PVAR estimation. Section 1.4 shows estimation outcomes with their interpretations. The final section summarizes, concludes, and highlights the study's implications.

1.2 Literature Review and Contribution

This section reviews the literature related to servicification issues in GVCs and emphasizes the contributions of this study. Discussions on servicification can be categorized into emerging patterns, causes, and impacts.

The emerging patterns of services in GVCs are illustrated by a large and increasing share of services in value-added trade (OECD, WTO and World Bank Group 2014; Johnson and Noguera 2017). Heuser and Mattoo (2017) demonstrated that services as a share of value-added trade increased from below 30% in 1980 to more than 40% in 2009, while gross exports have remained at approximately 20% since 1980. Asian and Central and Eastern European economies are no exception to this pattern (Baldwin et al. 2015; Kordalska and Olczyk 2021). From a sectoral perspective, some studies have verified the increasing role of digital services in GVCs dynamics (Blázquez et al. 2023; Baek et al. 2023). Service involvement in GVCs may be complex and not necessarily follow a linear trend. Qiu (2020) argued that while service inputs help develop manufacturing in proximate districts, they may hinder it in distant districts and that service inputs have an inverted U-shaped effect on GVC development.

[1] See the website: https://data-explorer.oecd.org/

The causes of servicification in GVCs have been explained by Baldwin et al. (2015) and Heuser and Mattoo (2017) as follows: (1) Reclassification—many services traditionally sourced in-house by manufacturing firms, thus classified as manufacturing, have been outsourced at arm's length and classified accordingly as services; (2) Task-composition shift: connecting services—GVC requires connections among geographically separated production sites, involving services links including telecommunications, transportation, and mailing; (3) Task-composition shift: changes in final goods—many manufactured goods have become more intensive in services such as software in cars and sophisticated design in machines; and (4) Task-relative price shift—the prices of service tasks have increased relative to those of manufacturing tasks because manufacturing tasks are easier to offshore to lower cost locations.

The impact of servicification on GVCs can be described by two key aspects of economic performance: productivity growth and the evolution of comparative advantages (Heuser and Mattoo 2017). Cheng and Xiao (2021) demonstrated that the growth of producer services for GVCs help improve the productivity of final goods and services and reduce the supply cost of producer services. Díaz-Mora et al. (2018) argued that the foreign services value-added content of exports positively contributes to export performance. Hansen et al. (2022) demonstrated the upgradation of their services through interviews and case studies of firms operating as suppliers of embedded services for wind and power projects in South Africa.

Regarding policy issues on GVCs servicification, Findlay and Roelfsema (2023) stated that restricting service trade is detrimental to GVC participation, especially for ASEAN members. Accordingly, they emphasized the need for policy actions to follow up on trade liberalization with a new round of lower restrictions on services trade.

Considering the literature mentioned above, this study focuses on the patterns of GVC servicification. However, the existing literature has just illustrated the increased presence of service sectors in GVCs as its patterns; no scientific studies have elucidated the mechanism of servicification in GVCs. The novelty is that this study clarifies the servicification mechanism by visualizing the endogenous interactions between gross exports and inputs in the business services and manufacturing sectors by checking their causalities using a PVAR framework.

1.3 Empirical Methods

This section empirically analyzes the service sector's involvement in GVCs, focusing on selected emerging and developing Asian economies. This study targets the following eight Asian economies: Cambodia, China, India, Indonesia, Malaysia, the Philippines, Thailand, and Vietnam. This section presents a descriptive analysis, followed by econometric methods that contain data on key variables and methodologies for the PVAR estimation.

1.3.1 Descriptive Analysis

Figure 1.1 shows the trends in the ratio of business service content to gross exports for the eight economies. The trend is computed using the "total business sector services" as an industrial origin of value added, divided by the "total gross exports" from the OECD TiVA database. These trends can be classified into three groups. Cambodia and Vietnam, the lower-middle incomers, show decreasing trends in their ratios; India and the Philippines show increasing trends; and China, Indonesia, Malaysia, and Thailand, the upper-middle incomers, display inverted U-shaped trends.[2] Thus, servicification has progressed in selected Asian economies, except for the lower-middle incomers, especially since the mid-2000s. This observation motivates us to conduct a PVAR model estimation to determine how service inputs have been linked to manufacturing and service exports and whether the service inputs have domestic or foreign origins.

1.3.2 Variables and Data

This subsection identifies the variables for the PVAR model estimation. The study samples include time-series data for the maximum data from 1995 to 2020 for all variables. Then, the study constructs panel data for the eight sample countries.

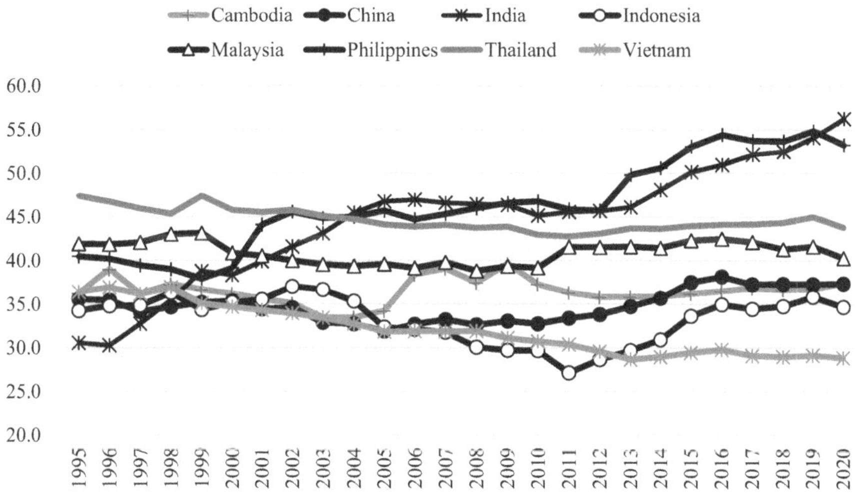

Fig. 1.1 Ratio of service content to gross exports. Source: Authors' calculation based on the OECD TiVA 2023 database

[2]The income classification is based on World Bank's classification. Please see https://datahelpdesk.worldbank.org/knowledgebase/articles/906519

Examining the interactions between service inputs and manufacturing exports and inputs requires the following variables: gross exports of manufacturing (*mex*), manufacturing value added as the domestic origin of *mex* (*modm*) and foreign origin of *mex* (*mofm*), and value added of "total business sector services" (hereafter, business services) as the domestic origin of *mex* (*mods*) and foreign origin of *mex* (*mofs*). Estimating the interactions between business service inputs and exports and manufacturing inputs requires the following variables: gross exports of business services (*sex*), manufacturing value added as the domestic origin of *sex* (*sodm*) and foreign origin of *sex* (*sofm*), business service value added as the domestic origin of *sex* (*sods*), and foreign origin of *sex* (*sofs*). The OECD TiVA 2023 database (in millions of US dollars) provided all value-added trade variables.

Real GDP per capita (*pcy*) is inserted as a control (exogenous) variable in the PVAR model estimation because the industrial structure might be affected by the development stage of an economy, according to Petty–Clark's law (Clark 1940). The data are retrieved from the United Nations Conference on Trade and Development (UNCTAD) Stat,[3] particularly the "GDP per capita, constant (2015) prices." Table 1.1 presents the list of the variables and data sources, and Table 1.2 presents their descriptive statistics.

The estimation adds the period dummy variable for 2006–2020 (*d06*) to identify the acceleration of servicification in the sample economies since the mid-2000s, as in Sect. 1.3.1. The dummy value takes one for 2006–2020 and is attached to the following service input variables: *mods*, *mofs*, *sods*, and *sofs*.

Table 1.1 List of variables and data sources

Variables	Description	Sources
mex	*Gross exports: manufacturing*	OECD TiVA
modm	*Domestic industrial origin of mex: manufacturing*	
mofm	*Foreign industrial origin of mex: manufacturing*	
mods	*Domestic industrial origin of mex: total business sector services*	
mofs	*Foreign industrial origin of mex: total business sector services*	
sex	*Gross exports: total business sector services*	
sodm	*Domestic industrial origin of sex: manufacturing*	
sofm	*Foreign industrial origin of sex: manufacturing*	
sods	*Domestic industrial origin of sex: total business sector services*	
sofs	*Foreign industrial origin of sex: total business sector services*	
pcy	*GDP* per capita, *constant (2015) prices*	UNCTAD

Sources: Authors' description
Note: The unit of TiVA data is millions of US dollars, and that of GDP per capita is US dollars

[3] See the website: https://unctadstat.unctad.org/datacentre/

Table 1.2 Descriptive statistics

Variables	Obs.	Median	Std. Dev.	Min.	Max
mex	208	56,786	388,832	447	2,022,223
modm	208	21,344	188,471	277	1,014,395
mofm	208	6780	27,719	48	134,602
mods	208	6519	79,633	39	435,281
mofs	208	7058	27,907	55	133,631
sex	208	29,186	89,403	304	439,994
sodm	208	1612	9237	11	44,836
sofm	208	1371	1960	32	9061
sods	208	18,884	68,295	196	345,943
sofs	208	2483	3550	38	15,818
pcy	208	2343	2622	383	11,115

Sources: Authors' description
Note: The unit of TiVA data is millions of US dollars, and that of GDP per capita is US dollars

1.3.3 Data Property

Before the PVAR model estimation, this study investigates the stationarity of the data by employing panel unit-root tests for each variable and, if required, a panel co-integration test for a set of variables. Panel unit-root tests are first conducted on the null hypothesis, suggesting that the level and first difference of the individual data have a unit root. If the unit-root tests reveal that each variable's data are not stationary at a given level but stationary in the first difference, the variables' data corresponds to the case of $I(1)$. Then, it can be further examined using a co-integration test for "level" data. If data for a set of variables are identified to have co-integration, using "level" data is justified for model estimation.

For the panel unit-root tests, this study applies the Levin, Lin, and Chu (LLC) test (Levin et al. 2002) as a common unit-root test; and the Fisher-ADF and Fisher-PP tests (Choi 2001; Maddala and Wu 1999); and the Im, Pesaran, and Shin tests (Im et al. 2003) as individual unit-root tests. The common unit-root test assumes a common unit-root process across cross-sections, whereas the individual unit-root test allows individual unit-root processes to vary across cross-sections. This study conducts a Johansen-Fisher panel co-integration test (Maddala and Wu 1999). All test equations contain individual intercepts and trends, automatically selecting the lag length.

Tables 1.3 and 1.4 present the test results. The common and individual unit-root tests do not reject the null hypothesis of a unit root in level data at conventional significance levels; however, the null hypothesis is rejected in the first differences for all variables (except for *pcy* in the Fisher-PP test). Therefore, the variables follow Case $I(1)$. Subsequently, a panel co-integration test is conducted on the combination of variables, and the results (trace and max-eigenvalues) suggest that the level series for variable data are co-integrated. Thus, this study utilized level data for subsequent estimations.

Table 1.3 Panel unit root tests

	Panel Unit Root Tests							
	Level				First Difference			
Variables	LLC	ADF Fisher	PP Fisher	Im et al.	LLC	ADF Fisher	PP Fisher	Im et al.
mex	0.542	7.178	6.679	1.734	−7.968***	75.609***	76.981***	−7.414***
modm	1.660	6.946	7.038	2.307	−7.308***	67.311***	67.793***	−6.600***
mofm	0.428	8.896	9.015	1.688	−8.870***	88.064***	148.860***	−8.606***
mods	−0.828	12.481	11.865	0.514	−5.588***	75.093***	80.565***	−7.345***
mofs	1.033	7.391	7.213	2.037	−6.140***	80.163***	111.282***	−7.878***
sex	2.515	2.830	2.837	4.390	−2.281**	54.946***	48.060***	−5.021***
sodm	2.554	5.914	6.279	1.814	−1.656**	50.151***	41.911***	−3.566***
sofm	0.720	9.189	7.411	1.096	−5.587***	65.944***	88.114***	−5.689***
sods	3.097	2.273	2.295	5.057	−2.092**	55.950***	50.652***	−5.219***
sofs	1.150	10.147	6.206	1.086	−2.557***	50.343***	66.033***	−4.436***
pcy	0.658	4.752	0.492	4.018	−1.383*	35.970***	19.740	−3.023***

Sources: Authors' estimation
Note: *, **, and *** denote statistical significance at the 10%, 5%, and 1% level, respectively

Table 1.4 Panel co-integration test

Johansen Fisher Panel Cointegration Test		
Group	Trace test	Max-Eigen test
mex, modm, mofm, mods, mofs	237.0***	130.8***
sex, sodm, sofm, sods, dofs	185.8***	128.2***

Sources: Authors' estimation
Note: *** denotes statistical significance at the 1% level

1.3.4 PVAR Model Specification

This study adopts a PVAR model to examine the quantitative interactions between service inputs and manufacturing exports and inputs and those between service inputs and service exports. Applying a PVAR model is justified by the comprehensive and data-driven approach to clarify the mechanism of servicification in GVCs in multiple countries. In addition, the key variables in this study—service and manufacturing exports and inputs—are interdependent. Thus, single-equation regressions would lead to biased and inconsistent estimators owing to variable endogeneity. Instead, a PVAR model allows for endogeneity among the estimated variables and allows the data to determine causality between the targeted variables. No scientific studies have elucidated the mechanism of servicification in GVCs using the PVAR model. The PVAR model can be specified for estimation as follows:

$$y_{it} = \mu + V_1 y_{it-1} + V_2 z_{it} + f_i + f_t + \varepsilon_t \quad (1.1)$$

where the subscripts i and t denote the eight sampled Asian economies and the period 1995–2020. y is a column vector of the endogenous variables, that is, y = (*mex*, *modm*, *mofm*, *mods*, *mods**d06*, *mofs*, *mofs**d06*) to examine the interactions between business service inputs and manufacturing exports and inputs, and y = (*sex*, *sodm*, *sofm*, *sods*, *sods***d06*, *sofs*, *sofs***d06*) to examine the interactions between business service inputs and exports and manufacturing inputs.

The other vectors are: y_{-1} is a vector of the one-year lagged endogenous variables rooted in a limited number of time-series data; z is the control variable of real GDP per capita (*pcy*); f_i and f_t represent time-invariant country-specific and country-invariant time-specific fixed effects, respectively; μ is a constant vector; V_1 and V_2 are coefficient matrices; and ε_t is a vector of the random error terms in the system. This panel estimation applies the fixed-effects model represented by f_i and f_t for the following reasons. From a statistical perspective, the Hausman specification test (Hausman 1978) is generally used to choose between fixed- and random-effects models. However, this study emphasizes exogenous factors affecting value-added trade. For instance, time-invariant factors such as political systems, institutional quality, technology-absorbing capacity, and economic strategies might differ widely among the sample economies, and these country-specific factors might be correlated with value-added trade. There are also country-invariant time-specific factors, namely, economic fluctuations caused by external shocks, such as the Asian financial crisis in 1997–1998 and the global financial crisis in 2008–2009. Accordingly, as these factors are correlated with the error term among the sample economies for a given sample period, simple pooled estimates that ignore this correlation may lead to inefficient estimations. Additionally, adopting a fixed-effects model can alleviate the endogeneity problem by absorbing unobserved heterogeneity among the sample countries. Thus, a fixed-effects model is adopted for all estimations in this study.

Based on these specifications, the analysis estimates the PVAR model and examines Granger causalities among the endogenous variables using a block exogeneity test. The block exogeneity test provides a data-driven toolkit to determine whether a variable should be included or excluded from an estimation model. This test justifies the inclusion of a variable based on Granger causality in the PVAR framework. Granger causality was identified by rejecting the null hypothesis that a variable is excluded from the PVAR model.

1.4 Estimation Results and Interpretations

Table 1.5 shows the PVAR model estimation results, and Table 1.6 presents the block exogeneity test results based on the PVAR model estimation. The estimation results are summarized in the following subsections.

1.4.1 Causalities Between Business Service Inputs and Manufacturing Exports and Inputs

Tables 1.5a and 1.6a confirm the Granger causalities with positive signs and conventionally significant levels: from foreign manufacturing inputs (*mofm*) to manufacturing exports (*mex*), from domestic manufacturing inputs (*modm*) to domestic

Table 1.5 PVAR model estimation results

(a) Interactions between business service inputs and manufacturing exports and inputs

	mex	*modm*	*mofm*	*mods*	*mods*d06*	*mofs*	*mofs*d06*
mex-1	1.401**	0.144	0.043	0.047	0.273**	0.070	0.185**
	[2.469]	[0.569]	[0.730]	[0.557]	[2.304]	[1.143]	[2.288]
modm-1	0.692	1.267***	0.012	0.226**	−0.020	0.005	−0.141
	[0.985]	[4.037]	[1.267]	[2.175]	[−1.138]	[0.060]	[−1.410]
mofm-1	7.943***	3.455***	1.650***	0.238	0.849	1.034***	1.250***
	[2.853]	[2.780]	[5.688]	[0.579]	[1.459]	[3.429]	[3.153]
mods-1	−5.405***	−2.572***	−0.341**	0.242	−0.323	−0.423***	−0.351*
	[−3.704]	[−3.948]	[−2.242]	[1.122]	[−1.058]	[−.2.674}	[−1.687]
mods d06-1*	2.458	1.428**	0.164	0.140	0.444	0.171	−0.012
	[1.525]	[2.116]	[1.038]	[0.625]	[1.405]	[1.045]	[−0.056]
mofs-1	−7.093	−2.527	−0.615	−0.344	−1.858	−0.142	−1.437*
	[−1.289]	[−1.029]	[−2.073]	[−0.423]	[−1.614]	[−0.237]	[1.833]
mofs d06-1*	−3.529	−1.840*	−0.337	−0.242	0.057	−0.304	0.519*
	[−1.665]	[−1.945]	[−1.526]	[−0.773]	[0.130]	[−1.323]	[1.718]
pcy	21.403**	10.113***	2.172**	2.104	2.465	2.030**	3.090**
	[2.449]	[2.592]	[2.385]	[1.628]	[1.349]	[2.144]	[2.482]
adj. R^2	0.992	0.993	0.982	0.996	0.991	0.981	0.968

(b) Interactions between business service inputs and exports and manufacturing inputs

	sex	*sodm*	*sofm*	*sods*	*sods*d06*	*sofs*	*sofs*d06*
sex-1	3.200***	0.328***	0.067**	1.352***	2.289***	0.175***	0.224***
	[4.908]	[4.319]	[2.498]	[3.099]	[4.102]	[3.702]	[4.090]
sodm-1	−4.308***	0.290**	−0.141***	−2.405***	−3.479***	−0.351***	−0.430***
	[−3.892]	[2.253]	0.960***	[−3.247]	[−3.672]	[−4.377]	[−4.626]
sofm-1	3.317	0.813**	[7.458]	1.284	0.486	0.267	0.158
	[1.063]	[2.240]	[4.711]	[0.615]	[0.182]	[1.181]	[0.603]
sods-1	−2.462***	−0.375***	−0.071**	−0.523	−2.040***	−0.175***	−0.226***
	[−3.666]	[−4.793]	[−2.550]	[−1.163]	[−3.548]	[−3.590]	[−4.012]
sods d06-1*	0.345*	0.060***	0.008	0.211	0.765***	0.011	0.009
	[1.766]	[2.625]	[0.949]	[1.616]	[4.573]	[0.797]	[0.568]
sofs-1	−5.567*	−0.985***	−0.169	−2.814	−3.758	0.325	−0.329
	[−1.730]	[−2.632]	[−1.276]	[−1.307]	[−1.365]	[1.394]	[−1.221]
sofs d06-1*	−3.407*	−0.502**	−0.116	−2.121*	−2.603*	−0.126	0.538***
	[−1.970]	[−2.493]	[−1.624]	[−1.833]	[−1.758]	[−1.008]	[3.710]
pcy	6.234***	1.057***	0.257***	3.517**	5.337***	0.245**	0.639***
	[2.870]	[4.181]	[2.867]	[2.420]	[2.871]	[2.188]	[3.505]
adj. R^2	0.989	0.986	0.961	0.992	0.987	0.963	0.959

Sources: Authors' estimation

Note: *, **, and *** denote rejection of the null hypothesis at 90%, 95%, and 99% levels, respectively. The *t*-statistics are shown in parentheses

Table 1.6 Block exogeneity test results

Dependent variable	Excluded	Chi-sq	*df*	Probability
(a) Causalities between business service inputs and manufacturing exports and inputs				
mex	*modm*	0.971	1	0.325
	mofm	8.141	1	0.004
	mods	13.716	1	0.000 (negative)
	mofs	1.661	1	0.198
modm	*mex*	0.323	1	0.570
	mods	15.589	1	0.000 (negative)
	mofs	1.058	1	0.304
mofm	*mex*	0.532	1	0.466
	mods	5.024	1	0.025 (negative)
	mofs	1.151	1	0.283
mods	*mex*	0.310	1	0.578
	modm	4.730	1	0.030
	mofm	0.179	1	0.672
*mods*d06*	*mex*	5.309	1	0.021
	modm	0.019	1	0.890
	mofm	2.130	1	0.144
mofs	*mex*	1.306	1	0.253
	modm	0.004	1	0.952
	mofm	11.757	1	0.001
*mofs*d06*	*mex*	5235.000	1	0.022
	modm	1.987	1	0.159
	mofm	9.939	1	0.002
(b) Causalities between business service inputs and exports and manufacturing inputs				
sex	*sodm*	15.150	1	0.001 (negative)
	sofm	1.130	1	0.288
	sods	13.439	1	0.000 (negative)
	sofs	2.993	1	0.083 (negative)
sodm	*sex*	18.651	1	0.000
	sods	22.970	1	0.000 (negative)
	sofs	6.929	1	0.009 (negative)
sofm	*sex*	6.240	1	0.013
	sods	6.504	1	0.011 (negative)
	sofs	1.627	1	0.202
sods	*sex*	9.602	1	0.002
*sods*d06*		16.829	1	0.000
sofs		13.708	1	0.000
*sofs*d06*		16.731	1	0.000

Sources: Authors' estimation

business service inputs (*mods*), from foreign manufacturing inputs (*mofm*) to foreign business service inputs and their cross-terms with a period dummy for 2006–2020 (*mofs* and *mofs*d06*), and from manufacturing exports (*mex*) to the cross-terms between domestic and foreign business service inputs and a period dummy for 2006–2020 (*mods*d06* and *mofs*d06*).

These results can be interpreted as follows: First, within manufacturing sectors, foreign manufacturing inputs drive manufacturing exports. Second, regarding the interactions between business service inputs and manufacturing exports and inputs, the estimation results suggest that business service inputs, including domestic and foreign inputs, have been facilitated by manufacturing exports and foreign manufacturing inputs since the mid-2000s. This implies that business services are actively involved in manufacturing GVC activities.

1.4.2 Causalities Between Business Service Inputs and Exports and Manufacturing Inputs

Tables 1.5b and 1.6b verify the Granger causalities with positive signs and conventionally significant levels as follows: from business service exports (*sex*) to domestic and foreign manufacturing inputs (*sodm* and *sofm*), and also from business service exports (*sex*) to domestic and foreign business service inputs and their cross-terms with a period dummy for 2006–2020 (*sods*, *sods*d06*, *sofs*, and *sofs*d06*). These results suggest that, first, both domestic and foreign manufacturing inputs are induced by business service exports. Second, within business service sectors, business service inputs (domestic or foreign) have been facilitated by business service exports. These trends have also accelerated since the mid-2000s. This finding implies the active involvement of business services in business service GVC activities.

1.4.3 Summary of Findings and Policy Implications

In the block exogeneity tests, all combinations between gross exports and inputs in the business service and manufacturing sectors were comprehensively examined in terms of causalities in Sects. 1.4.1 and 1.4.2 based on Table 1.6. Thus, no significant results regarding the mechanism of servicification in GVCs are unanalyzed. The key findings of the test results (Fig. 1.2) are as follows. First, reciprocal interactions between the business services and manufacturing sectors are confirmed. Thus, manufacturing exports induce business service inputs, whereas business service exports induce manufacturing inputs. Second, foreign manufacturing inputs facilitate foreign business service inputs. Third, business service inputs are promoted by business service exports. These trends in the involvement of business services have accelerated since the mid-2000s. These findings to support servicification in GVCs

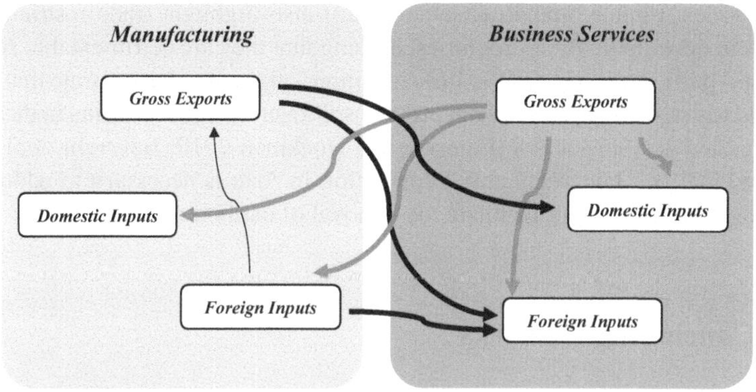

Fig. 1.2 Key findings of causalities between manufacturing and business services. Source: Authors' description

are consistent with the existing literature on servicification such as OECD, WTO, and World Bank Group (2014), Johnson and Noguera (2017), Heuser and Mattoo (2017), Baldwin et al. (2015), Blázquez et al. (2023), and Baek et al. (2023). However, this study differs from earlier studies, in that it provided deep insights on the mechanism of servicification in GVCs by quantifying the interactions between gross exports and inputs in the business service and manufacturing sectors. This finding implies that "Task-composition shift: changes in final goods" as one of causes of servicification (Baldwin et al. 2015; Heuser and Mattoo 2017) has been significantly working so that servicification can contribute to productivity growth and comparative advantage.

The policy implication is that there should be room to create better environments for trade in services, especially considering that servicification in the GVC processes has accelerated in Asian economies. Heuser and Mattoo (2017) proposed the following two types of policy issues inhibiting the enhanced role of services in GVCs: explicit restrictions on foreign services and service suppliers and regulatory divergence across countries, which reduce the inter-compatibility of goods, services, and service components needed for fragmenting production across countries. The World Bank provides the Service Trade Restrictions Index, which represents the restrictiveness of service trade policies across countries.[4] This index is based on data collected between 2008 and 2010 from 103 countries and ranges from 0 (completely open) to 100 (completely closed). Focusing on the sample economies in this study, the index scores of China (36.6), India (65.7), Indonesia (50.0), Malaysia (46.1), the Philippines (53.5), Thailand (48.0), and Vietnam (41.5) exceed the world sample average (28.4) (only Cambodia's index, 23.7, is below the average). This observation suggests that even Asian economies that have reaped huge benefits from trade liberalization and investment in goods continue to restrict foreign presence in

[4] See the website: https://www.worldbank.org/en/research/brief/services-trade-restrictions-database

their services. Findlay and Roelfsema (2023) also highlight trade restrictions on services in developing Asian countries, arguing that they are detrimental to ASEAN members' participation in GVCs. Instead, empirical studies demonstrate that reducing trade restrictions on service can provide spillover benefits for firms in the manufacturing and service sectors (Francois and Hoekman 2010; Beverelli et al. 2017; Shepherd 2019). Thus, regulatory cooperation in Asia is necessary to address the regulatory divergence and facilitate the removal of explicit restrictions.

1.5 Concluding Remarks

This study investigated the involvement of service sectors in GVCs in selected emerging and developing Asian economies by examining the quantitative interactions between service inputs and manufacturing exports and inputs, and those between service inputs and service exports, using a PVAR model based on the OECD TiVA 2023 database. This study's aimed to visualize the endogenous interactions of value-added trade variables related to the service sectors by checking their causalities in a PVAR framework, especially considering that previous studies have failed.

The main findings are: First, reciprocal interactions between business services and the manufacturing sector were confirmed. Therefore, manufacturing exports induce foreign business service inputs, whereas business service exports induce manufacturing inputs. Second, foreign manufacturing facilitates foreign business service inputs. Third, business service inputs are promoted by business service exports. These trends in the involvement of business services in GVC activities have accelerated since the mid-2000s in all aspects, and are expected to expand in the post-COVID-19 era.

A policy implication is that there should be room to create better environments for service trade following the post-COVID-19 era because servicification in GVC processes has accelerated in Asian economies. Since Asian economies having reaped huge benefits from trade liberalization and investment in goods have continued to maintain restrictions on foreign presence in services, regulatory cooperation in the Asian region is necessary to address regulatory divergence and facilitate the removal of explicit restrictions.

A limitation of this study is the lack of detailed and in-depth analyses of servicification in GVCs in Asian economies. By conducting case studies on individual sectors and countries to examine the complexity of servicification in Asian GVCs and how regulatory divergence has hindered their services in trade, it would be possible to validate the evidence found in this study and to develop more concrete recommendations for facilitating servicification in Asian GVCs.

References

Alvarez JB, Baris KV, Crisostomo MCR et al (2021) Recent trends in global value chains. In: Asian Development Bank (ed) Global value chain development report 2021: beyond production. ADB, The Research Institute for Global Value Chains at the University of International Business and Economics, The World Trade Organization, The Institute of Developing Economies – Japan External Trade Organization, and The China Development Research Foundation

Baek N, Chahande K, Eklou KM et al (2023) ASEAN-5: further harnessing the benefits of regional integration amid fragmentation risks. IMF Working Papers, WP/23/191

Baldwin R, Forslid R, Ito T (2015) Unveiling the evolving sources of value added in exports. IDE–JETRO Joint Research Program Series 161

Beverelli C, Fiorini M, Hoekman B (2017) Services trade policy and manufacturing productivity: the role of institutions. J Int Econ 104(C):166–182

Blázquez L, Díaz-Mora C, González-Díaz B (2023) Slowbalisation or a 'new' type of GVC participation? The role of digital services. J Ind Bus Econ 50:121–147. https://doi.org/10.1007/s40812-022-00245-x

Cheng D, Xiao Z (2021) Producer services and productivity: a global value chain perspective. Rev Income Wealth 67(2):418–444

Choi I (2001) Unit root tests for panel data. J Int Money Finance 20(2):249–272

Clark C (1940) The conditions of economic progress. Macmillan, New York

Díaz-Mora C, Gandoy R, González-Díaz B (2018) Looking into global value chains: influence of foreign services on export performance. Rev World Econ 154:785–814. https://doi.org/10.1007/s10290-018-0326-4

Findlay C, Roelfsema H (2023) Services trade in the ASEAN region and participation in GVCs. J Asia Pacific Econ 28(3):986–1006

Francois J, Hoekman B (2010) Services trade and policy. J Econ Lit 48(3):642–692

Hansen UE, Nygaard I, Morris M et al (2022) Servicification of manufacturing in global value chains: upgrading of local suppliers of embedded services in the South African market for wind turbines. J Dev Stud 58(4):787–808

Hausman JA (1978) Specification tests in econometrics. Econometrica 46:1251–1272

Heuser C, Mattoo A (2017) Services trade and global value chains. In: World Bank, Institute of Developing Economies – Japan External Trade Organization, Organization for Economic Cooperation and Development, University of International Business and Economics, and World Trade Organization (ed) Global value chain development report 2017: measuring and analyzing the impact of GVCs on economic development. World Bank Group, Washington, DC, p 141.I

Im KS, Pesaran MH, Shin Y (2003) Testing for unit roots in heterogeneous panels. J Econ 115(1):53–74

Johnson RC, Noguera G (2017) A portrait of trade in value added over four decades. Rev Econ Stat 99(5):896–911

Kimura F (2006) International production and distribution networks in East Asia: eighteen facts, mechanics, and policy implications. Asian Econ Pol Rev 1:326–344

Koopman R, Wang Z, Wei S (2014) Tracing value-added and double counting in gross exports. Am Econ Rev 104(2):459–494. https://doi.org/10.1257/aer.104.2.459

Kordalska A, Olczyk M (2021) Linkages between services and manufacturing as a new channel for GVC development: evidence from CEE countries. Struct Change Econ Dyn 58:125–137

Levin A, Lin CF, Chu CSJ (2002) Unit root tests in panel data: asymptotic and finite-sample properties. J Econ 108(1):1–24

Maddala GS, Wu S (1999) A comparative study of unit root tests with panel data and a new simple test. Oxf Bull Econ Stat 61(S1):631–652

Nano E, Stolzenburg V (2021) The role of global services value chains for services-led development. In: Asian Development Bank (ed) Global value chain development report 2021: beyond production. ADB, The Research Institute for Global Value Chains at the University

of International Business and Economics, the World Trade Organization, the Institute of Developing Economies – Japan External Trade Organization, and the China Development Research Foundation
OECD (Organization for Economic Cooperation and Development), WTO (World Trade Organization), World Bank Group (2014) Global value chains: challenges, opportunities, and implications for policy. G20 Trade Ministers Meeting, Sydney, Australia
Qiu Y (2020) Promotion or hindrance? The threshold effect of services on global value chains. Appl Econ Lett 27(5):406–411
Shepherd B (2019) Services policies and manufacturing exports. In: Helble M, Shepherd B (eds) Leveraging services for development: prospects and policies. Asian Development Bank Institute, Tokyo
Taguchi H, Thet MS (2021) Quantitative linkage between global value chains' backward participation and logistics performance in the host country: a structural gravity model analysis of emerging ASEAN economies. Asia-Pac J Reg Sci 5:453–475
World Bank (2020) World development report - trading for development in the age of global value chains. World Bank, Washington, DC
World Trade Organization (WTO) (2021) World trade report 2021: economic resilience and trade

Chapter 2
Economic Impact of Foreign Direct Investment, Gross Capital Formation, and Trade Openness on ASEAN Economies: The Matter of the COVID-19 Epidemic and the Global Financial Crisis

Htwe Ko, George Randolph Dirth, Chukiat Chaiboonsri, and Nattapan Kongbuamai

Abstract This study aimed to investigate the impact of foreign direct investment (FDI), gross fixed capital formation (GCF), trade openness (TOP), the COVID-19 pandemic, and the global financial crisis on the economic growth of the Association of Southeast Asian Nations (ASEAN) countries from 2000 to 2023. It employs panel fixed and random effects, and also panel autoregressive distributed lag (P-ARDL) models to analyze the relationship between independent and dependent variables. We found that FDI and TOP have a significant positive effect, and GCF has an insignificant positive effect on economic growth. Thus, unemployment rates, exchange rates, inflation rates, and the global financial crisis did not have a significant impact while the pandemic had significant negative effects on the economic growth. Further analysis using the P-ARDL model corroborates these findings, revealing that in both the short and long run, trade openness and GCF significantly and positively impact economic growth. Interestingly, FDI has a positive effect in the short run but a negative effect in the long run. Unemployment, exchange, and inflation rates remain insignificant across both the short and long runs. The pandemic had a greater detrimental impact on economic growth from 2000 to 2023 than the global financial crisis.

Keywords FDI · Gross capital formation · Trade openness · GDP per capita · The COVID-19 pandemic · Panel fixed effects · Panel random effects · Panel autoregressive distributed lag model · ASEAN

H. Ko · G. R. Dirth · C. Chaiboonsri
Faculty of Economics, Chiang Mai University, Chiang Mai, Thailand

N. Kongbuamai (✉)
Tourism, Hospitality, and Event (TH&E) Research Group, School of Management, Mae Fah Luang University, Chiang Rai, Thailand
e-mail: nattapan.kon@mfu.ac.th

© The Author(s), under exclusive license to Springer Nature Singapore Pte Ltd. 2025
H. Taguchi (ed.), *Sustainability of Economic Growth in East Asia*,
New Frontiers in Regional Science: Asian Perspectives 82,
https://doi.org/10.1007/978-981-96-3731-7_2

2.1 Introduction

The Association of Southeast Asian Nations (ASEAN) was founded in 1967 in Bangkok, Thailand (ASEAN Secretariat 2014). During the 1970s, ASEAN economies began to grow, becoming one of the world's most important economic blocs (Hicklin et al. 1997; World Bank 2024). Over the next four decades, ASEAN experienced rapid economic growth, positioning itself among the fastest-growing regions globally (Hicklin et al. 1997; Vinayak et al. 2014; ASEAN Secretariat 2019; World Bank 2024). By 1999, ASEAN had expanded to include 10 member-states, and in 2015, the ASEAN community was formally established (ASEAN Secretariat 2012). As a result, it became a significant driver of global economic growth (ASEAN Secretariat 2019). In 2023, ASEAN countries are estimated to house 685.36 million people, accounting for approximately 8% of the global population (World Bank 2024). The ASEAN region is projected to become the world's fourth-largest economy by the year 2050 (Vinayak et al. 2014; ASEAN Secretariat 2019); this region spans approximately 4,817,000 km^2 (National Committee of Indonesia's Chairmanship in ASEAN 2023). In economic terms, ASEAN's combined Gross Domestic Product (GDP) reached 3.78 trillion USD in 2023, representing approximately 3.5% of the global GDP (World Bank 2024). In 2023, excluding Myanmar, ASEAN exports and imports of goods and services totaled 2.32 trillion USD (7.5% of global exports) and 2.11 trillion USD (6.9% of global imports), respectively (World Bank 2024).

Recently, however, it has faced significant challenges, including internal issues, such as slower economic growth, rising inflation rates, weather disruptions, and political unrest. Additionally, external influences like the global economic downturn, geopolitical tensions, stricter monetary policies in the United States and Europe, and the rise of the BRICS countries have impacted the region (Asian Development Bank 2023). Furthermore, the ASEAN economy is still in slow recovery from the 2008–2009 global financial crisis (GFC) (Hossain et al. 2022) and the COVID-19 pandemic (ASEAN 2020; D'Aloia and Gugler 2024). The GFC, which lasted from mid-2007 to early 2009, was one of the most severe economic downturns since the Great Depression of the 1930s (Temin 2010). The COVID-19 outbreak, originating in Wuhan, China, in December 2019, spread to 203 countries, infecting millions and causing millions of deaths worldwide. On March 11, 2020, the World Health Organization declared COVID-19 as a global pandemic, and it resulted in widespread disruption of economic activities worldwide (ASEAN 2020).

To drive regional growth, ASEAN members focused on increasing GDP by promoting foreign direct investment (FDI), international trade, domestic capital investment, and so on (Asian Development Bank 2023). These efforts aimed to create jobs, reduce poverty, improve overall well-being, and contribute to the United Nations (UN) Sustainable Development Goals.

This study primarily aimed to investigate the impact of FDI, gross fixed capital formation (GCF), and trade openness (TOP) on economic growth in ASEAN countries from 2000 to 2023, accounting for the effects of the GFC and the COVID-19 pandemic. To achieve this, this study employed panel fixed effects, random effects, and pooled mean group (PMG) panel autoregressive distributed lag (P-ARDL) models. This study provides empirical evidence of how FDI, GCF, and TOP contribute to economic growth in the ASEAN countries and offers policy implications for fostering growth and development.

2.2 Literature Review

Theoretical perspectives highlight the significant roles of FDI, GCF, and trade liberalization in driving economic growth (Romer 1994; Foss 1998; Singh 2010). Table 2.1 summarizes recent empirical studies from different regions. The main findings demonstrate a range of results and methodologies. For FDI and economic growth nexus, many studies, including those by Karahan and Çolak (2024) and Malik and Sah (2024), examined the causality between FDI and economic growth. Karahan and Çolak (2024) identified an asymmetric causality between FDI and GDP per capita in Regional Comprehensive Economic Partnership (RCEP) countries, whereas Malik and Sah (2024) reported a short-run relationship between FDI inflows and growth in BRIC countries. Furthermore, studies have noted FDI's positive impact consistently in several regions, such as high-income Asian economies (Sugözü and Dorbonova 2024), the Middle East and North Africa (Ben Abdallah 2024), and Algeria (Kaddouri and Benelbar 2024). However, Sugözü and Dorbonova (2024) observed a negative impact in low- and middle-income Asian economies. Several studies, while exploring the nexus between trade liberalization and economic growth, have explored how TOP affects economic growth (Hossain et al. 2022; Ko 2024; Nam and Yu 2024). Ko (2024) reported that TOP positively affected Myanmar's economy, while Hossain et al. (2022) observed a positive relationship between TOP and economic growth in 30 Asian nations. Another study by Nam and Yu (2024) found that, although high trade volume promotes export-led growth in ASEAN, TOP does not directly correlate with economic development. The aforementioned studies highlight the complexity of these correlations. Owing to the limited research on these dynamics and a dearth of studies conducted on ASEAN countries and the COVID-19 effect, this study specifically aimed to focus on examining these factors within ASEAN economies.

2.3 Data and Methodology

This study sourced all data from the World Bank's World Development Indicators (World Bank 2024). Per capita GDP growth rate (PGDP) served as the dependent variable in this study. The independent variables included FDI, GCF, and TOP. The control variables were unemployment rates (UNEMP), exchange rates (EXR), inflation rates (INF), the global financial crisis (GFC), and the COVID-19 pandemic

Table 2.1 Recent empirical literature studies

Authors (year)	Methodology	Main findings
Nam and Yu (2024)	FE and FE-2SLS regression models	TOP has a varying effect on ASEAN countries from 2000 to 2022. It does not have any association with economic development. Interestingly, high trade volume promotes export-led growth.
Karahan and Çolak (2024)	Hatemi-J Cointegration test	Asymmetric causality between FDI and GDP per capita was found in RCEP countries from 1980 to 2020.
Sugözü and Dorbonova (2024)	Panel fixed effect and random effect regression	FDI inflows, TOP, and GCF positively correlate with economic growth in high-income Asian economies from 2000 to 2021; however, FDI inflows and TOP negatively affect economic growth in low- and middle-income Asian economies.
Hakim and Budi (2024)	Panel random effect	FDI inflows mediate the indirect effects of political stability and government effectiveness on economic growth in ASEAN, highlighting the need for political stability to attract FDI.
Ai-Jun et al. (2024)	Panel VECM	Found a causal link between FDI inflows and economic growth across six sectors in Bangladesh from 2007–2008 to 2018–2019.
Malik and Sah (2024)	Bayesian VAR	Only a short-run relationship exists between FDI inflows and economic growth in BRIC countries from 1991 to 2020.
Ben Abdallah (2024)	ARDL and VECM	FDI inflows and TOP positively impacted economic growth in the Middle East and North Africa from 1990 to 2012.
Epor et al. (2024)	ARDL	FDI and TOP have had a positive but insignificant impact on economic growth in Brazil, Nigeria, and Vietnam from 1990 to 2021.
Mose and Kipchirchir (2024)	ARDL and the Granger causality test	FDI inflows result in both short- and long-run economic growth in Kenya from 1990 to 2021.
Bakpa and Yeboah (2024)	GMM and Durbin–Watson	FDI inflows and gross capital formation positively impacted economic growth in Ghana from 1998 to 2017.
Ghazalian (2024)	Dynamic panel-data analysis	Economic growth attracts more FDI inflows.
Kaddouri and Benelbar (2024)	ARDL	FDI positively correlates with economic growth in Algeria from 1990 to 2023.
Ko (2024)	Linear and nonlinear regression models	Trade openness had a positive effect while FDI inflows had a negative effect on economic growth in Myanmar from 1990 to 2022.
Wang et al. (2023)	Panel GLS approach	FDI inflows increased income inequality in developed economies but reduced it in emerging economies from 1974 to 2019.
Sanusi and Eita (2023)	Fixed effect, random effect, and Dumitrescu–Hurlin causality test	No evidence of FDI impact on economic growth in the Southern African Development Community from Q1:1970 to Q1:2022.
Minh and Trinh (2023)	Threshold and GMM	FDI inflows positively affect GDP per capita in 60 developing nations from 1995 to 2019.

(continued)

Table 2.1 (continued)

Authors (year)	Methodology	Main findings
Sobirova et al. (2023)	Panel PMG-ARDL	Higher FDI inflows and trade openness positively impact long-term economic growth in CIS countries from 2000 to 2020.
Mwakabungu and Kauangal (2023)	ARDL and Granger causality test	Both short- and long-term impacts of FDI inflows on GDP growth were observed in Tanzania from 1990 to 2020.
Mohamed and Abdulle (2023)	NARDL	Short- and long-term asymmetric impacts of FDI inflows, trade openness, and gross capital formation on economic development were found in Somalia from 1971 to 2021.
Rashid et al. (2023)	ARDL-ECM	FDI inflows had a positive but insignificant effect on economic growth in India from 1991 to 2020.
Chude and Chude (2023)	ECM	Both foreign aid and FDI inflows significantly impacted economic growth in Nigeria from 1981 to 2021.
Hossain and Hossain (2023)	VAR model	Economic growth attracted FDI inflows in China from 1981 to 2020.
Budhia and Kaur (2029)	Panel fixed effect model	FDI inflows enhanced economic growth in BRIC economies from 2001 to 2017.
Aashiq and Sharma (2023)	ANOVA test	FDI significantly and positively affects economic growth in BRICS countries, excluding South Africa, from 2000 to 2020.
Emmanuel Obiora Nwakeze et al. (2023)	Regression analysis	FDI inflows significantly impacted economic growth in ten selected countries from 2018 to 2022.
Hossain et al. (2022)	PCSE, GMM, and Granger causality test	FDI and TOP positively affected GDP growth in 30 Asian nations from 1991 to 2017.

Note: *GDP*, gross domestic product; *FDI*, foreign direct investment; *TOP*, trade openness; *VAR*, vector auto-regression; *ARDL*, autoregressive distributed lag; *NARDL*, nonlinear autoregressive distributed lag; *ARDL-ECM*, autoregressive distributed lag-error correction mechanism; *ECM*, error correction mechanism; *ANOVA*, analysis of variance; *GLS*, generalized least squares; *PCSE*, panel corrected standard error; *GMM*, generalized method of moments

(COVID). Based on data availability, data from eight counties in the ASEAN region (Brunei Darussalam, Cambodia, Indonesia, Malaysia, the Philippines, Thailand, Singapore, and Vietnam) were collected from 2000 to 2023. For the units of these data, PGDP, FDI, GCF, and TOP are (1) the percentage of GDP per capita growth, (2) the percentage of GDP, (3) the percentage of GDP, and (4) the sum of total imports and total exports divided by GDP, respectively. For control variables, UNEMP is measured as a percentage of the total labor force, EXR as per US dollar against local currencies, and INF as the inflation rate; GFC and COVID-19 are represented by dummy variables.

Figure 2.1 illustrates the trends in PGDP, FDI, GCF, and TOP across the eight ASEAN countries from 2000 to 2023. The data showed that all variables generally followed similar trends with fluctuations. Additionally, the figure highlights the effects of the global financial crisis (2008–2009) and COVID-19 pandemic (2020),

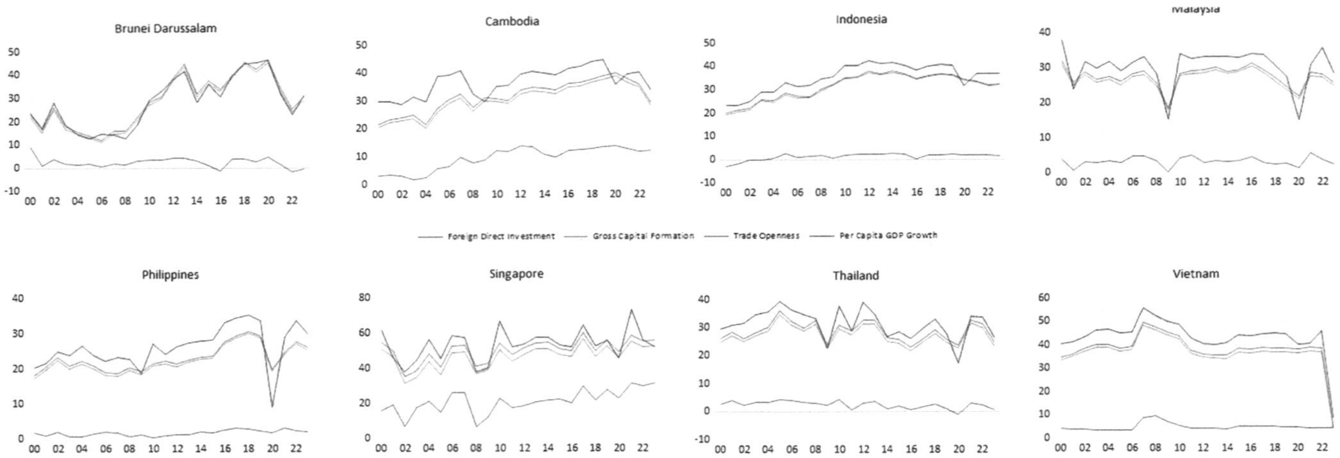

Fig. 2.1 Trends in four economic indicators in ASEAN economies (2000–2023)

Table 2.2 Data description of variables used in this study

Test	PGDP	FDI	GCF	TOP	UNEMP	EXR	INF	GFC	COVID-19
Mean	3.1582	5.87128	25.4085	1.32347	3.30994	4240.94	3.25927	0.08377	0.08377
Median	3.79614	3.28080	24.6185	1.10937	3.43400	42.4462	2.66825	0.00000	0.00000
Standard deviation	3.37486	7.02859	6.14542	0.92798	2.10132	6807.49	3.61518	0.27777	0.27777
Skewness	−0.71494	1.94914	0.24332	1.84192	0.48714	1.48729	2.56984	3.00482	3.00482
Kurtosis	5.04587	6.22209	2.72002	5.42797	2.60562	3.92051	13.6447	10.0289	10.0289
Observations	191	191	191	191	191	191	191	191	191

Note: *PGDP*, per capita; *GDP*, growth rate; *FDI*, Foreign Direct Investment; *GCF*, gross capital formation; *TOP*, trade openness; *UNEMP*, unemployment rate; *EXR*, exchange rate; *INF*, inflation rate; *GFC*, global financial crisis; *COVID-19*, COVID-19 pandemic

both of which caused significant declines in all indicators. Following each crisis, a gradual recovery in PGDP and GCF was observed, reflecting economic adaptation in the ASEAN economies. Although the trends were broadly similar, the recovery speeds varied among countries. A summary of common tests, including mean, median, standard deviation, skewness, and kurtosis, for data description is provided in Table 2.2.

We conducted a panel analysis to examine the economic impact of FDI, GCF, TOP, unemployment, and exchange rates, inflation, global financial crisis, and the COVID-19 pandemic on economic growth in ASEAN countries from 2000 to 2023. The empirical panel models used in this study comprise panel fixed effects (P-FE), panel random effects (P-RE), and panel autoregressive distributed lag (P-ARDL) models. In this model, FDI, GCF, and TOP were treated as fixed production proportions. Additionally, the UNMEP, EXR, INF, and dummy variables for the GFC and COVID-19 were included as control variables. These relationships can be expressed as follows:

$$\text{GDP per capita} = f\left(\text{FDI,GCF,TOP,UNEMP,EXR,INF,GFC,COVID}\right) \quad (2.1)$$

Equation (2.1) can be rewritten in regression form as follows:

$$\begin{aligned} Y_t &= \alpha + \beta_1\text{FDI}_t + \beta_2\text{GCF}_t + \beta_3\text{TOP}_t + \beta_4\text{UNEMP}_t \\ &+ \beta_5\text{EXR}_t + \beta_6\text{INF}_t + \beta_7\text{GFC}_t + \beta_8\text{COVID}_t + \varepsilon_t \end{aligned} \quad (2.2)$$

where Y represents per capita GDP; $\beta_1 - \beta_8$ are coefficients to be estimated, and ε represents the error term.

The fixed effects model (FEM) assumes individual differences using different intercepts for all units and time periods. Unlike the FEM, the random effects model (REM) is based on maximum likelihood or Generalized Least Squares (GLS) rather than Ordinary Least Squares (OLS) (Park 2005). One advantage of REM is that it eliminates heteroskedasticity. However, both models estimate the panel data attributes.

Both the FEM and REM are regression models shown in Eqs. (2.3) and (2.4), respectively.

$$\text{FEM,} \qquad Y_{it} = \alpha_i + \beta_i X_{it} + \varepsilon_{it} \tag{2.3}$$

$$\text{REM,} \qquad Y_{it} = \alpha_i + \beta_i X_{it} + \mu_i + \varepsilon_{it} \tag{2.4}$$

where i (number of individuals or cross section) = 1,2,…,N., t (time periods) = 1,2,…,T., μ_i = individual residuals, and ε_{it} = residuals of error terms (sum of cross section or time series).

The Hausman test is commonly used to assess whether fixed- or random-effects yield reliable results. The REM was considered more appropriate if the p value was >0.05, and the FEM was selected. Unit root and cointegration tests must first be performed to estimate the PMG P-ARDL, which can provide short- and long-term coefficients. This method is a likelihood-based estimation developed by Pesaran and Smith (1995) and Pesaran et al. (1997). The full panel ARDL-ECM is expressed as follows:

$$\begin{aligned}\Delta\text{PGDP}_{it} &= \beta_i + \theta_i \text{ECM}_{i,t-1} + \sum_{j=1}^{p}\beta_1\Delta\text{PGDP}_{i,t-j} + \sum_{j=1}^{q}\beta_2\Delta\text{FD}I_{i,t-j} \\ &+ \sum_{j=1}^{q}\beta_3\Delta\text{GCF}_{i,t-j} + \sum_{j=1}^{q}\beta_4\Delta\text{TOP}_{i,t-j} + \sum_{j=1}^{q}\beta_5\Delta\text{UNEMP}_{i,t-j} + \sum_{j=1}^{q}\beta_6\Delta\text{EXR}_{i,t-j} \\ &+ \sum_{j=1}^{q}\beta_7\Delta\text{INF}_{i,t-j} + \sum_{j=1}^{q}\beta_8\text{GFC}_{i,t-j} + \sum_{j=1}^{q}\beta_9\text{COVID}_{i,t-j} + \delta_2\text{FDI}_{i,t-j} + \delta_3\text{GCF}_{i,t-j} \\ &+ \delta_4\text{TOP}_{i,t-j} + \delta_5\text{UNEMP}_{i,t-j} + \delta_6\text{EXR}_{i,t-j} + \delta_7\text{INF}_{i,t-j} + \delta_8\text{GFC}_{i,t-j} \\ &+ \delta_9\text{COVID}_{i,t-j} + \varepsilon_{it}\end{aligned} \tag{2.5}$$

where Δ denotes first difference, θ_i denotes the adjustment to long-run equilibrium, $\beta_1 - \beta_9$ signifies short-term coefficients, and $\delta_2 - \delta_9$ signifies long-term coefficients.

2.4 Main Findings

The results of the panel unit root tests reveal that most variables are integrated of order $I(0)$, as Table 2.3 shows. Variables such as TOP, UNEMP, and EXR must be differenced to achieve stationarity in a valid regression analysis. These results suggest that FEM and REM use the first-differenced variables for TOP, UNEMP, and EXR, whereas other variables can be used in their current forms to avoid spurious results.

The cointegration tests (Table 2.4), including the Panel V-statistic, Panel RHO-statistic, Panel PP-statistic, Panel ADF-statistic, Group RHO-statistic, Group PP-statistic, Group ADF-statistic, and Kao ADF-statistic, all indicate the existence of a long-term equilibrium relationship among the variables. Notably, the panel and group PP statistics and ADF statistics are significant, supporting the conclusion that

Table 2.3 Panel unit root results (cross sectionally independent)

Variable/Test	Levin, Lin, and Chu t*		Im, Pesaran, and Shin W-stat		ADF-Choi Z-stat	
	I(0)	I(1)	I(0)	I(1)	I(0)	I(1)
PGDP	−8.71(0.0000)	−8.76(0.0000)	−7.34(0.0000)	−10.70 (0.0000	−6.73(0.0000)	−9.01(0.0000)
FDI	−3.12(0.0009)	−8.70(0.0000)	−4.08(0.0000)	−9.26(0.0000)	−3.88(0.0001)	−8.09(0.0000)
GCF	−1.78(0.0373)	−10.39(0.0000)	−2.57(0.0051)	−9.75(0.0000)	−2.62(0.0044)	−8.50(0.0000)
TOP	−0.91(0.1812)	−10.58(0.0000)	−1.27(0.1015)	−9.78(0.0000)	−1.18(0.1182)	−8.39(0.0000)
UNEMP	−1.04(0.1493)	−8.35(0.0000)	−0.53(0.2981)	−8.67(0.0000)	−0.42(0.3362)	−7.55(0.0000)
EXR	−0.86(0.1946)	−7.58(0.0000)	0.32(0.6276)	−6.75(0.0000)	0.38(0.6475)	−6.41(0.0000)
INF	−6.27(0.0000)	−15.18(0.0000)	−5.50(0.0000)	−14.98(0.0000)	−5.29(0.0000)	−11.3(0.0000)
GFC	–	12.44(0.0000)	−5.66(0.0000)	−10.95(0.0000)	−5.70(0.0000)	−9.38(0.0000)
COVID-19	–	–	–	–	–	–

* 90 %, (P = 0.10)

Note: *PGDP*, per capita; *GDP*, growth rate; *FDI*, Foreign Direct Investment; *GCF*, gross capital formation; *TOP*, trade openness; *UNEMP*, unemployment rate; *EXR*, exchange rate; *INF*, inflation rate; *GFC*, global financial crisis; *COVID-19*, COVID-19 pandemic; *ADF-Choi-Z-stat*, Augmented Dickey–Fuller (ADF) Unit Root Test by Choi Z-statistics

Table 2.4 Panel cointegration results

Test	*t*-statistic (prob.)
Panel V-stat.	−0.383191 (0.6492)
Panel ROH-stat.	1.484615 (0.9312)
Panel PP-stat.	−7.010198 (0.0000)
Panel ADF-stat.	−3.497505 (0.0002)
Group ROH-stat.	2.828249 (0.9977)
Group PP-stat.	−8.864815 (0.0000)
Group ADF-stat.	−3.300369 (0.0005)
Kao ADF-stat	−3.506092 (0.0002)

Note: *stat*, statistics

Table 2.5 Panel analysis results

	Fixed effects model	Random effects model
Variable	Coefficient (Prob.)	Coefficient (Prob.)
C	2.376***(0.0447)	2.300***(0.0732)
FDI	0.159***(0.0199)	0.122***(0.0291)
GCF	0.008***(0.8395)	0.015***(0.7179)
D(TOP)	0.073***(0.0001)	0.071***(0.0001)
D(UNEMP)	−0.677***(0.1135)	−0.741***(0.0840)
D(EXR)	−0.0003**(0.5836)	−0.0002**(0.7098)
INF	−0.006***(0.9207)	0.032***(0.6423)
GFC	−0.487***(0.5131)	−0.638***(0.4011)
COVID-19	−4.328***(0.0000)	−4.193***(0.0000)
R-squared	*0.476090*	*0.228043*
F-statistic	*10.11714*	*8.479251*
Durbin–Watson	*2.108798*	*1.463462*
Hausman Test		*P = 1.0000*

Note: ** and *denote significance at the 5% and 10% levels, respectively
Note: *FDI*, foreign direct investment; *GCF*, gross capital formation; *TOP*, trade openness; *UNEMP*, unemployment rate; *EXR*, exchange rate; *INF*, inflation rate; *GFC*, global financial crisis; *COVID-19*, COVID-19 pandemic

a stable long-term relationship exists among GDP, FDI, GCF, TOP, and other macroeconomic variables. This suggests that, despite short-term fluctuations, these variables move together in the long run. The mix order of $I(0)$ and $I(1)$ and the presence of long-term cointegration rationalize that PMG P-ARDL modeling is appropriate for this study.

The panel fixed effects estimation (Table 2.5) reveals that FDI and TOP had significant and positive impacts on economic growth in ASEAN countries. Specifically, FDI had a coefficient of 0.1599 (p-value = 0.0199) and TOP, of 0.0730 ($p = 0.0001$), indicating that both variables contributed positively to economic growth. For FDI, this is similar to the finding in developing countries (Minh and Trinh 2023), Tanzania (Mwakabungu and Kauangal 2023), Kenya (Mose and Kipchirchir 2024), Ghana

(Bakpa and Yeboah 2024), BRICS (Chude and Chude 2023), and 30 Asian countries (Hossain et al. 2022), among others; while studies conducted in Myanmar (Ko 2024), Commonwealth of Independent States (CIS) countries (Sobirova et al. 2023), and so on show a different pattern. The current study confirmed similar positive findings in Myanmar (Ko 2024), 30 Asian countries (Hossain et al. 2022), and CIS countries (Sobirova et al. 2023), and so on. However, certain findings were entirely the opposite of the findings of some studies conducted in South Asia (Rahman et al. 2020), low- and middle-income Asian economics (Sugözü and Dorbonova 2024). However, the COVID-19 pandemic had a substantial negative effect, with a coefficient of −4.3285 (p-value = 0.0000). Some studies, however, lacked data for analysis regarding COVID-19 and economic growth in ASEAN countries (D'Aloia and Gugler 2024). Contrastingly, GCF, UNEMP, EXR, INF, and GFC were found to be insignificant, with coefficients of 0.0087 (p value = 0.8395), −0.6779 (p value = 0.1135), −0.0003 (p value = 0.5836), −0.0069 (p value = 0.9207), and −0.4880 (p value = 0.5131), respectively. Some studies have found a negative relationship between GFC and economic growth in 30 Asian economies (Hossain et al. 2022).

In the panel random effects estimation for the same period (Table 2.5), FDI and TOP also showed significant positive impacts on economic growth, with coefficients of 0.1223 (p = 0.0291) and 0.0711 (p = 0.0001), respectively. The COVID-19 pandemic exhibited a significant negative effect, with a coefficient of −4.1932 (p-value = 0.0000). Contrastingly, GCF, UNEMP, EXR, INF, and GFC were insignificant, with coefficients of 0.0152 (p-value = 0.7179), −0.7415 (p-value = 0.0840), −0.0002 (p-value = 0.7098), 0.0322 (p-value = 0.6423), and −0.6386 (p-value = 0.4011), respectively. The model statistics for the fixed effects estimation included a coefficient of determination (R-squared) of 0.4761, an F-statistic of 10.1171, and a Durbin–Watson statistic of 2.1088. For the random effects model, the R-squared value was 0.2280, the F-statistic was 8.4793, and the Durbin–Watson statistic was 1.4635. The Hausman test suggested that the random effects model was more appropriate (p = 1.0000).

The P-ARDL (1,1) model results for the long run (Table 2.6) revealed that GCF and TOP had significantly and positively impacted economic growth. The coefficients for GCF and for TOP were 0.1567 (p = 0.0000) and 0.0278 (p = 0.0000), respectively. These results indicate that increases in GCF and TOP significantly contribute to economic growth in ASEAN countries. Contrastingly, FDI showed an insignificant and negative effect, with a coefficient of −0.0209 (p = 0.7303). This suggests that over the long term, changes in FDI did not significantly influence economic growth in ASEAN countries. Interestingly, UNEMP also demonstrated an insignificant and positive relationship, with a coefficient of 0.1383 (p = 0.2852), indicating that fluctuations in unemployment rates did not significantly impact economic growth. Both EXR and INF exhibit insignificant and negative effects, with coefficients of −4.41E−05 (p = 0.3055) and −0.0363 (p = 0.2446), respectively.

In the short run, FDI had a significant and positive impact on economic growth, with a coefficient of 0.3265 (p = 0.0072). This implies that in the short term, FDI positively contributes to economic growth in ASEAN countries. Conversely, GCF,

Table 2.6 PMG panel ARDL (p, q) estimation

Variable	Coefficient	Std. Error	Prob.	Relationship
		Long Run		
FDI	−0.020949	0.060615	0.7303	Insignificant and Negative
GCF	0.156726	0.026919	**0.00**	Significant and Positive
TOP	0.027849	0.004872	**0.0000**	Significant and Positive
UNEMP	0.138270	0.128712	0.2852	Insignificant and Positive
EXR	−4.41E-05	4.29E-05	0.3055	Insignificant and Negative
INF	−0.036318	0.031040	0.2446	Insignificant and Negative
		Short Run		
Cointeq-	−1.018845	0.131566	0.0000	–
D(FDI)	0.326495	0.119086	**0.0072**	Significant and Positive
D(GCF)	0.046357	0.069137	0.5040	Insignificant and Positive
D(TOP)	0.044807	0.041744	0.2856	Insignificant and Positive
D(UNEMP)	−1.013651	0.629178	0.1102	Insignificant and Negative
D(EXR)	−4.349932	3.329723	0.1943	Insignificant and Negative
D(INF)	0.101406	0.173264	0.5596	Insignificant and Positive
GFC	−1.202802	1.096557	0.2752	Insignificant and Negative
COVID-19	−3.870861	1.129832	**0.0009**	Significant and Negative
C	−4.047684	1.599606	0.0129	–
		Model Performance		
	RMSE	1.522387		
	MAE	1.040274		
	Normality test	23.85**(0.0000)		

Note: *FDI*, foreign direct investment; *GCF*, gross capital formation; *TOP*, trade openness; *UNEMP*, unemployment rate; *EXR*, exchange rate; *INF*, inflation rate; *GFC*, global financial crisis; *COVID-19*, COVID-19 pandemic

TOP, UNEMP, EXR, and INF were insignificant in the short run. The coefficients are 0.0464 ($p = 0.5040$) for GCF, 0.0448 ($p = 0.2856$) for TOP, −1.0137 ($p = 0.1102$) for UNEMP, −4.3499 ($p = 0.1943$) for EXR, and 0.1014 ($p = 0.5596$) for INF. While both the global financial crisis (GFC) and COVID-19 pandemic were negatively correlated with per capita GDP, the COVID-19 pandemic had a more pronounced effect on the economic stability of ASEAN countries.

The analysis demonstrates that FDI and TOP are significant drivers of economic growth in ASEAN countries, with trade openness showing consistently positive effects in both the short and long run. The pandemic has significantly negatively impacted economic stability.

Table 2.7 presents the short-run cross-section coefficients for each selected ASEAN country within the PMG-ARDL model. Each row corresponds to a specific country while the columns show various economic variables including intercept and cointegration term (C and Cointeg01), foreign direct investment (D(FDI)), gross capital formation (D(GCF)), trade openness (D(TOP)), unemployment rate (D(UNEMP)), exchange rate (D(EXR)), inflation rate (D(INF)), and two dummy variables for financial crisis and COVID-19 pandemic (GFC and COVID). The

Table 2.7 Cross section short-run coefficients for selected ASEAN within PMG ARDL

Variable/ country	Cointeq01	D(FDI)	D(GCF)	D(TOP)	D(UNEMP)	D(EXR)	D(INF)	GFC	COVID-19	*C*
Brunei	−0.280** (0.0010)	−0.026* (0.40450	0.005* (0.3909)	−10.241* (0.8164)	−0.842* (0.2870)	−11.081* (0.8911)	−0.621** (0.0030)	−2.071* (0.3577)	−0.993* (0.6970)	−2.20* (0.3598)
Cambodia	−0.955** (0.0000)	0.238** (0.0183)	−0.011* (0.7071)	15.592* (0.7960)	0.865* (0.8147)	−0.001** (0.0011)	0.057** (0.0106)	1.338* (0.7309)	−7.621** (0.0286)	−0.598* (0.4221)
Indonesia	−1.557** (0.0000)	−0.179** (0.0048)	−0.134** (0.0005)	4.715*(0.6864)	−0.243* (0.0932)	−0.0003** (0.0000)	0.027** (0.0064)	1.287** (0.0245)	−5.835** (0.0004)	−3.062* (0.6597)
Malaysia	−0.850** (0.0000)	0.335** (0.0007)	0.326** (0.0002)	4.144* (0.6462)	−4.950** (0.0032)	2.484* (0.0853)	0.089** (0.0075)	1.565** (0.0485)	−1.789* (0.1610)	−2.863** (0.0171)
Philippines	−1.107** (0.0003)	0.676* (0.0987)	0.371** (0.0136)	27.103* (0.8816)	−0.272* (0.937)	−0.400** (0.0005)	−0.032* (0.6311)	0.551* (0.8766)	−6.278* (0.2261)	−1.858* (0.2183)
Singapore	−1.317** (0.0001)	0.190** (0.0011)	−0.019* (0.7574)	−2.786* (0.8851)	−0.629* (0.7354)	−25.35* (0.9358)	1.164** (0.0424)	−7.327* (0.5459)	1.726* (0.8430)	−14.863* (0.2885)
Thailand	−1.087** (0.0000)	0.719** (0.0021)	−0.018* (0.7075)	−0.098* (0.9975)	−1.972* (0.3743)	−0.445** (0.0021)	0.068* (0.2504)	−1.387* (0.3447)	−5.743* (0.0999)	−4.727** (0.0328)
Vietnam	−0.995** (0.0000)	0.658** (0.0000)	−0.148** (0.0002)	−2.583** (0.0335)	−0.065* (0.1534)	6.460** (0.0000)	0.058** (0.0000)	−3.579** (0.0065)	−4.433** (0.0000)	−2.204* (0.2797)

Note: ** and *denote significance at the 5 percent and 10% levels, respectively

Note: *FDI*, foreign direct investment; *GCF*, gross capital formation; *TOP*, trade openness; *UNEMP*, unemployment rate; *EXR*, exchange rate; *INF*, inflation rate; *GFC*, global financial crisis; *COVID-19*, COVID-19 pandemic

results indicated significant relationships between these variables and economic growth, with asterisks denoting statistical significance. For example, in Brunei, the coefficient of D(TOP) −10.241 is statistically significant at 10% level (indicated by *).

2.5 Conclusion Remarks, Policy Recommendation, and Limitations

This study analyzed the economic impact of FDI inflows, GCF, and TOP in ASEAN-8 countries, accounting for other key macroeconomic variables from 2000 to 2023. Although this study is limited by data availability for certain ASEAN countries, specifically Lao People's Democratic Republic (PDR) and Myanmar, and the constraints of the chosen econometric models, the findings remain significant. The P-ARDL analysis confirms that FDI and TOP are essential drivers of the economic growth in the ASEAN countries. Overall, the results from both the panel regression and ARDL analyses align with theoretical perspectives and previous studies.

The use of panel fixed effects and random effects models shows a strong association between increases in FDI and TOP and higher per capita GDP. However, the COVID-19 pandemic has had profound detrimental effects on economic stability. The GCF as a percentage of GDP, currency devaluation (EXR), consumer price inflation, UNEMP, and the global financial crisis did not significantly affect economic growth during the study period. We found that GCF and TOP continue to positively influence economic growth in the long run, whereas FDI has a positive short-term effect, but less impact over time. Currency devaluation, unemployment, and inflation rates are insignificant in both terms. We found that the negative impact of the pandemic was more severe than that of the Global Financial Crisis.

Based on these findings, ASEAN countries should focus on several key areas to boost their economic growth. First, they should increase their FDI by offering tax incentives and simplifying the regulatory processes to attract foreign capital. Furthermore, they can also expand their TOP. It can be deduced that reducing trade barriers and promoting trade agreements can help integrate ASEAN economies deeper into the global market. Moreover, investing in GCF through infrastructure and capital projects supports long-term growth, and strengthening healthcare systems is important to build resilience against future crises. Finally, encouraging innovation and diversification will support sustainable economic growth and contribute to achieving the Sustainable Development Goal 8.1.

This study has several limitations. First, the data were incomplete for certain ASEAN countries, specifically Lao PDR and Myanmar. This data gap may affect the generalizability of the findings and their applicability to all ASEAN countries. Second, the choice of econometric model used in the analysis may have influenced the robustness and reliability of the results. Different models and methodologies may provide alternative insights into the relationships examined. Third, the study does not specify the sources of FDI inflows or the interest rates associated with projects connected to these inflows. This lack of detail could affect the interpretation of the influence of FDI on economic growth. Finally, the focus on specific crises, namely, the COVID-19 pandemic and the GFC, may not fully capture other external shocks or policy changes that could affect economic growth in the selected ASEAN countries. Future research should thus aim to improve this by using more complete data, different econometric models, and clarifying FDI sources and interest rates. Additionally, incorporating a wider array of external shocks and policy changes could offer a deeper understanding of the ASEAN economic development dynamics.

References

Aashiq FP, Sharma G (2023) Impact of foreign direct investment on BRICS countries economic growth. Int J Res Appl Sci Eng Technol 11:2272–2281. https://doi.org/10.22214/ijraset.2023.49972

Ai-Jun G, Mohsin AKM, Ahmed SF et al (2024) Exploring the nexus between FDI inflows and economic growth: a sectoral level analysis. PLoS One 19:13–17. https://doi.org/10.1371/journal.pone.0301220

ASEAN (2020) Economic impact of Covid-19 outbreak on ASEAN. Jakarta

ASEAN Secretariat (2012) Cebu declaration on the acceleration of the establishment of an ASEAN community by 2015. https://asean.org/cebu-declaration-on-th-acceleration-of-the-establishment-of-an-asean-community-by-2015/. Accessed 7 Oct 2019

ASEAN Secretariat (2014) About ASEAN. https://asean.org/about-us/. Accessed 1 Oct 2024

ASEAN Secretariat (2019) ASEAN integration report 2019. Jakarta, Indonesia

Asian Development Bank (2023) Asian Development Outlook September 2023 - Southeast Asia. Manila

Bakpa EK, Yeboah JA (2024) The role of foreign direct investment on Ghana's economic growth: a Durbin Watson analysis. Afr J Econ Sustain Dev 7:197–208. https://doi.org/10.52589/ajesd-bq9gapya

Ben Abdallah A (2024) The relationship between trade openness, foreign direct investment inflows, and economic growth in middle east and north of Africa region: autoregressive distributed lag model vs. vector error correction model. J Knowl Econ 15:1118–1141. https://doi.org/10.1007/s13132-023-01099-x

Budhia D, Kaur TP (2029) Foreign direct investment led economic growth: an analysis of BRICS economies using panel data. World Rev Entrep Manag Sustain Dev 19:379–388

Chude NP, Chude DI (2023) Effect of international capital inflows on economic growth of Nigeria. Int J Innov Sci Eng Technol 10:112–125. https://doi.org/10.51386/25815946/ijsms-v2i1p102

D'Aloia F, Gugler P (2024) Impact of Covid-19 on the economic growth of ASEAN countries: convergence or divergence? Int J Glob Bus Compet 19:83–95. https://doi.org/10.1007/s42943 024 00098-2

Epor SO, Yua H, Terhemba Iorember P (2024) Foreign direct investment and economic growth in developing countries: the role of international trade and foreign debt. Mod Finance 2:1–17. https://doi.org/10.61351/mf.v2i1.87

Foss NJ (1998) The new growth theory: some intellectual growth accounting. J Econ Methodol 5:223–246. https://doi.org/10.1080/13501789800000014

Ghazalian PL (2024) Does economic growth attract FDI inflows? A dynamic panel analysis. Economies 12:1–19. https://doi.org/10.3390/economies12010001

Hakim DR, Budi S (2024) Governance and economic growth: the mediating role of FDI inflows. Inst Econ 16:1–25. https://doi.org/10.22452/IJIE.vol16no3.1

Hicklin J, Robinson D, Singh A (1997) Macroeconomic issues facing ASEAN countries. International Monetary Fund, Washington, DC

Hossain MK, Hossain MS (2023) Causal interaction between foreign direct investment inflows and China's economic growth. Sustainability 15:1–18. https://doi.org/10.3390/su15107994

Hossain R, Roy CK, Akter R (2022) The effects of foreign direct investment and trade openness on economic growth amid crises in Asian economies. Econ J Emerg Mark 14:231–243. https://doi.org/10.20885/ejem.vol14.iss2.art7

Kaddouri N, Benelbar M (2024) The impact of foreign direct investment on economic growth: empirical evidence. Int Res J Finance Econ 73:123–132. https://doi.org/10.22610/imbr.v7i4.1166

Karahan Ö, Çolak O (2024) The causality relationship between foreign direct investment and economic growth in RCEP countries. J Econ Adm Sci 40:95–110. https://doi.org/10.1108/JEAS-04-2022-0112

Ko H (2024) Linear and non-linear regression analysis of trade openness and FDI on economic growth of Myanmar (1990-2022). Inya Econ J 3:58–85

Malik A, Sah AN (2024) Does FDI impact the economic growth of BRICS economies? Evidence from Bayesian VAR. J Risk Financ Manag 17. https://doi.org/10.3390/jrfm17010010

Minh VTH, Trinh PTT (2023) The impact of FDI on economic growth in developing countries: the role of FDI inflow and trade openness. Econ Finance Lett 10:216–229. https://doi.org/10.18488/29.v10i3.3519

Mohamed AN, Abdulle AY (2023) The asymmetric effects of foreign direct investment inflow on economic growth: fresh evidence from Somalia. J Law Sustain Dev 11:1–21. https://doi.org/10.55908/sdgs.v11i7.416

Mose N, Kipchirchir E (2024) Foreign direct investment and economic growth in Kenya: a comprehensive analysis. Asian J Econ Bus Account 24:1–13. https://doi.org/10.9734/ajeba/2024/v24i21215

Mwakabungu BHP, Kauangal J (2023) An empirical analysis of the relationship between FDI and economic growth in Tanzania. Cogent Econ Financ 11. https://doi.org/10.1080/23322039.2023.2204606

Nam H-J, Yu D (2024) Does trade openness promote economic growth in developing countries? J Int Financ Mark Inst Money 93. https://doi.org/10.1016/j.intfin.2024.101985

National Committee of Indonesia's Chairmanship in ASEAN (2023) Interesting facts of the ASEAN region in numbers. https://asean2023.id/en/news/interesting-facts-of-the-asean-region-in-numbers. Accessed 10 Oct 2024

Nwakeze EO, Orajekwe JC, NmaSylvanus A et al (2023) Nexus between foreign direct investment (FDI) and economic growth (EG): a study of 10 countries of the world (2018 - 2022). World J Adv Res Rev 19:1511–1522. https://doi.org/10.30574/wjarr.2023.19.1.1491

Park HM (2005) Linear Regression models for panel data using SAS, STATA, LIMDEP, and SPSS

Pesaran MH, Smith R (1995) Estimating long-run relationships from dynamic heterogeneous panels. Elsevier Science S.A

Pesaran H, Shin Y, Smith RP (1997) Pooled estimation of long-run relationships in dynamic heterogeneous panels. Cambridge

Rahman MM, Saidi K, Ben MM (2020) Economic growth in South Asia: the role of CO_2 emissions, population density and trade openness. Heliyon 6. https://doi.org/10.1016/j.heliyon.2020.e03903

Rashid M, Ansari S, Khan A, Amir M (2023) The impact of FDI and export on economic growth in India: an empirical analysis. Asian J Econ Financ Manag 9:33–41. https://doi.org/10.51386/25815946/ijsms-v6i5p106

Romer PM (1994) The origins of endogenous growth. J Econ Perspect 8:3–22. https://doi.org/10.4324/9780203443965.ch26

Sanusi KA, Eita JH (2023) Trade openness, foreign direct investment and economic growth: case of Southern African Development Community. Cuad Econ 46:64–74
Singh T (2010) Does international trade cause economic growth? A survey. World Econ 33:1517–1564. https://doi.org/10.1111/j.1467-9701.2010.01243.x
Sobirova Y, Jeong JY, ugli Karimov MU, Bekjanov D (2023) Do FDI and trade openness matter for economic growth in CIS countries? Evidence from Panel ARDL. J East-West Bus 29:345–374. https://doi.org/10.1080/10669868.2023.2242854
Sugözü İH, Dorbonova İ (2024) Do FDI and trade openness affect economic growth differently across income groups? Case studies from Asian countries. Selçuk Üniversitesi Sos Bilim Mesl Yüksekokulu Derg 27:308–320. https://doi.org/10.29249/selcuksbmyd.1446206
Temin P (2010) The great recession & the great depression. Daedalus 1:115–124. https://doi.org/10.1162/DAED_a_00048
Vinayak H, Thompson F, Tonby O (2014) Understanding ASEAN: seven things you need to know. McKinsey & Company, New York
Wang W, Xu T, Xiaoyi L, Sun Y (2023) FDI inflows and income inequality: a Schumpeterian economic growth. Int Rev Econ Finance 83:805–820. https://doi.org/10.1016/j.iref.2022.10.023
World Bank (2024) Data. https://data.worldbank.org/. Accessed 10 Oct 2024

Chapter 3
Effects of Structural Reforms on Labor Productivity of Selected Southeast Asian Countries

Hidekatsu Asada

Abstract Structural reforms involve the development of infrastructure and human capital, external openness, efficient and well-developed financial systems, deliberate fiscal policy frameworks, and sound economic institutions that promote competition. Theoretically and empirically, these policy measures have been found to increase productivity growth. The severe economic downturn during the COVID-19 pandemic has amplified the significance of enhancing resilience and ensuring sound economic growth through structural reforms. This study aims to examine the effects of various structural reform measures on productivity growth in Southeast Asian countries, including Indonesia, Malaysia, the Philippines, Thailand, and Vietnam, from 2001 to2019. The effects of the policy measures are examined using the fully modified least squares and dynamic ordinary least squares estimators. The econometric analysis reveals that the effects of these countries' structural reform measures on labor productivity growth are inconclusive. From 2001 to 2019, structural reforms such as infrastructure and financial market development positively contributed to labor productivity growth. Macroeconomic instability and the possible deterioration of public sector governance negatively contributed to labor productivity growth. However, the effect of human capital development remains unclear.

Keywords Structural reforms · Labor productivity · Selected Southeast Asian Countries

H. Asada (✉)
Graduate School of Humanities and Social Sciences, Saitama University, Saitama, Japan
e-mail: asada@mail.saitama-u.ac.jp

© The Author(s), under exclusive license to Springer Nature Singapore Pte Ltd. 2025

H. Taguchi (ed.), *Sustainability of Economic Growth in East Asia*,
New Frontiers in Regional Science: Asian Perspectives 82,
https://doi.org/10.1007/978-981-96-3731-7_3

3.1 Introduction

Countries in Southeast Asia, such as Indonesia, Malaysia, the Philippines, Thailand, and Vietnam, have experienced rapid and dynamic economic growth compared with developed countries and emerging economies. This growth is significantly attributed to structural transformation, which involves shifting resources from low-productivity to high-productivity sectors (McMillan et al. 2014). A critical question is: What elements enabled these Southeast Asian countries to achieve economic development and what policy measures should be prioritized to maintain their growth momentum?

Structural transformation is driven by capital accumulation and technology transfer from advanced countries, embodied in foreign direct investment (FDI). Additionally, reallocating labor to sectors with higher labor productivity, particularly the export-oriented and labor-intensive manufacturing sectors, is crucial to this transformation. An increase in exports contributes to creating a basis for economic growth, which results in easing the constraints of importing advanced intermediate and capital goods.

However, as discussed in the concept of the "middle-income trap" (Gill and Kharas 2007; Kharas and Gill 2020), the effects of accumulating production factors such as capital and labor on economic growth gradually diminish. The positive effects of imported technology and "learning-by-doing" diminish as a country approaches the global technological frontier. These countries need to increase labor productivity to mitigate the negative impacts of diminishing returns on factor inputs. From this perspective, structural reforms aimed at enhancing labor productivity are required to escape the middle-income trap and promote convergence to higher income levels (World Bank 2024).

Another important aspect of labor productivity growth is its contribution to inclusive growth, which promotes a more equitable pattern of economic development. A study of the inclusive growth of Southeast Asian countries reveals that labor productivity growth contributed to reducing inequality through per capita income growth from 1992 to 2019 (Alekhina and Ganelli 2020).

There has been considerable debate regarding desirable policy measures that ensure long-term economic growth. Although no one-size-fits-all policy prescriptions exist, the common goal is to facilitate factor accumulation and alleviate regulatory, institutional, and structural bottlenecks to growth. A growing consensus suggests that structural reforms can improve resource allocation, productivity, and growth. These reforms include the development of infrastructure and human capital, external openness, efficient and well-developed financial systems, deliberate fiscal policy frameworks, and sound economic institutions that promote competition. These policy measures have been found to increase productivity growth (Dabla-Norris et al. 2013).

Governments of Southeast Asian countries have recognized the significance of promoting structural reforms and have taken steps to enhance economic resilience by addressing both supply- and demand-side constraints and strengthening regional cooperation. The establishment of the Association of Southeast Asian Nations

(ASEAN) Economic Community in 2016 initiated a regional program to reduce trade barriers, improve connectivity, enhance competitiveness, improve the regulatory framework, and attract more investment in the region. The severe economic downturn during the COVID-19 pandemic has highlighted the significance of enhancing resilience and ensuring sound economic growth through structural reforms.

Against this backdrop, this study examines the effects of several structural reforms on labor productivity growth in selected Southeast Asian countries. It provides insights into how these structural reform measures have affected productivity growth in countries that have not been well examined. This study reveals that the effects of these countries' structural reform measures are inconclusive. From 2001 to 2019, structural reforms such as infrastructure and financial market development positively contributed to labor productivity growth. Macroeconomic instability and the possible deterioration of public sector governance negatively contribute to labor productivity growth. However, the effect of human capital development remains unclear.

The remainder of this paper is organized as follows. Section 3.2 reviews the literature related to the nexus of structural reforms and labor productivity. Section 3.3 presents the model, methodology, and data, followed by the analysis results in Sect. 3.4. Finally, Sect. 3.5 provides conclusions and policy implications.

3.2 Literature Review

Several studies have identified structural reform as a crucial determinant of labor productivity growth. This reform is achieved by promoting efficient resource allocation such as capital and labor, reducing market rigidities, liberalizing capital flows, and boosting trade (Spilimbergo et al. 2009; Dabla-Norris et al. 2013; Christiansen et al. 2013; Prati et al. 2013; Konté et al. 2021).

Structural reform measures aimed at boosting labor productivity include pro-competition reforms in product markets such as human capital development, infrastructure development, macroeconomic stability, domestic financial system enhancement, and regulatory framework improvement.

Theoretical and empirical studies elucidate the potential determinants of labor productivity growth. These studies highlight human capital development, infrastructure development, inflation, financial sector development, and the quality of the regulatory framework.

3.2.1 Human Capital Development

Human capital development is a crucial driver of growth in endogenous growth theory. It facilitates the development of higher value-added industries by absorbing new technologies and can enhance labor productivity through technological diffusion between firms (Barro 2001). Improving educational attainment is essential for human capital development, as it enhances the capacity to adopt new technologies and facilitates the diffusion of acquired technologies and skills. Empirical evidence suggests that, for developing countries, improving enrolment and the quality of primary and secondary education affects the ability to adapt to advanced technology. However, for countries approaching the technology frontier, tertiary education has a more significant impact on innovation capabilities (Aghion and Howitt 2006). Mankiw et al. (1992) employ the secondary-school enrolment rate as a proxy for the investment rate in human capital. By examining data from 98 developing countries in 1985, they conclude that human capital differences explained 50% of the income differences.

3.2.2 Infrastructure Development

Adequate infrastructure, such as a stable energy supply and well-functioning transportation and telecommunications networks, are essential elements affecting firms' productivity. A higher stock of public capital in infrastructure would increase the productivity of other inputs, such as labor and private capital, through economies of scale, network externalities, and enhanced competition (Agénor and Moreno-Dodson 2006; Dabla-Norris et al. 2013). For developing countries, reducing infrastructure bottlenecks encourages a shift in resources toward more productive sectors.

3.2.3 Macroeconomic Instability (Inflation)

Existing literature argues that greater macroeconomic instability, particularly a higher inflation rate, tends to negatively affect labor productivity growth (Miller and Upadhyay 2000; Berument et al. 2011; Loko and Diouf 2009). A higher inflation rate is detrimental to allocative efficiency, thereby reducing productivity. By contrast, low and stable inflation encourages long-term investment by fostering confidence in the real value of nominal assets and reducing the uncertainty surrounding returns on productive investment, which is an essential source of productivity growth. Furthermore, low and stable inflation could contribute to financial sector stability and, consequently, macroeconomic stability. It also facilitates the maintenance of low long-term nominal interest rates, thereby reducing the costs of long-term investments. Stable inflation also reduces the risk for financial intermediaries holding long-term nominal assets.

3.2.4 *Financial Sector Development*

Both theoretical and empirical studies suggest a positive interaction between financial development and productivity growth, emphasizing that the development of financial markets is a critical and inextricable element of the growth process (Levine 2004). Financial sector development enables channel savings and spurs more efficient allocation of capital across firms and industries. Additionally, it expands access to credit by lowering costs, enabling firms to finance new capital goods, adopt new technologies, and promote innovation. It also enables effective risk management and diversification (Levine et al. 2000; Gehringer 2014; Heil 2017).

3.2.5 *Quality of Regulatory Framework*

Recent studies on economic development have emphasized the importance of improving public sector governance to promote productivity and long-term growth (Acemoglu et al. 2014). Improving regulatory frameworks contributes to productivity growth through several channels. First, streamlining unnecessary regulations improves allocative efficiency by encouraging competition and reducing economic rents. Second, enhanced competition increases production efficiency. With increased competition, firms are compelled to allocate underutilized resources such as capital and labor more efficiently. Finally, promoting competition incentivizes dynamic efficiency by encouraging innovation to reduce production costs (Loko and Diouf 2009; Konté et al. 2021).

Structural reform encompasses various policy measures. Practically, these measures are implemented holistically, for example, following a country's development planning. Nonetheless, numerous studies have examined the impact of structural reform measures in isolation, concentrating on trade and investment liberalization, financial sector reform, human capital development, and institutional reform.

Studies examining the impact of these measures on labor productivity in emerging countries, particularly in Southeast Asia, from a holistic perspective, remain limited. For example, Dabla-Norris et al. (2016) examine the impact of structural reform measures, such as banking systems, trade reforms, institutions, agricultural sectors, business regulations, and the labor market, on labor productivity in 108 emerging and developing countries from 1970 to 2011. They conclude that the impact of these reforms depends on the income levels of the countries. Lower-income countries benefit the most from trade and investment liberalization and agricultural sector reforms, such as the removal of price controls. For emerging market economies, larger productivity gains result from improvements in the efficiency of banking systems, capital market development, and improving the business environment. Konté et al. (2021) examine the effects of structural reform measures, including trade, product market, and financial sector reforms, in 30 developing countries from 1975 to 2015. They demonstrate that financial sector reform had greater effects on labor productivity growth than trade and product market reforms.

Drawing on the aforementioned literature, this study examines the effects of structural reform measures on labor productivity growth in some selected Southeast Asian countries from 2001 to 2019.

3.3 Model, Methodology, and Data

3.3.1 *Model Specification*

This study examines the impact of various structural factors, such as FDI, trade openness, human capital development, infrastructure development, and regulatory reform, on the labor productivity growth of some selected Southeast Asian countries from 2001 to 2019. The analysis includes five countries: Indonesia, the Philippines, Malaysia, Thailand, and Vietnam. Following previous studies such as Prati et al. (2013) and Konté et al. (2021), the model for the empirical analysis is specified in Eq. (3.1):

$$\begin{aligned} \ln LP_{it} &= \alpha_1 + \alpha_2 \ln HRD_{it} + \alpha_3 INFL_{it} + \alpha_4 \ln INFRA_{it} \\ &+ \alpha_5 \ln FDV_{it} + \alpha_6 \ln GOV_{it} + \varepsilon_{it} \end{aligned} \tag{3.1}$$

where *LP* is labor productivity. *HRD* refers to human capital development. *INFL* is the inflation rate as a proxy for macroeconomic stability. *INFRA* refers to infrastructure development. *FDV* represents financial sector development. *GOV* represents the quality of governance. ε is the error term. The subscripts i and t denote country and year, respectively. *ln* is the natural logarithm.

To examine the long-term relationship among the variables, the model is estimated using the panel fully modified ordinary least squares (FMOLS) proposed by Phillips and Moon (1999) and the panel dynamic ordinary least squares (DOLS) proposed by Kao and Chiang (2000). These methods correct for endogeneity and serial correlation in the cointegrating regressions, thereby providing unbiased estimates of the cointegrating coefficients.

3.3.2 *Data and Descriptive Statistics*

The variables for the analysis are as follows. Labor productivity (*LP*): LP is defined as the annual value-added per hour worked, calculated as real GDP divided by total work hours. The GDP data are for the 2019 constant prices. Data on man-hour labor productivity are sourced from the APO Productivity Database 2020 Version 1 provided by the Asian Productivity Organization.

Human capital development (*HRD*): Human capital development is measured using the gross secondary education enrolment rate. Secondary education is a critical step to the education ladder because it lays the foundation for access to higher educational opportunities. Data are obtained from the World Bank's World Development Indicators.

Infrastructure development (*INFRA*): Annual electricity generation is used as a proxy for infrastructure development because its supply is critical to firm productivity (Straub 2008). The data are obtained from the EIA energy database.

Inflation rate (*INFL*): The annual inflation rate is used as a proxy for macroeconomic stability, as discussed in Sect. 3.2. Data are obtained from the World Bank's World Development Indicators.

Financial development (*FDV*): To measure financial development, the International Monetary Fund's financial development index is applied. The index is a relative ranking of countries' financial institutions and financial markets in terms of depth (size and liquidity), access (the ability of individuals and firms to access financial services), and efficiency (the ability of financial institutions to provide financial services at a low cost with sustainable revenue and the level of capital market activity) (Svirydzenka 2016).

Quality of public sector governance *(GOV)*: The regulatory quality index of the World Bank's Worldwide Governance Indicators (WGI) provides data on the quality of public sector governance in industrial and developing countries. The data for the WGI are obtained by summarizing the views of a large number of enterprises, citizens, and expert survey respondents on the quality of governance. The regulatory quality index in the WGI captures perceptions of the government's ability to formulate and implement sound policies and regulations that permit and promote private sector development (Kaufmann et al. 2010).

These data are presented in Tables 3.1 and 3.2 presents the correlations between the variables.

3.3.3 Panel Unit Root Tests

Panel unit root tests are conducted to examine the stationarity of the variables, with the null hypothesis that a series has a unit root. Four different tests are conducted: the Levin, Lin, and Chu (LLC) test (2002), which assumes a common unit root process; the Im, Pesaran, and Shin (IPS) test (2003); Fisher-ADF test (Maddala and Wu 1999); and Fisher-PP test (Maddala and Wu 1999), which assume individual unit root processes. The results of these tests are listed in Table 3.3. At this level, not all the variables are stationary. However, after taking the first difference, all

Table 3.1 Descriptive statistics

	lnLP	*lnHRD*	*lnINFRA*	*INFL*	*lnFDV*	*lnGOV*
Mean	4.250	4.400	4.733	0.042	−0.840	3.870
Median	4.016	4.407	4.788	0.035	−0.994	3.950
Maximum	5.445	4.875	5.648	0.208	−0.301	4.330
Minimum	3.253	4.041	3.421	−0.009	−1.309	3.041
Std. Dev.	0.697	0.150	0.495	0.035	0.316	0.334

Note: Observation numbers are 95. *ln* is the natural logarithm of each variable

Table 3.2 Correlations between variables

	lnLP	*lnHRD*	*lnINFRA*	*INFL*	*lnFDV*	*lnGOV*
lnLP	1.000	0.544	0.044	−0.287	0.020	0.320
lnHRD	0.544	1.000	0.483	−0.427	0.417	0.462
lnINFRA	0.044	0.483	1.000	−0.144	0.337	0.276
INFL	−0.287	−0.427	−0.144	1.000	−0.461	−0.562
lnFDV	0.020	0.417	0.337	−0.461	1.000	0.694
lnGOV	0.320	0.462	0.276	−0.562	0.694	1.000

Note: *ln* is the natural logarithm of each variable

Table 3.3 Results of the panel unit root tests

Variables	LLC	IPS	Fisher-ADF	Fisher-PP
Level				
lnLP	0.661	3.515	1.151	1.149
lnHRD	−5.392***	−1.818**	20.010**	19.102**
lnINFRA	−3.032***	−0.271	17.241	34.708***
INFL	−5.195***	−4.136***	34.767***	34.428***
lnFDV	−2.486***	−0.979	12.068	10.182
lnGOV	−0.919	−1.165	14.961	14.026
First difference				
lnLP	−7.028***	−6.208***	51.813***	58.924***
lnHRD	−5.040***	−5.302***	44.750***	62.114***
lnINFRA	−10.078***	−10.078***	84.032***	74.169***
INFL	−11.271***	−10.384***	88.574***	291.608***
lnFDV	−9.753***	−8.780***	73.990***	110.661***
lnGOV	−7.393***	−7.678***	64.560***	57.438***

Note: Tests are conducted using individual intercepts and no trends. *** and ** denote rejection of the null hypothesis of non-stationary at the significance level at 1% and 5%, respectively. Schwarz's Bayesian criterion is used to select the lag length

variables become stationary, as the null hypothesis is rejected at the 1% significance level. Because all the variables are integrated in order one or $I(1)$, cointegration is tested as a prerequisite for the FMOLS and DOLS methodologies.

3.3.4 Cointegration Test

This section examines the long-run relationships among the variables using panel cointegration tests. The Pedroni cointegration test (Pedroni 2004) is performed using within-dimension (panel cointegration) and between-dimension (mean panel) tests, allowing for heterogeneity in the panel both in the short-run dynamics and long-run slope and intercept coefficients. The panel cointegration tests comprising panel v-statistics, panel rho-statistics, panel PP-statistics, and panel ADF-statistics are based on pooling and averaging the test statistics for cointegration across the

Table 3.4 Pedroni residual cointegration test

3.4-1 Within-dimension

			Weighted	
	Statistic	*p*-value	Statistic	*p*-value
Panel v-Statistic	0.254	0.400	−0.208	0.582
Panel rho-Statistic	1.665	0.952	0.975	0.835
Panel PP-Statistic	−2.633	0.004	−4.174	0.000
Panel ADF-Statistic	−3.106	0.001	−4.269	0.000

3.4-2 Between-dimension

	Statistic	*p*-value
Group rho-Statistic	2.127	0.983
Group PP-Statistic	−4.056	0.000
Group ADF-Statistic	−4.282	0.000

Table 3.5 Kao residual cointegration test

	Statistic	*p*-value
ADF	−3.239	0.000

within-dimensions of the panel. Additionally, four other values of the same tests are computed as weighted statistics. The mean panel tests comprising the group rho-statistic, group PP-statistic, and group ADF-statistic are based on pooling the regression residuals along the between-dimension of the panel.

The results of the Pedroni cointegration test are presented in Table 3.4. Most tests (6 out of 11) rejected the null hypothesis of no cointegration. These results confirm that the variables in the model are cointegrated in the long run.

Additionally, the Kao residual cointegration test (Kao 1999), which assumes homogeneous coefficients (i.e., the relationship between the variables is the same across all cross-sections), is conducted. The results are summarized in Table 3.5. These results conform to those of the Pedroni cointegration test.

3.4 Results of the Analysis

Table 3.6 presents the results of the FMOLS and DOLS estimations of the impact of various structural factors on labor productivity growth in the selected Southeast Asian countries. In both the FMOLS and DOLS models, infrastructure and financial market development positively contributed to labor productivity growth. These findings are consistent with the theoretical framework and empirical studies reviewed in Sect. 3.2. The inflation rate negatively contributed to labor productivity growth, indicating that macroeconomic instability from 2001 to 2019 hindered labor

Table 3.6 Results of FMOLS and DOLS estimations

	FMOLS	DOLS
lnHRD	0.168 (0.115)	0.168 (0.261)
lnINFRA	0.452*** (0.000)	0509*** (0.000)
INFL	−0.811*** (0.001)	−1.037** (0.013)
lnFDV	0.481*** (0.000)	0.319** (0.022)
lnGOV	−0.204*** (0.009)	−0.167*** (0.003)

Note: *p*-values are in parentheses. *, **, and *** denote rejection of the null hypothesis of non-stationary at the significance level at 10%, 5%, and 1%, respectively

productivity growth. This is consistent with the existing studies, as reviewed in Sect. 3.2. Additionally, the impact of the quality of governance on labor productivity growth is negative. This result could imply a deterioration in the quality of governance across countries in this period. However, the effect of human capital development remains unclear.

3.5 Conclusion

This study aims to provide insights into the effects of various structural reform measures on productivity growth in Southeast Asian countries, including Indonesia, Malaysia, the Philippines, Thailand, and Vietnam, from 2001 to 2019. The effects of the policy measures were examined using the FMOLS and DOLS estimators.

The econometric analysis reveals that the effects of these countries' structural reform measures on labor productivity growth are inconclusive. From 2001 to 2019, structural reforms such as infrastructure and financial market development positively contributed to labor productivity growth. However, the effect of human capital development remains unclear. Macroeconomic instability and the possible deterioration of public sector governance negatively contributed to labor productivity growth.

These results confirm that a holistic plan for structural reform measures and firm implementation is necessary to achieve further labor productivity growth in Southeast Asian countries. Labor productivity in Southeast Asian countries grew by 3.0% on average annually from 1971 to 2018. A significant portion of labor productivity growth in these countries was attributable to capital deepening, while contributions of total factor productivity and human capital were relatively limited (The ASEAN Secretariat 2021b).

The governments of Southeast Asian countries have recognized the significance of promoting structural reforms to shift their growth patterns from being led by factor accumulation to being driven by productivity growth. Therefore, these countries have adopted region-wide collective actions to boost productivity. Beginning in 2016, the ASEAN Economic Community has implemented a regional program to further reduce trade barriers, improve connectivity, enhance competitiveness, improve the regulatory framework, and attract more investment in the region. The program's orientation is consistent with the theoretical framework, advocating the benefits of structural reforms. However, in assessing the ASEAN Secretariat, the implementation of the program was not sufficient, prompting the need for accelerated policy measures (The ASEAN Secretariat 2021a).

Existing literature argues that the sectoral effects of structural reforms are heterogeneous (Helble et al. 2019; Konté et al. 2021). Future studies could expand this analysis to examine the impact of structural reform measures on a sectoral basis, such as agriculture, manufacturing, and services. This analysis would further offer insight into the effects of policy measures and guide the policy priorities of countries in the Southeast Asian region.

References

Acemoglu D, Gallego FA, Robinson JA (2014) Institutions, human capital, and development. Annu Rev Econ 6:875–912. https://doi.org/10.1146/annurev-economics-080213-041119

Agénor PR, Moreno-Dodson B (2006) Public infrastructure and growth: new channels and policy implications. World Bank Policy Research Working Paper 4064(November)

Aghion P, Howitt P (2006) Appropriate growth policy: a unifying framework. J Eur Econ Assoc 4(2–3):269–314. https://doi.org/10.1162/jeea.2006.4.2-3.269

Alekhina V, Ganelli G (2020) Determinants of inclusive growth in ASEAN. IMF Working Papers 20(118). https://doi.org/10.5089/9781513549194.001

Barro RJ (2001) Human capital and growth. Am Econ Rev 91(2)

Berument H, Dincer NN, Mustafaoglu Z (2011) Total factor productivity and macroeconomic instability. J Int Trade Econ Dev 20(5):605–629. https://doi.org/10.1080/09638190903365930

Christiansen L, Schindler M, Tressel T (2013) Anchoring growth: the Schindler, and T. Tressel. Growth and structural reforms: a new assessment. J Int Econ 89(2):347–356. https://doi.org/10.1016/j.jinteco.2012.07.008

Dabla-Norris E, Giang H, Kalpana K, Annette K, Robert T (2013) Anchoring growth: the importance of productivity-enhancing reforms in emerging market and developing economies. International Monetary Fund Staff Discussion Note 13(08)

Dabla-Norris E, Ho G, Kyobe A (2016) Structural reforms and productivity growth in emerging market and developing economies. IMF Working Papers 16(15). https://doi.org/10.5089/9781498306560.001

Gehringer A (2014) Financial liberalization financial development and productivity growth—an overview. Int J Monet Econ Finance 7(1):40–65. https://doi.org/10.1504/IJMEF.2014.063841

Gill I, Kharas H (2007) An east Asian renaissance: ideas for economic growth. World Bank

Heil M (2017) Finance and productivity: a literature review OECD economics department working papers 1374, vol 1374. OECD Economics Department Working Papers. Organisation for Economic Co-operation and Development. https://doi.org/10.1787/41194fea-en

Helble M, Trinh L, Le T (2019) Sectoral and skill contributions to labor productivity in Asia. ADBI Working Paper Series, 929 (March). https://doi.org/10.2139/ssrn.3374794

Im KS, Pesaran MH, Shin Y (2003) Testing for unit roots in heterogeneous panels. J Econ 115(1):53–74. https://doi.org/10.1016/S0304-4076(03)00092-7

Kao C (1999) Spurious regression and residual-based tests for cointegration in panel data. J Econ 90(1):1–44. https://doi.org/10.1016/S0304-4076(98)00023-2

Kao C, Chiang MH (2000) On the estimation and inference of a cointegrated regression in panel data. In: Advances in econometrics, vol 45. Emerald Publishing

Kaufmann D, Kraay A, Mastruzzi M (2010) The worldwide governance indicators: methodology and analytical issues. World Bank Policy Research Working Paper, 5430 (September). http://documents1.worldbank.org/curated/en/630421468336563314/pdf/WPS5430.pdf

Kharas H, Gill IS (2020) Growth strategies to avoid the middle-income trap. Duke Global Working Paper, no. Paper 17 (January). https://doi.org/10.2139/ssrn.3526261

Konté M, Kouamé WA, Mensah EB (2021) Structural reforms and productivity growth in developing countries: intra- or inter-reallocation channel? Policy Research Working Papers. The World Bank. https://doi.org/10.1596/1813-9450-9733

Levin A, Lin CF, Chu CSJ (2002) Unit root tests in panel data: asymptotic and finite-sample properties. J Econ 108(1):1–24

Levine R (2004) Finance and growth: theory and evidence 10766. NBER working paper. National Bureau of Economic Research, Cambridge, MA. https://doi.org/10.3386/w10766

Levine R, Beck T, Maksimovic V (2000) Financial structure and economic development: firm, industry, and country evidence. Policy research working papers. The World Bank. https://doi.org/10.1596/1813-9450-2423

Loko B, Diouf MA (2009) Revisiting the determinants of productivity growth: what's new? IMF Working Papers 09(225). https://doi.org/10.5089/9781451873726.001

Maddala GS, Wu S (1999) A comparative study of unit root tests with panel data and a new simple test

Mankiw NG, Romer D, Weil DN (1992) A contribution to the empirics of economic growth. Q J Econ 107(2):407–437

McMillan M, Rodrik D, Verduzco-Gallo Í (2014) Globalization, structural change, and productivity growth, with an update on Africa. World Dev Forum 63(November):11–32. https://doi.org/10.1016/j.worlddev.2013.10.012

Miller SM, Upadhyay MP (2000) The effects of openness, trade orientation, and human capital on total factor productivity. J Dev Econ 63(2):399–423. https://doi.org/10.1016/S0304-3878(00)00112-7

Pedroni P (2004) Panel cointegration: asymptotic and finite sample properties of pooled time series tests with an application to the PPPP hypothesis. Econ Theory 20(03). https://doi.org/10.1017/S0266466604203073

Phillips PCB, Moon HR (1999) Linear regression limit theory for nonstationary panel data. Econometrica 67(5):1057–1111. https://doi.org/10.1111/1468-0262.00070

Prati A, Onorato MG, Papageorgiou C (2013) Which reforms work and under what institutional environment? Evidence from a new data set on structural reforms. Rev Econ Stat 95(3):946–968. https://doi.org/10.1162/REST_a_00307

Spilimbergo A, Prati A, Ostry JD (2009) Structural reforms and economic performance in advanced and developing countries. Occasional Papers. International Monetary Fund, Washington, D.C. https://doi.org/10.5089/9781589068186.084

Straub S (2008) Infrastructure and growth in developing countries: recent advances and research challenges. Policy research working papers. The World Bank. https://doi.org/10.1596/1813-9450-4460

Svirydzenka K (2016) Introducing a new broad-based index of financial development. IMF Working Papers 16(05). https://doi.org/10.5089/9781513583709.001

The ASEAN Secretariat (2021a) Mid-term review: ASEAN economic community blueprint 2025. The ASEAN Secretariat. https://asean.org/launched-asean-mid-term-review-of-the-aec-blueprint-2025/

The ASEAN Secretariat (2021b) Regional study on labour productivity in ASEAN. The ASEAN Secretariat. https://asean.org/regional-study-on-labour-productivity-in-asean/

World Bank (2024) World development report 2024. Washington, DC

Chapter 4
The Progress of the Division of Labor in the Automobile Industry in the ASEAN Region in the Post-COVID-19 Era

Kenji Nozaki

Abstract This study aims to clarify the progress of the division of labor in the automobile industry within the context of the Association of Southeast Asian Nations (ASEAN) region, assess the effects of the advancement of the economic integration in this region, and discuss the effects of the COVID-19 pandemic. This study confirmed that intra-regional trade of parts and components in the transportation industry in ASEAN increased and raised its share of total trades with progress of ASEAN economic integration. Although the share is stable in recent years, not only Thailand and Indonesia, which are main automobile assembler, but also the Philippines and Vietnam export their goods into the region. When observing detailed information of parts and components item, specific characteristics are found. Although there are some differences, key components such as engines and some other items are exported from core automobile assembler, Indonesia and Thailand. However, some other items are mutually exported inside ASEAN. In this case, even the Philippines, which is a lagged automobile assembler, exports parts and components to Indonesia and Thailand. These facts are supported by two different ideas. In general, progress of economic integration has facilitated regional procurement of parts. However, we should consider the protectionist policy measures in the Philippines, and Vietnam may support the parts industry in these countries. Further study would be necessary. As for the influence of pandemic by COVID-19, the negative impact of pandemic seems to have been more serious than other main automobile assembler, such as Japan, the United States, and China. However, in the post-pandemic years, production in ASEAN recovered and the intra-regional trade in parts and components in automobile industry, at least strengthening of division of labor continues and no negative change is observed.

Keywords Division of labor · Automobile industry · ASEAN region

---

K. Nozaki (✉)
Faculty of Economics, Takasaki City University of Economics, Takasaki, Gunma, Japan

© The Author(s), under exclusive license to Springer Nature Singapore Pte Ltd. 2025

H. Taguchi (ed.), *Sustainability of Economic Growth in East Asia*,
New Frontiers in Regional Science: Asian Perspectives 82,
https://doi.org/10.1007/978-981-96-3731-7_4

4.1 Introduction

This paper firstly aims to clarify the progress of the division of labor in the automobile industry within the context of the Association of Southeast Asian Nations (ASEAN) region. The second purpose of this paper is to assess the effects of the advancement of the economic integration in this region. In addition to that, the author tries to discuss the effects of the COVID-19 pandemic.

Although the circumstances of the automobile industry in ASEAN countries are changing with the progress and increasing popularity of electric vehicles (EV), the automobile industry remains key for industrialization. For example, the 13th National Economic and Social Development Plan (2023–2027) of Thailand admits that the automobile industry continues to be important at the national level, albeit it also emphasizes the necessity of the industry to shift toward new pathways and newer technology focused on EVs. Under such policy directions, the conventional automobile industry can be understood as being a first target of industrialization. In addition, although the conventional engines should be substituted by electric technology, many automotive parts can be utilized for EV production. Considering that ASEAN countries are in different stages of development of EV technology, we can look at automobile production in the context of regional economic integration.

The ASEAN Economic Community (AEC) was established in the end of 2015 to promote the economic integration of ASEAN countries, while the ASEAN Trade in Goods Agreement (ATIGA) was founded in 2009 to advance regional good trade agreements under the ASEAN Free Trade Agreement (AFTA), which in turn started in 1992. Regarding tariff reductions, which is often a key process for economic integration, almost all tariff barriers were eliminated in the region in 2018, including among latecomer ASEAN countries. Both the importance of the automobile industry for the ASEAN region as a whole and the recent progress of the AEC render this study, which attempts to measure the effects of regional production integration (i.e., division of labor of production) surrounding the automobile industry, meaningful.

The remainder of this chapter is structured as follows. Section 4.2 focuses on reviewing the recent literature and analytical measures used in the study. Section 4.3 comprises three subsections (i.e., automobile production in ASEAN countries; trade in the transportation sector; details of automobile components and parts) and the main portion of the text, describing the major results of the analyses. Section 4.4 discusses and concludes the study.

4.2 Literature Review and Data

4.2.1 Theoretical Research

Various empirical studies have used the Grubel and Lloyd Index (GL-index), developed by Grubel and Lloyd (1971), to measure the progress of intra-regional trade. The GL-index is expressed as follows,

$$\mathrm{GL}_i = \frac{(X_i + M_i) - |X_i - M_i|}{X_i + M_i}.$$

where X_i presents the exports of a country to a partner country for item i, and M_i represents the imports from the partner country. The GL-index runs from 0 to 1; when there is no intra-industrial trade, the score is 0, while active mutual intra-industrial trade leads to scores close to 1. Importantly, the GL-index is influenced by aggregation affects, as delineated by Greenaway and Milner (1983), implying the need to collect data that is as detailed as possible. When we find mutual trades in some items of a given industry, we need to first grasp whether the phenomenon involves the horizontal or the vertical division of labor. Greenaway et al. (1995) suggests a way to analyze trade figures using unit prices; specifically, if the gap in unit prices of each exporting good is within 25% (either positive or negative), the transaction represents a horizontal division of labor, while if it is over 25%, it represents a vertical division of labor. However, we should also pay attention when observing items with similar unit prices. For example, if the investigation is about a finalized car (e.g., passenger car or a light commercial vehicle (LCV)), it represents a horizontal division of labor, whereas a discussion about car parts and components will imply differences in the details of the specifications of the product or in the remaining aggregation affects.

4.2.2 Empirical Research

Shimizu (2011) analyzed the automobile industry in the ASEAN region since the 1980s. This cited author describes that the progress of economic integration among ASEAN countries led to the concentration of automobile production in Thailand and Indonesia, while the production of specific automobile parts and components also became concentrated in these countries, and a mutual procurement process started taking place among Thailand and Indonesia. The consequence was, according to Shimizu (2011), that transmission production (e.g., car gearbox) already started to take place in the Philippines in the 1980s. The cited author then described two possibilities for furthering regional economic integration, as follows: the first was for each country to develop the production of specific automobile parts utilizing each their own relative competitive advantages; the second was concentrating the production of car parts in Thailand and Indonesia, considering that automobile assemblers are already concentrated in these two countries and that supporting industries would be established close to their parent firms. Shimizu (2011) also suggested that economic partnerships between ASEAN countries and other countries/regions would influence the parts procurement structure.

Shimizu continued to advance the idea initiated in Shimizu (2011) in a subsequent study (Shimizu 2019), proposing that the emergence of the Comprehensive and Progressive Agreement for Trans-Pacific Partnership (CPTPP), Regional Comprehensive Economic Partnership (RCEP), and other multilateral economic integration plans require us to consider influences from outside the ASEAN region. Meanwhile, among ASEAN countries, the Philippines and Vietnam—considered latecomers in automobile production—introduced protectionism measures, the first with the 2016 Comprehensive Automotive Resurgence Strategy (CARS) Program focused on promoting domestic automobile production and the latter by introducing non-tariff measures to protect domestic automobile assembling (i.e., after the elimination of tariffs to ASEAN members in 2018). Although these measures conflicted with the economic integration project in the ASEAN region, foreign direct investments for automobile parts industry were induced to invest to both countries. It is because automobile assemblers should procure substantial amounts of parts within these two countries in order to make them local product under the local content criteria. In light of these discussions, Shimizu (2019) suggested two possibilities for the automobile parts industry in the ASEAN region, as follows: the first is to promote regional economic integration through concentrating the automobile parts industry within Thailand and Indonesia, seeing that automobile assembly processes and firms already concentrates in both countries; the second is to increase parts production in the Philippines and Vietnam, which have their protection measures in place. Other studies also provide suggestions. For instance, Sukegawa (2021) pointed that even if the tariffs were eliminated in the ASEAN region, the non-tariff measures in Vietnam entail that liberalization in the country will not really progress and that the economic integration of ASEAN countries with other countries and multilateral organizations (e.g., RCEP) should be considered.

Kobayashi (2016, 2018) probed into the production and trade of automobile parts with a focus on the Philippines and Vietnam, which have an inferior competitive position within the ASEAN region when it comes to automobile production. As automobile assembly is concentrated in Thailand and Indonesia, automobile parts firms have also gathered around these two countries. Accordingly, although acknowledging that the Philippines and Vietnam cannot become key regional automobile assemblers, Kobayashi (2016) pointed out that both countries may be able to secure competitive advantages owing to their industrial structures and to uphold a certain status in automobile parts production. For example, the Philippines has had an important role in the supply of transmission parts, which is a core component of automobiles. Kobayashi (2016) further described the existence of signs of a gradual increase in the number of automobile parts products in the Philippines and Vietnam, although both are expected to improve their positions as parts suppliers under the liberalization efforts in the ASEAN region. Kobayashi (2018) also analyzed the new situation of the Philippines, reporting a focus on the CARS program—like was described in the study by Shimizu (2019)—and that the automobile parts industry had room to develop and promote the automobile industry in the country as local content rule (i.e., to produce final cars, the assembler needs to clear the minimum standard of domestic parts requirement) was applied. However, when the study by Kobayashi (2018) was written, the exports of automobile parts from the Philippines could not yet cover the imports of assembled cars. Kobayashi (2018) suggests the necessity to wait and see the possibility to increase the exports of parts from the Philippines supported by CARS Program.

4.2.3 Data

The Research Institute of Economy, Trade, and Industry provides export data (RIETI-TID2022) according to the production categories proposed by both the Standard International Trade Classification (also known as SITC) and the Harmonized System (HS). Nonetheless, the HS-based data set covers data only after 2017, and thus this study uses the SITC data set, wherein the transportation industry is categorized as SITC 11. Figures are also further divided into law material, parts and components, capital goods, and consumption goods. In this research, which focuses on the transport industry, the capital goods are commercial vehicles and the consumption goods are passenger cars.

To confirm the existence of aggregation affects, we need detailed trade figures for individual items. UN-Comtrade provides trade data according to the HS-6 digit. The transportation industry is categorized as HS-87 in the HS system, and this study uses automobile products and their parts and components from this category. Furthermore, HS-84 includes engines, which are a very important part of automobiles, and thus the study uses automobile engines from this category. It is clear that the automobile industry uses other items and parts outside those mentioned here (e.g., electric cables and plastic materials), but since these items belong to categories wherein it would be hard to distinguish whether the parts being mentioned relate to automobiles or other products, these other automobile items were omitted from this study.

4.3 Observations

4.3.1 Automobile Production in ASEAN Countries

Worldwide, automobile production increased from 58.4 million units in 2000 to 93.5 million units in 2023, and although the largest contribution to this increase stems from China (i.e., 2.1 to 30.2 million units, respectively), five ASEAN countries (i.e., Thailand, Indonesia, Malaysia, the Philippines, and Vietnam) also increased their production (Table 4.1; i.e., 1.0 to 4.3 million units, respectively). Meanwhile, the United States of America and Japan, who were the largest assemblers in the past, decreased their production. The consequence was the share of the global market which ASEAN countries accounted for going from 1.6% in 2000 to 4.6% in 2023. Thailand is the front-runner in terms of automobile production among ASEAN countries (accounting for approximately 2 million units in recent years), followed by Indonesia (above 1 million units). According to the 13th National Economic and Social Development Plan (2023–2027), the Thai government corroborates these numbers by having described Thailand as a core automobile producer among ASEAN countries.

However, if we separate passenger cars and commercial vehicles, the landscape shifts. While the main products produced in Thailand are LCVs (1.3 million units, accounting for 68.5% of the 1.8 million units produced in the five aforementioned ASEAN countries in 2023), most products in Indonesia are passenger cars (1.2 million units, accounting for 84.6% of the 1.4 million units produced in the five aforementioned ASEAN countries in 2023). These numbers demonstrate that passenger car production in Indonesia has already overcome that in Thailand, which in turn remains the largest automobile producer for commercial vehicles.

Regarding the influence of the COVID-19 pandemic, automobile production dropped worldwide by as much as 15.7% from 2019 to 2020 (91.9 to 77.4 million units, respectively). Nonetheless, the numbers recovered year after year since the onset of the pandemic and recently surpassed pre-pandemic levels (i.e., 93.5 million in 2023). Regarding production in the five ASEAN countries, total production dropped by 31.6% in 2020, and if we take this percentage in light of the decrease of 2.0% in China, 16.7% in Japan, and 19.0% in the United States of America, one may propose that ASEAN countries are in a vulnerable position in the market. Thailand and Indonesia, as leading assemblers among ASEAN countries, also saw a drop of 29.1% and 46.4% in production, respectively. It remains that, similar to the

Table 4.1 Total number of automobile production (Unit: 1000)

	2000	2005	2010	2015	2019	2020	2021	2022	2023
Indonesia	293	501	703	1,099	1,287	690	1,122	1,470	1,396
Malaysia	285	563	568	615	572	485	482	702	775
Philippines	42	45	66	99	95	67	86	92	110
Thailand	326	1,123	1,645	1,912	2,014	1,427	1,686	1,884	1,842
Vietnam	7	32	42	172	176	166	168	232	177
Sum of ASEAN5	952	2,264	3,023	3,896	4,143	2,835	3,543	4,381	4,300
Japan	10,144	10,800	9,629	9,278	9,685	8,068	7,837	7,836	8,997
China	2,069	5,708	18,265	24,567	25,751	25,225	26,122	27,021	30,161
USA	12,800	1197	7743	12,106	10,893	8,821	9,157	10,053	10,612
Germany	5,527	5,758	5,906	6,033	4,664	3,515	3,096	3,480	4,109
World	58,374	66,482	77,584	90,955	91,858	77,439	80,005	84,830	93,547

(Data) Website of International Organization of Motor Vehicle Manufacturers (OICA)

situation in the rest of the world, these drops were temporary, with production numbers recovering to pre-pandemic levels by 2023.

4.3.2 Intra-Regional Trade in the Transportation Industry

Passenger Cars and LCVs

Regarding passenger car production in the ASEAN region, Indonesia has the lead, and trades from Indonesia and Thailand are also at the forefront. Specifically, over half of all traded passenger cars among the five aforementioned ASEAN countries come from Indonesia, and around one-third come from Thailand. The Philippines and Vietnam are currently mostly importing countries and provide very few exports; the situation regarding exports is similar in Malaysia, as the country provides just a very small amount of passenger cars. Regarding bilateral relationships, both the Philippines and Vietnam simply import these goods from both Indonesia and Thailand, and the GL-index is rather high between Indonesia and Thailand (Tables 4.2 and 4.3).

Regarding LCV production in the ASEAN region, Thailand is nearly the sole exporter, with an export share in the region of over 70%. Although some mutual trades seem to happen between Indonesia and the Philippines, Thailand is at the core of the regional production of LCVs. Importantly, while the previous subsection expounds upon Malaysia, the Philippines, and Vietnam becoming automobile producers, their production is mainly focused on their respective domestic market, and no so much on exports.

Table 4.2 Exports of consumption goods in the transportation industry in 2022 (unit: mil.USD)

Import Export	Indonesia	Malaysia	Philippines	Thailand	Vietnam
Indonesia	–	109.5	2781.7	513.9	1197.1
Malaysia	26.7	–	50.5	237.1	70.0
Philippines	0.4	0.0	–	5.5	2.7
Thailand	155.4	103.9	896.1	–	1335.8
Vietnam	104.2	21.6	100.4	216.4	–

(Note) The author calculated by using the data of RIETI "TID"

Table 4.3 Exports of capital goods in the transportation industry in 2022 (unit: mil.USD)

Import Export	Indonesia	Malaysia	Philippines	Thailand	Vietnam
Indonesia	–	15.0	249.9	78.0	36.1
Malaysia	56.8	–	30.1	33.4	3.5
Philippines	121.4	0.0	–	0.5	0.0
Thailand	485.5	596.1	1203.7	–	160.3
Vietnam	0.8	0.1	0.1	31.6	–

(Note) The author calculated by using the data of RIETI "TID"

Parts and Components

Before discussing bilateral procurement in the ASEAN region, the author would like to provide an overview of the origins of procurement in both Thailand and Indonesia. These are the main regional automobile producers (Figs. 4.1 and 4.2), and they show common trends in recent years, which are a decrease of procurement from Japan and an increase from China. Regarding intra-regional procurement, both countries increased their import shares, albeit Thailand does not show an increase as drastic as that in Indonesia. Specifically, in Thailand, the share of imported automobile parts and components from the other four ASEAN countries was 9.0% in 2000 and 13.2% in 2022, while the figures in Indonesia were 4.9% and 24.5%, respectively. Thus, there has been a clear increase in the total volume of imports in both countries that accompanied the increase in automobile production throughout the 2000–2022 period, but the situation for intra-regional procurement shares seems to not be increasing in recent years. The cause here may have been the increase in

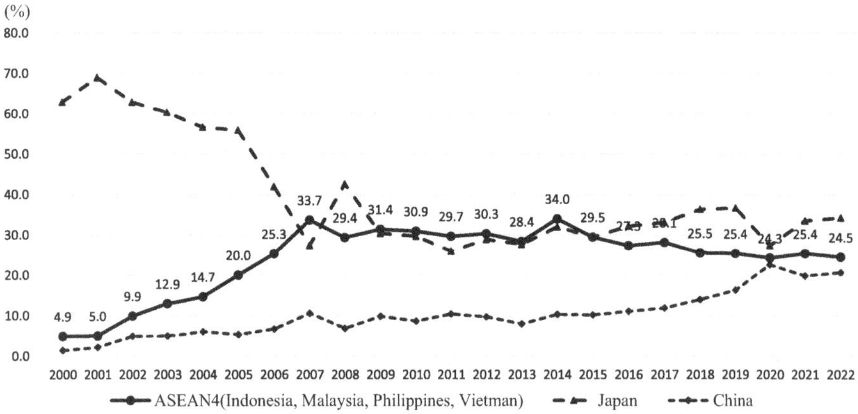

Fig. 4.1 Imports of parts and components into Indonesia

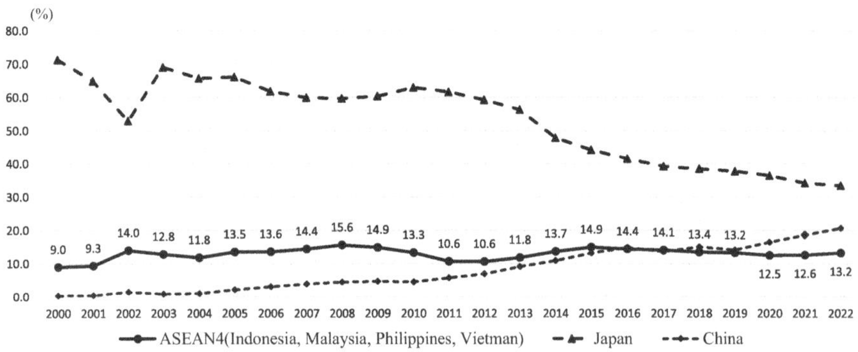

Fig. 4.2 Imports of parts and components into Thailand

procurement from China. As China increased its automobile production capacity, the supporting industry has also developed substantially. This situation in China in recent years may be similar to the situation of ASEAN countries in the early 2000s, in that as they strengthened their automobile production, the supporting industry followed.

Based on prior literature, one of the reasons why intra-rational procurement among ASEAN countries is not increasing is that the progress of Free Trade Agreements (FTA) and Economic Partnership Agreements (EPA) with countries outside of the ASEAN region makes it easier for ASEAN countries to import. However, the situation becomes more complex when we observe actual tariff rates. Tables 4.4 and 4.5 show the preferable tariff rate for some automobile parts items. Since the AEC is not a customs union like the European Union, tariff rates are different across ASEAN countries, with one example being that a type of engine (HS-840732) can be imported from ASEAN countries without tariff. Nonetheless, if the import is from Japan, while there is no tariff in Indonesia, there is a 10% tariff (i.e., the Most Favored Nation tariff according to the World Trade Organization rates) in Thailand. Additionally, while Thailand also imposes this 10% tariff to China, the United States of America, and Germany, Indonesia applies a preferable rate of 5% to China. A similar tariff structure is applied in these two ASEAN countries for other automobile parts and accessories (HS-870899). What follows is that the productivity required to overcome the tariff barrier is more influential for exports

Table 4.4 Tariff rates for item HS-840732

	Indonesia	Malaysia	Philippines	Thailand	Vietnam
MFN	10%	30%	1%	10%	30%
ASEAN	Free	Free	Free	Free	Free
Japan	Free	Free	Free	10%	3.7%
China	5%	Free	Free	10%	30%
USA	10%	30%	1%	10%	30%
Germany	10%	30%	1%	10%	11.2%

(Data) FedEx Trade Networks 'World Tariff'
(Note) HS-840732 is the code for Engines; reciprocating piston engines, of a kind used for the propulsion of vehicles of chapter 87, of a cylinder capacity exceeding 50 cc but not exceeding 250 cc. In detail, capacity 50 cc–110 cc and not for tractor, if specified by each country

Table 4.5 Tariff rates for item HS-870899

	Indonesia	Malaysia	Philippines	Thailand	Vietnam
MFN	10%	5%	1%	30%	15%
ASEAN	Free	Free	Free	Free	Free
Japan	Free	Free	Free	30%	Free
China	5%	Free	1%	30%	Free
USA	10%	5%	1%	30%	15%
Germany	10%	5%	1%	30%	5.6%

(Data) FedEx Trade Networks 'World Tariff'
(Note) HS-870899 is the code for Vehicles; parts and accessories. In detail, HS-870799.11

Table 4.6 Exports of parts and components in the transportation industry in 2022 (unit: mil.USD)

Import Export	Indonesia	Malaysia	Philippines	Thailand	Vietnam
Indonesia	–	376.9	136.9	426.1	141.9
Malaysia	89.2	–	30.9	115.6	45.0
Philippines	60.2	15.2	–	300.1	6.4
Thailand	1071.8	1027.8	133.7	–	511.2
Vietnam	101.5	59.0	20.5	267.8	–

(Note) The author calculated by using the data of RIETI "TID"

than the enjoyment of low or zero tariffs. For example, although Japan enjoys the privilege of zero tariffs from Indonesia, its export shares are decreasing, and while China faces the Most Favored Nation tariff in Thailand, its export shares are increasing. Of course, we should also consider means of economic integration, like non-tariff barriers and/or smooth implementation, besides tariffs.

Returning to the status of the procurement of automobile parts in the ASEAN region, despite some variations across countries, the progress in mutual procurement is clear. Regarding the transportation figures, almost all countries export automobile parts and components to each other, amounting to a trade value of over 10 million USD in 2022 (Table 4.6), with the exception being exports from the Philippines to Vietnam—and even in this exception the value is still over 6 million USD. Furthermore, Thailand, Indonesia, and the Philippines (i.e., the latter being a latecomer in automobile production in the region) mutually export automobile parts and components, leading to rather high GL indexes for all combinations of ASEAN countries. However, when we consider the products of passenger cars and LCVs, the situation shifts.

4.3.3 Characteristics of Specific Items

The previous subsection delineates that there is a somewhat large mutual trade of automobile parts and components among ASEAN countries. To confirm whether aggregation affects exist and whether the mutual trade in the region represents a vertical or a horizontal division of labor, the author collected data on both export value and volume of related items. The following subsections will explore, in the engines and transportation categories, items with a trade value of more than 10 million USD when considering various bilateral relationships between the ASEAN countries in 2022.

Engines

Regarding actual engines, small engines (250–1000 cc) and rotary engines accounted for a small number of transactions. Engines with over 1000 cc are mainly exported from Indonesia to Malaysia, the Philippines, and Vietnam, as well as from Thailand

Table 4.7 Trade value of HS-840734 in 2022 (unit: mil. USD)

Import Export	Indonesia	Malaysia	Philippines	Thailand	Vietnam
Indonesia	–	104.2	45.0	4.8	41.4
Malaysia	0.4	–	0.4	3.6	na
Philippines	na	na	–	na	na
Thailand	0.1	38.1	7.0	–	64.1
Vietnam	na	na	na	na	–

(Note) 1. HS-840734 is the item of reciprocating piston engines, whose cylinder capacity are exceeding 1000cc
2. Calculated by using the UN Comtrade data

Table 4.8 GL-index of HS-840734 in 2022

	Malaysia	Philippines	Thailand	Vietnam
Indonesia	0.008	0.000	0.024	0.000
Malaysia		0.000	0.171	na
Philippines			0.000	0.000
Thailand				0.001

(Note) 1. HS-840734 is the item of reciprocating piston engines, whose cylinder capacity are exceeding 1000cc
2. Calculated by using the UN Comtrade data

to Vietnam (Table 4.7). Although the trade value of these items recorded over 10 million USD in 2022, most of the trades here are one-way trades and have low GL-indexes (Table 4.8). That is, regional automobile production countries such as Indonesia and Thailand have export capacity for engines with over 1000 cc, and Indonesia, which produces more passenger cars, has a stronger competitiveness than Thailand. Regarding diesel engines, these are mainly exported from Thailand to the other four ASEAN countries, which seems to reflect Thailand's LCV production capacity.

Regarding engine parts, there are differences depending on whether it is a diesel or a gasoline engine. There is mutual trade for gasoline engines, with the trade value of the following trades being over 10 million USD in 2022: exports from Indonesia to Thailand; from Thailand to Indonesia, Malaysia, and Vietnam; from Vietnam to Thailand. Accordingly, the GL-indexes between Indonesia and Thailand and between Thailand and Vietnam are rather high. Upon comparing unit prices, we observe that the prices in Thailand are higher than those in Indonesia and Vietnam; this, when coupled with the fact that Thailand exports more to these two countries than it imports, suggests that Thailand can produce products with greater added value. Regarding diesel engines, Indonesia exports much more diesel engine parts to Thailand than the other way around, and this is even if the trade value of Thai exports to Indonesia also recorded more than 10 million USD in 2022; as the unit price of diesel engines from Indonesia is cheaper than that of Thailand, the first may have a comparative advantage over the latter.

Parts and Components other than Engines

Since there are many items among automobile parts and components in the HS-87 category, we need to select items which were actively traded among ASEAN countries in recent years. To confirm these actively traded items, the author collected intra-regional trade data for 2022 from UN-Comtrade, finding five items with a one-way transaction value of 10 million USD or more, which were gearbox (HS-870840), axel (HS-870850), wheel (HS0870870), steering wheel (HS-870894), and airbag (HS-870895). Their export values and GL-indexes are shown in Tables 4.9, 4.10, 4.11, 4.12, 4.13, 4.14, 4.15, 4.16, 4.17, and 4.18. The following subsections provide detailed analyses for each item, focusing on bilateral trades between Indonesia and Thailand (i.e., the two countries with the most advanced automobile

Table 4.9 Trade value of HS-870840 in 2022 (unit: mil. USD)

Import Export	Indonesia	Malaysia	Philippines	Thailand	Vietnam
Indonesia	–	49.1	2.1	133.9	16.3
Malaysia	0.4	–	0.1	3.1	0.0
Philippines	15.2	6.2	–	195.6	2.8
Thailand	81.7	48.7	62.1	–	49.4
Vietnam	0.3	1.1	0.0	29.0	–

(Note) 1. HS-870840 is the item of gear boxes for vehicles and parts
2. Calculated by using the UN Comtrade data

Table 4.10 GL-index of HS-870840 in 2022

	Malaysia	Philippines	Thailand	Vietnam
Indonesia	0.015	0.239	0.758	0.037
Malaysia	–	0.019	0.121	0.018
Philippines		–	0.482	0.021
Thailand			–	0.739

(Note) 1. HS-870840 is the item of gear boxes for vehicles and parts
2. Calculated by using the UN Comtrade data

Table 4.11 Trade value of HS-870850 in 2022 (unit: mil. USD)

Import Export	Indonesia	Malaysia	Philippines	Thailand	Vietnam
Indonesia	–	10.3	15.0	25.8	13.1
Malaysia	5.3	–	0.0	9.6	0.0
Philippines	1.5	0.0	–	47.6	0.0
Thailand	95.4	33.3	6.2	–	26.4
Vietnam	0.0	0.0	0.0	0.0	–

(Note) 1. HS-870850 is the item of axel for vehicles and parts
2. Calculated by using the UN Comtrade data

Table 4.12 GL-index of HS-870850 in 2022

	Malaysia	Philippines	Thailand	Vietnam
Indonesia	0.683	0.177	0.426	0.000
Malaysia	–	0.000	0.449	0.000
Philippines		–	0.230	na
Thailand			–	0.000

(Note) 1. HS-870850 is the item of axel for vehicles and parts
2. Calculated by using the UN Comtrade data

Table 4.13 Trade value of HS-870870 in 2022 (unit: mil. USD)

Import Export	Indonesia	Malaysia	Philippines	Thailand	Vietnam
Indonesia	–	27.7	0.8	5.3	1.1
Malaysia	0.5	–	1.1	4.1	6.9
Philippines	0.0	0.0	–	0.3	0.0
Thailand	9.7	25.1	5.3	–	0.0
Vietnam	0.1	1.5	0.0	3.1	–

(Note) 1. HS-870870 is the item of wheel for vehicles and parts
2. Calculated by using the UN Comtrade data

Table 4.14 GL-index of HS-870870 in 2022

	Malaysia	Philippines	Thailand	Vietnam
Indonesia	0.033	0.000	0.710	0.235
Malaysia	–	0.000	0.279	0.354
Philippines		–	0.115	na
Thailand			–	0.524

(Note) 1. HS-870870 is the item of wheel for vehicles and parts
2. Calculated by using the UN Comtrade data

Table 4.15 Trade value of HS-870894 in 2022 (unit: mil. USD)

Import Export	Indonesia	Malaysia	Philippines	Thailand	Vietnam
Indonesia	–	8.4	0.7	6.3	7.9
Malaysia	10.8	–	0.0	11.9	6.9
Philippines	14.8	1.1	–	9.1	0.0
Thailand	72.7	94.6	15.6	–	0.9
Vietnam	0.1	0.1	0.0	4.3	–

(Note) 1. HS-870894 is the item of steering wheel for vehicles and parts
2. Calculated by using the UN Comtrade data

assembly capacity in the region), and exports from the Philippines and Vietnam to Thailand (i.e., two countries with a less advanced automobile assembly capacity exporting to a country with an advanced automobile assembly capacity).

Table 4.16 GL-index of HS-870894 in 2022

	Malaysia	Philippines	Thailand	Vietnam
Indonesia	0.875	0.094	0.159	0.019
Malaysia	–	0.038	0.224	0.034
Philippines		–	0.738	0.000
Thailand			–	0.324

(Note) 1. HS-870894 is the item of steering wheel for vehicles and parts
2. Calculated by using the UN Comtrade data

Table 4.17 Trade value of HS-870895 in 2022 (unit: mil. USD)

Import Export	Indonesia	Malaysia	Philippines	Thailand	Vietnam
Indonesia	–	1.0	0.9	0.2	1.2
Malaysia	7.8	–	0.0	15.0	0.5
Philippines	1.2	1.4	–	2.8	1.0
Thailand	33.3	26.8	3.6	–	1.1
Vietnam	11.7	1.7	0.0	25.1	–

(Note) 1. HS-870895 is the item of air bag for vehicles and parts
2. Calculated by using the UN Comtrade data

Table 4.18 GL-index of HS-870895 in 2022

	Malaysia	Philippines	Thailand	Vietnam
Indonesia	0.229	0.857	0.012	0.185
Malaysia	–	0.010	0.717	0.479
Philippines		–	0.874	0.000
Thailand			–	0.751

(Note) 1. HS-870895 is the item of air bag for vehicles and parts
2. Calculated by using the UN Comtrade data

(a) ***Gearbox***

The mutual trade between Indonesia and Thailand started to increase from Indonesia in the mid-2000s, which was followed by an increase in exports from Thailand after 2010. The GL-index has been high since the mid-2010s (Fig. 4.3), and the unit price difference is consistently around ±25%, suggesting a horizontal division of labor with some differences in product quality (Table 4.19).

A notable feature of gearbox trade is that the Philippines has been exporting this automobile part since the early 2000s (Fig. 4.4), reporting trade values of 77.5 million USD when exporting to Thailand and 10.4 million USD to Japan in 2000. This showcases that the capacity of gearbox production and trade has been developing in the Philippines for a long time. These findings are consistent with those in the studies by Shimizu (2011) and Kobayashi (2016). Therefore, despite the Philippines being a latecomer in automobile assembly, it has been contributing to the industry in the region with a very important item. Regarding Vietnam, it started to increase

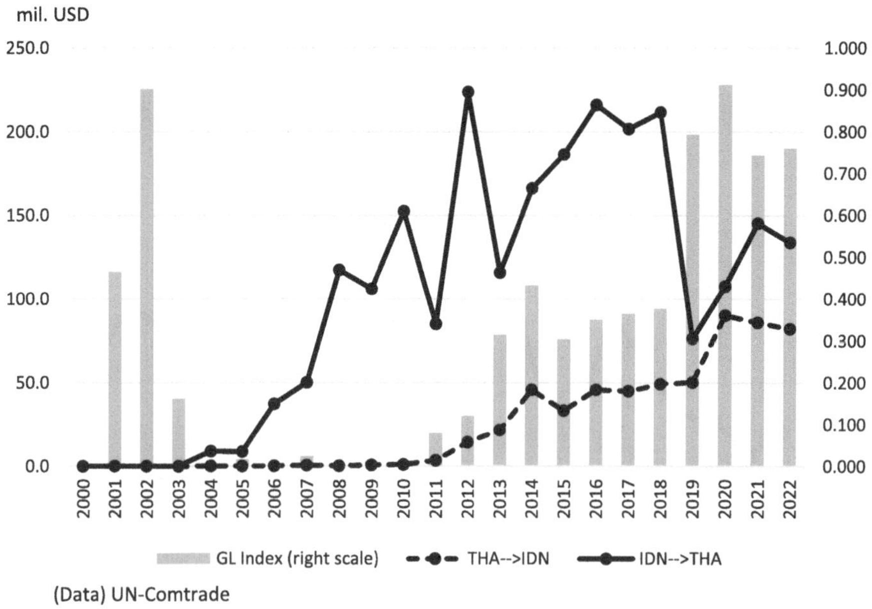

Fig. 4.3 HS870840 (Gear box): Thailand and Indonesia

Table 4.19 Unit value comparison between Thailand and Indonesia

Year	HS-870840 (gear box)	HS-870850 (axel)	HS-870870 (wheel)
2000	–	–	19.869
2001	–	2.875	–
2002	–	–	0.701
2003	0.083	–	0.563
2004	0.079	0.537	0.465
2005	2.730	0.922	0.445
2006	2.460	1.164	0.634
2007	0.701	2.646	0.578
2008	1.386	2.725	0.482
2009	3.187	2.816	0.598
2010	1.455	2.711	0.750
2011	1.168	1.272	0.793
2012	1.019	2.436	0.750
2013	1.215	2.424	0.718
2014	1.401	1.713	0.549
2015	1.369	1.306	0.370
2016	1.250	0.917	0.352
2017	1.235	1.127	0.465
2018	1.416	1.024	0.530
2019	2.269	0.901	0.484
2020	1.298	0.794	0.386
2021	1.256	0.815	0.385
2022	1.156	0.828	0.366

(Note) 1. Figures are (Indonesian export price)/(Export prices). Export prices are FOB (free on board) value (USD) divided by amount (kg)
2. Calculated by the author using data from UN-Comtrade

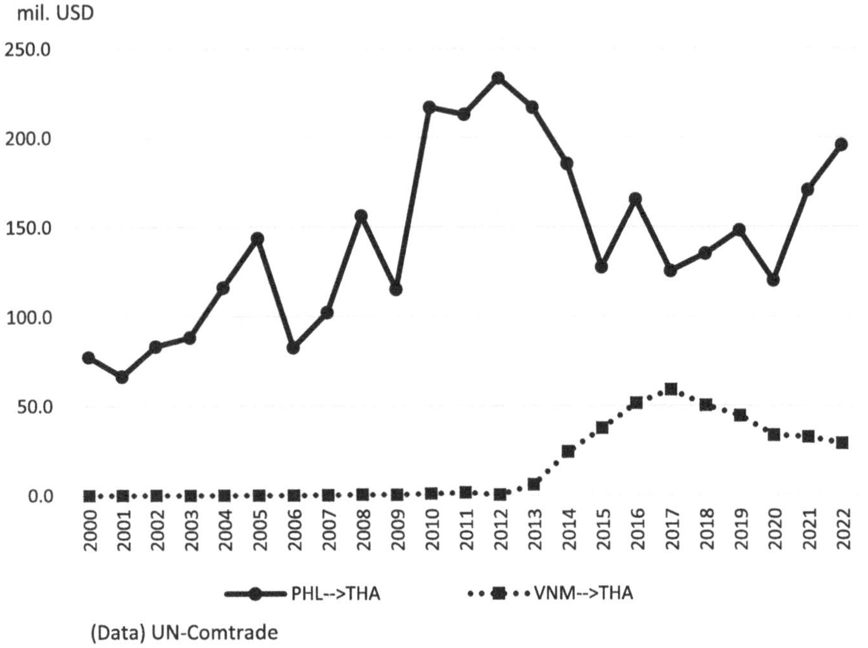

Fig. 4.4 HS870840 (Gear box): Philippines and Vietnam to Thailand

exports of gearboxes to Thailand since the early 2010s. Accordingly, although the export value of Vietnam in 2022 was lower than that of the Philippines and the export amounts are small, the country upholds a steady car gearbox export to Thailand.

Pertaining to the impact of the COVID-19 pandemic on car gearboxes, both exports between Indonesia and Thailand did not decrease in 2020. Exports between the Philippines and Thailand decreased in 2020, but went on to recuperate to almost pre-pandemic levels in 2022. Regarding Vietnam, its competitiveness seems to have decreased in recent years, as since 2017 its exports to Thailand have tended toward a decrease, and the COVID-19 seems not to have strongly impacted these trades. Collectively, these pieces of information showcase that the pandemic had some impact only in the trade between the Philippines and Thailand owing to its negative effects on automobile production, but as the automobile production industry recovered, so did the regional trades.

(b) ***Axel***

Mutual exports of car axel between Indonesia and Thailand have been underway since the mid-2000s (Fig. 4.5), and while exports from the latter consistently increased, exports from the first were slow at the beginning and started to increase more substantially since the mid-2010s. Following this increase in Indonesian exports, the GL-index raised to some extent, but it did not exceed 0.5 owing to

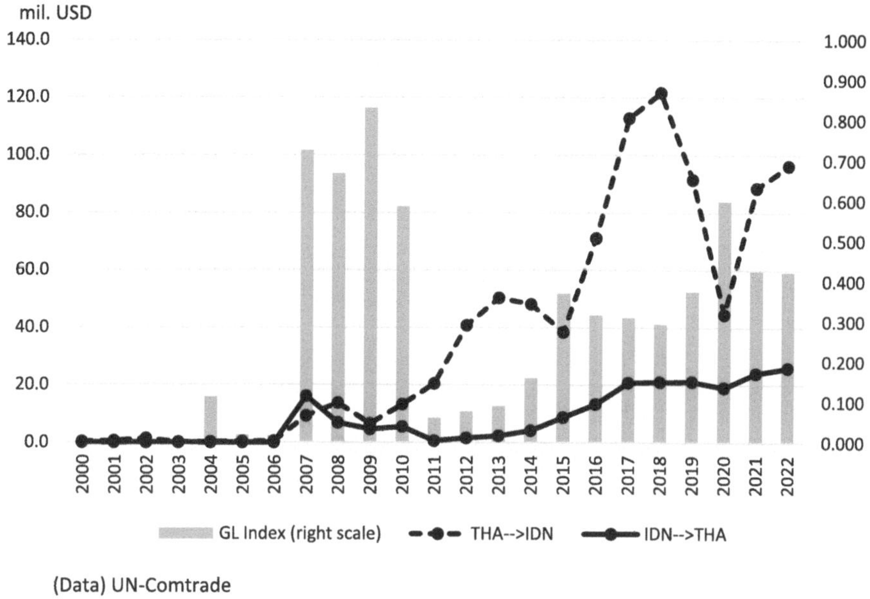

Fig. 4.5 HS870850 (Axel): Thailand and Indonesia

Thailand's exports increasing even more than Indonesia's; the exception here was the year 2019, when exports from Thailand decreased. Regarding unit price differences, they have remained around ±25% since 2015, and the mutual trade in this scenario indicates the presence of a horizontal division of labor (Table 4.19).

The value of exports to Thailand from both the Philippines and Vietnam was small until the mid-2010s (Fig. 4.6) while the value of exports from the Philippines to Thailand started to increase in 2015, and exports from Vietnam were still low until very recently. Regarding the effect of the CARS program in the Philippines, the onset of the increase in its exports occurred just before the program's beginning; still, even if the program has supported the increase in exports to some extent, the Philippines already had the potential to become an important supplier of car axels prior to the program. Regarding the impact of the COVID-19 pandemic on car axel exports, all ASEAN countries showed a decline in exports, either small or large, in 2020, but the general observation is that the pandemic had little impact on the trade of this automobile part, as the exports recovered in the following 1 or 2 years after the onset of the public emergency.

(c) ***Wheel***

The value of exports from both Indonesia and Thailand seems to have followed similar trends, increasing from the 2000s to 2015 and peaking in 2015 (Fig. 4.7). This may mean that both countries started to procure this item from countries outside the ASEAN region. Just focusing on bilateral trades, the unit price of car wheels

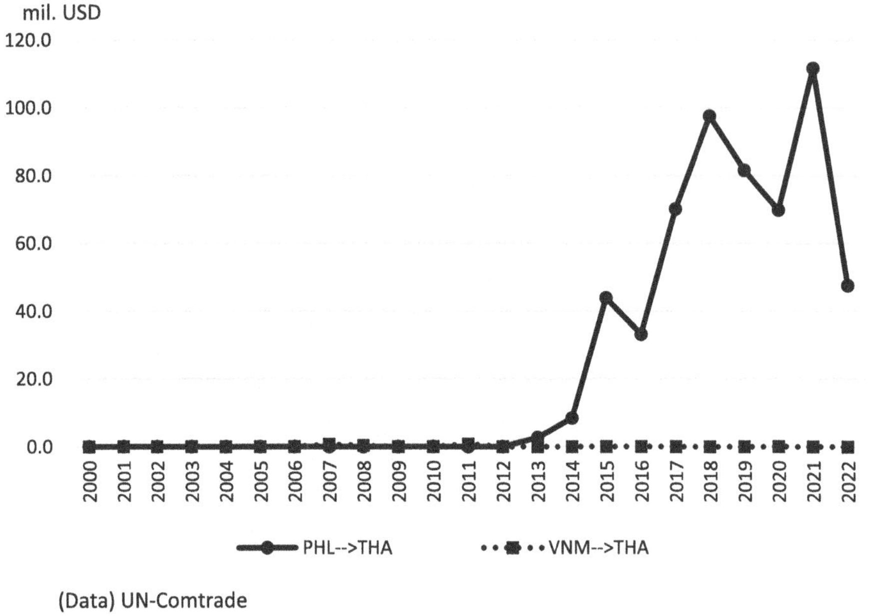

Fig. 4.6 HS870850 (Axel): Philippines and Vietnam to Thailand

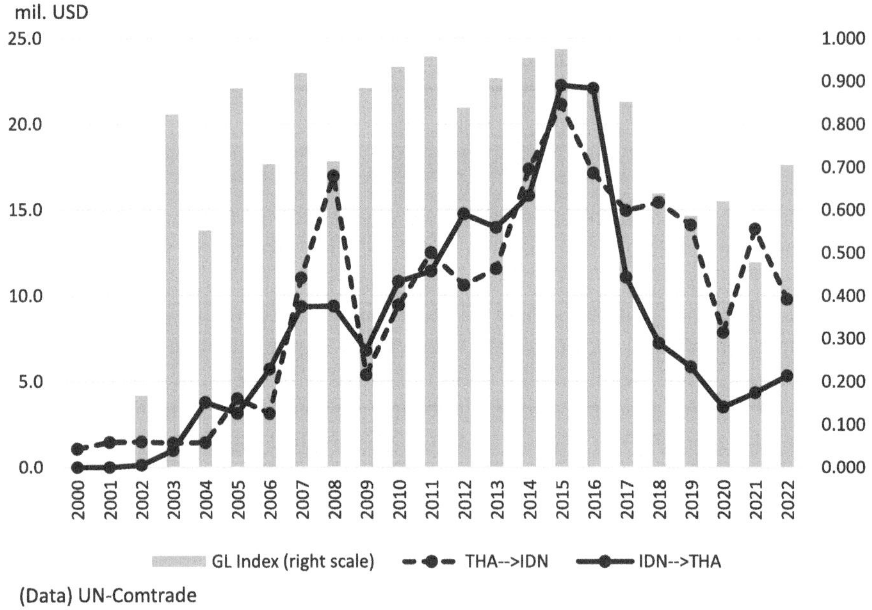

Fig. 4.7 HS870870 (Wheel): Thailand and Indonesia

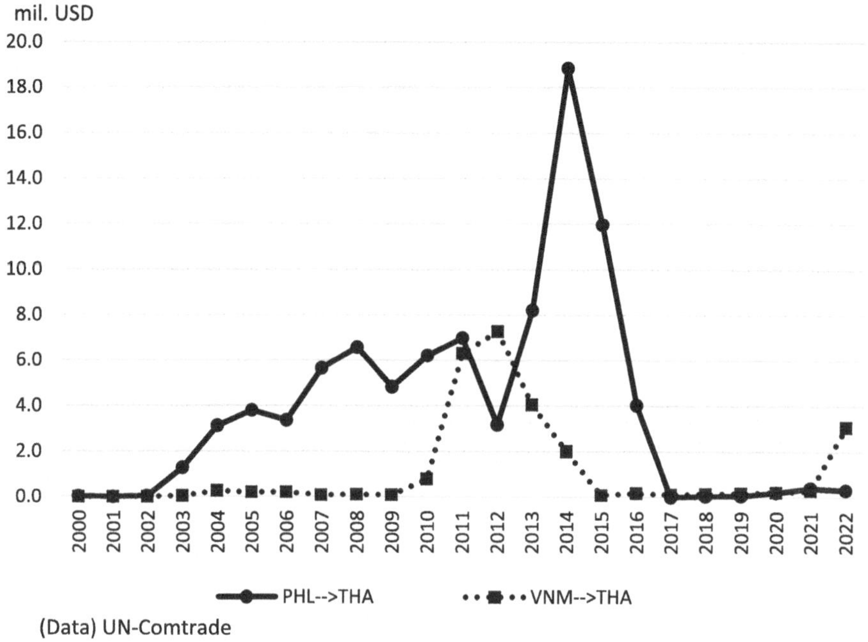

Fig. 4.8 HS870870 (Wheel): Philippines and Vietnam to Thailand

in Thailand is 25% higher than that of Indonesia (Table 4.19), indicating that this may represent a vertical division of labor.

Regarding export trends, they were similar for exports from the Philippines to Thailand and for the mutual trade between Indonesia and Thailand, increasing throughout the mid-2010s, peaking in 2015 (Fig. 4.8), decreasing after 2015, and recently recording very low amounts. This also entails that the CARS program did not influence automobile wheel production in the Philippines. Regarding exports from Vietnam to both the Philippines and Thailand, they showed similar trends and increased in 2022, hence improving at a different time than the other countries. The non-tariff protectionist measures in Vietnam may have played a role in these differences.

Regarding the impact of the COVID-19 pandemic on wheel exports, although the exports of both Indonesia and Thailand decreased in 2020 and recovered afterward, the peak in 2015 and the decrease in recent years seem to have been more important. The exports from the Philippines and Vietnam were small in 2019, making it difficult to expound upon the topic of the impact of the pandemic on these two countries.

(d) ***Steering Wheel***

Exports from Indonesia to Thailand are not as active as those of Thailand to Indonesia (Fig. 4.9), and we can observe one-way transactions from Thailand to

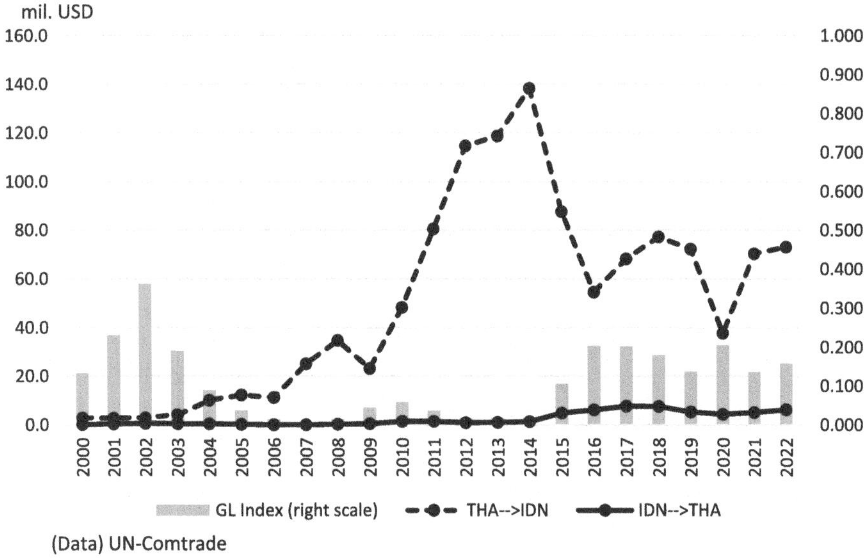

Fig. 4.9 HS870894 (Steering wheel): Thailand and Indonesia

Indonesia. The strengthening of the ASEAN regional integration resulted on the concentration of the capacity for producing automobile steering wheels in Thailand. Although exports from Thailand remained high in 2022, they seem to have peaked in 2015.

Exports from the Philippines to Thailand have increased since the mid-2010s, while Vietnam started to increase its exports to Thailand only in recent years (Fig. 4.10). There is a possibility that the CARS program in the Philippines influenced the increase in automobile steering wheels. Vietnam may also have induced foreign direct investment in this field through the use of its protectionist measures (e.g., non-tariff barriers), but it is not certain whether these protectionist measures were effective. Regardless of these situations, Vietnam seems to have achieved high productivity of car steering wheels recently.

Regarding the impact of the COVID-19 pandemic on steering wheel trade, there is space for discussion only regarding exports from Thailand to Indonesia and those from the Philippines to Thailand; both decreased in 2020 and recovered afterward, with this trend being very clear in the exports of Thailand to Indonesia.

(e) ***Airbag***

The HS code for airbag was assigned only in the HS 2007 standard, which entails that the airbag item belonged to another category before 2007, and there are no statistics for the item prior to 2007. Accordingly, this study used only the numbers after 2007. In the context of the mutual trades between Indonesia and Thailand, Indonesia did not have the capacity to export this item (Fig. 4.11), and thus only

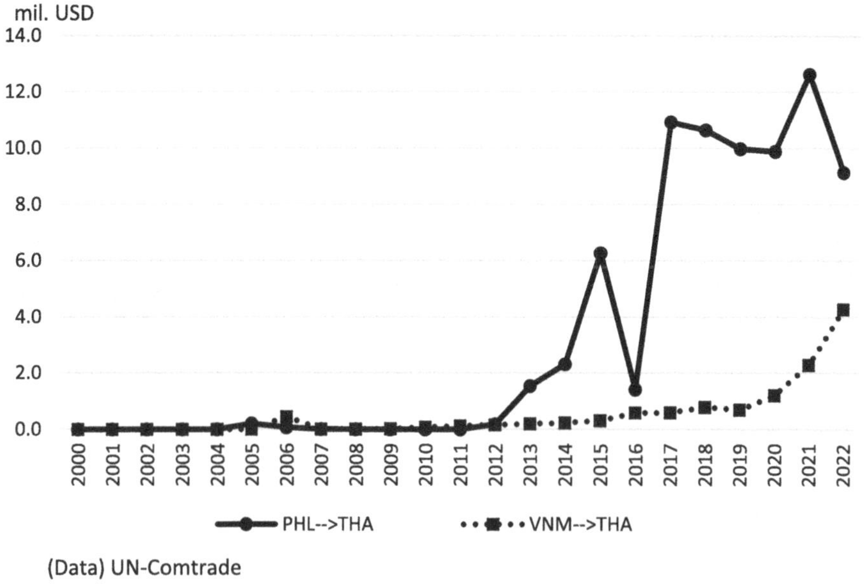

Fig. 4.10 HS870894 (Steering wheel): Philippines and Vietnam to Thailand

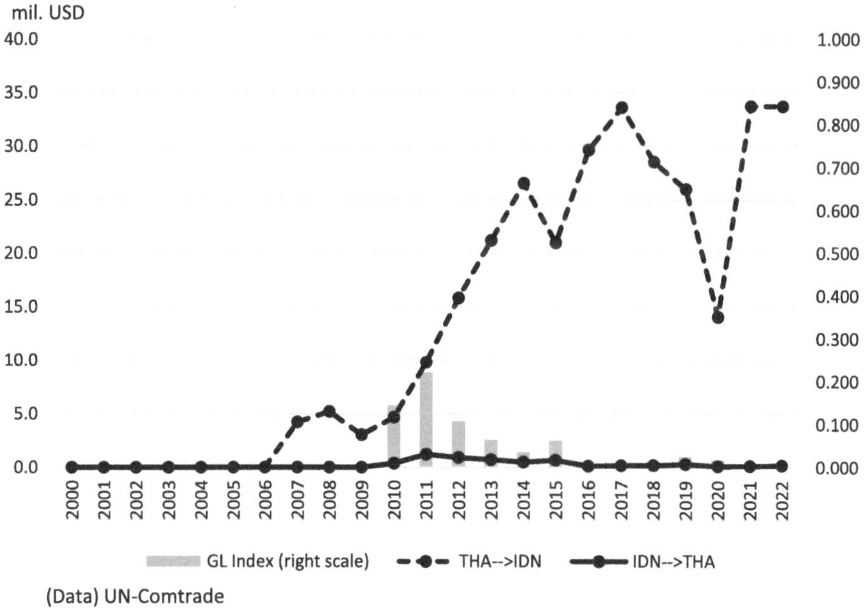

Fig. 4.11 HS870895 (Airbag): Thailand and Indonesia

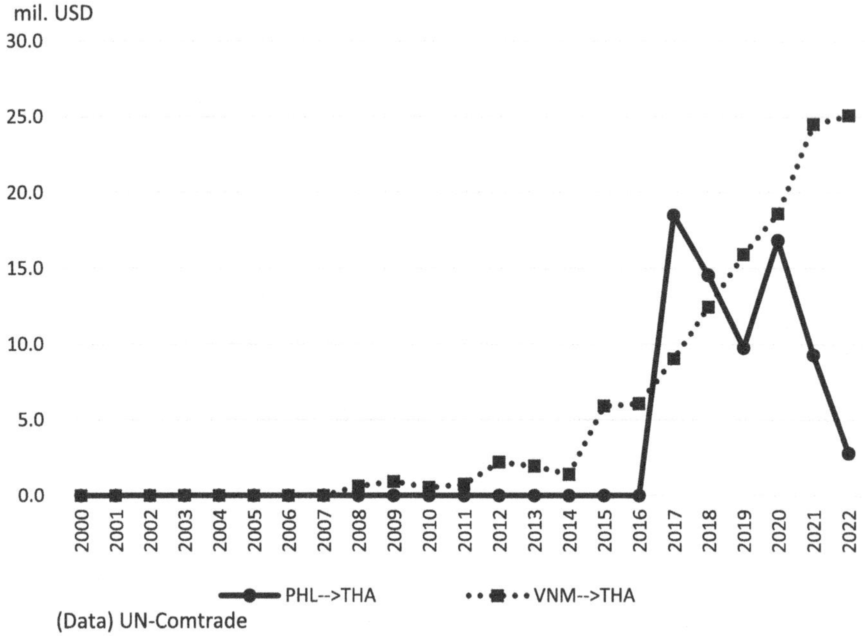

Fig. 4.12 HS870895 (Airbag): Philippines and Vietnam to Thailand

Thailand has been actively exporting it, its exports have increased throughout the 2010s, and they have continued so up to recent years.

Exports from the Philippines surged in 2017 and fluctuated after that, but it is difficult to pinpoint clearly whether the exports decreased in 2021 and 2022 (Fig. 4.12) owing to the sampling period being relatively short. The CARS program may have had an influence on these exports. Regarding exports from Vietnam to Thailand, they differed from the trends that can be observed for the exports of the Philippines, as Vietnam has steadily increased its exports to Thailand throughout the early 2010s and eventually overcame the export value of the Philippines. Therefore, Vietnam seems to have achieved competitiveness in airbag production before 2018, and this seems to have been unrelated to the protectionist measures in the country after the tariff reductions.

Regarding the impact of the COVID-19 pandemic on airbag trade, only Thailand was negatively influenced in 2020 but recovered afterward, while the Philippines saw an increase in 2020 and a subsequent decrease, and Vietnam was seemingly not influenced.

In summary, this subsection shows trends both between ASEAN countries advanced in automobile assembly, such as Thailand and Indonesia, and between latecomer countries such as the Philippines and Vietnam. The relationship between Thailand and Indonesia is characterized by a prevalence of Thailand exports, and while Indonesia simply does not export various automobile parts, the ones in which it is proficient, it does export them to Thailand more than Thailand does so to

Indonesia, and the two countries are undergoing an increase in segregation regarding their bases of production. Moreover, while there is a vertical division of labor for some automobile parts like wheels, wherein some elements of automobile parts are exported to Thailand so that the latter can then produce the complete version of the components, other automobile parts like gearboxes and axels are mutually exported owing to differences in details of the designs. As for the protectionist policies of the Philippines and Vietnam, the author could not find thorough evidence of these efforts having led to an increase in automobile parts production at the national level, but there are indications that this increase may be happening in both countries. The COVID-19 pandemic seems to have negatively influenced the exports of some countries, but most recovered after a few years, and Vietnam seems not to have been damaged by the pandemic.

4.4 Conclusion

This paper tried to clarify the progress of the regional economic integration and intra-regional trade in the transportation industry, specifically regarding automobile parts and components, among ASEAN countries. Although the share of imports in Thailand and Indonesia has stabilized in recent years, the total value is increasing, and the Philippines and Vietnam, as latecomers in automobile assembly, have increased their export amounts in the region.

When looking at detailed data of each item among the various automobile parts and components, it became clear that only the regional advanced automobile assemblers (i.e., Indonesia and Thailand) can export some specific items and key components (e.g., engines), albeit there are some differences. It also seems that ASEAN countries engage in mutual exports for some items. This suggests that the efforts at regional integration have facilitated the concentration of the automobile parts industry around the two core automobile assemblers in the region. The author also found that even the Philippines and Vietnam export automobile parts and components to Indonesia and Thailand. Previous studies suggested that both liberalization and protectionism efforts served as reasons for these regional latecomer countries in respect to automobile assembly (i.e., the Philippines and Vietnam) to have undergone an increase in the production of automobile parts and components. The author tried to investigate whether it is liberalization or protectionism that is having the prevailing influence over the increase, but this was ultimately a challenging endeavor; it seems that the region is being influenced by both liberalization and protectionism, at least when observing the trends in each of the items under scrutiny in this study.

Regarding future phenomena in the region, there are two topics that can be discussed. First, the promotion of liberalization in the latecomer countries, with an example being efforts at ensuring the gradual elimination of the non-tariff barrier in Vietnam. The continuation of this barrier generally goes against ASEAN regional integration, and Vietnam having accepted the tariff reduction entails that there is no reason for the country to maintain the non-tariff barrier ad infinitum. For the time being, we should keep on cautiously observing the related movements from the involved countries. Second, there could be efforts to broaden the economic integration measures to countries outside the ASEAN region and to other multilateral agreements, including the CPTPP and RCEP. Examples of related efforts include Vietnam eliminating the tariffs associated with the finished vehicle market by 2030 under the CPTPP scheme. At this point, it is unclear whether Vietnam will also introduce other non-tariff measures to deal with this situation, but what is clear is that the automobile production structure in Vietnam will be influenced, which in turn will influence automobile parts production.

Regarding the influence of the COVID-19 pandemic, its negative impact seems to have been stronger among ASEAN countries than in other main automobile assembler countries worldwide, such as Japan, the United States, and China. However, production and intra-regional trade among ASEAN countries regarding the automobile parts and components industry recovered in subsequent years, with the strengthening of the division of labor continuing in the region and no major negative change being observed.

References

Greenaway D, Milner C (1983) On the measurement of intra-industry trade. Econ J 93(372):900–908

Greenaway D, Hine R, Milner C (1995) Vertical and horizontal intra-industry trade: a cross industry analysis for the United Kingdom. Econ J 105(433):1505–1518

Grubel HG, Lloyd PJ (1971) The empirical measurement of intra-industry trade. Econ Rec 47(4):494–517

Kobayashi T (2016) What kind of influence did ASEAN free trade agreement have on the automobile industry of Philippine and Vietnam? Josai Keizai Gakkaishi 37:173–194. (in Japanese)

Kobayashi T (2018) A study on the trade structure of the Philippine automotive parts industry. Ann Josai Grad Sch Econ 31:43–61. (in Japanese)

Shimizu K (2011) ASEAN Regional Economic Cooperation and Auto Parts Complementation Scheme. Ann Soc Ind Stud Jpn 26:65–77

Shimizu K (2019) ASEAN economic integration and automobile industry. J Econ (Chuo University) 60(1):57–77. (in Japanese)

Sukegawa S (2021) ASEAN's initiatives for free trade in East Asia under AEC. J Contemp East Asia Stud 10(1):42–64

Chapter 5
Cross-Border Trade Between Thailand and Myanmar in the Post-COVID Era

Yasuhito Asami and Nattapan Kongbuamai

Abstract Covid-19 undoubtedly affected Thailand's border trade, though not in a uniform way; some aspects of border trade declined while others increased. In some cases, the direction of the impact changed over time. For example, the spread of Covid-19 caused a sharp decline in Myanmar's land exports to Thailand but a rapid growth in its sea exports to Thailand in 2020. However, in the following years, this pattern reversed. Such fluctuations in preferred trade routes imply a substitutional relation between land and sea trade. External shocks such as the spread of Covid-19 affect traders' choice of trade routes. This study also analyzes why Thai–Myanmar border trade remained robust against the impact of Covid-19, with a focus on methods used to transport commodities across the border (where truck drivers tend to remain largely within their own national territories). This robustness mitigated the potentially much more severe negative impact of Covid-19 on border trade in the region.

Keywords Border trade · Transit trade · Thailand · Myanmar · Border economy

5.1 Introduction, Research Methodology, and Reliability of Data

Among Thailand's 77 provinces, 31 have geographic borders with neighboring countries, with a total length of 5656 km. According to the Department of Local Administration under the Thailand Ministry of Interior, there are 12 provinces

Y. Asami
Department of Global Politics, Faculty of Law, Hosei University, Tokyo, Japan
e-mail: asami@hosei.ac.jp

N. Kongbuamai (✉)
Tourism, Hospitality, and Event (TH&E) Research Group, School of Management, Mae Fah Luang University, Chiang Rai, Thailand
e-mail: nattapan.kon@mfu.ac.th

© The Author(s), under exclusive license to Springer Nature Singapore Pte Ltd. 2025

H. Taguchi (ed.), *Sustainability of Economic Growth in East Asia*,
New Frontiers in Regional Science: Asian Perspectives 82,
https://doi.org/10.1007/978-981-96-3731-7_5

bordering the Laos (1810 km), 10 provinces bordering Myanmar (2401 km), 7 provinces bordering Cambodia (798 km), and 4 provinces bordering Malaysia (647 km) (Department of Local Administration 2014; Department of Treaties and Legal Affairs 2022).

The impact of Covid-19 on Thailand's border trade with different trading partners varied considerably. Table 5.1 compares changes in the volume of border trade between Thailand and its four neighboring countries between 2018 and 2022.

As shown in Table 5.1, in terms of total volume, Thailand's land exports to Malaysia were not seriously affected by Covid-19, though its imports were much more severely affected. Meanwhile, Covid-19's impact on border trade with Laos and Cambodia was quite the opposite. That is, Thailand's exports to Laos and Cambodia were negatively affected while its imports from these two countries were unaffected. Thailand's imports from Laos and Cambodia increased in 2020 and 2021, the years in which Thailand and its neighboring countries were severely affected by Covid-19.

As for Thailand's border trade with Myanmar, Table 5.1 shows that both exports and imports declined by more than 10% in 2020 due to Covid-19. These negative impacts were, however, short-lived. Border trade with Myanmar recovered quickly in 2021; by 2022, it far exceeded pre-Covid levels.

Despite its economic and geopolitical importance, in-depth analysis of Thailand's border trade is lacking, primarily due to a paucity of reliable data. Although Thailand's Department of Foreign Trade (DFT) and the Customs Office publish monthly data on border trade in their websites, these data do not include informal border trade. If we assume that such informal border trade occupies a stable share of Thailand's total border trade, we could potentially conduct an analysis using only the official figures. However, our field research in Thailand's border areas suggests that the share of informal border trade changes frequently in response to external shocks, such as the spread of Covid-19 or severe political and military conflict in Myanmar.

Thailand's official border trade figures are also unreliable due to the murky distinction between "border trade" and "transit trade." The DFT defines "border trade" as exports to and imports from Thailand's four neighboring countries, namely, Malaysia, Myanmar, Laos, and Cambodia through its land border, and it also says that exporting goods to and importing from the third countries through the four neighboring countries via border trading points under the Border Transport Agreement are also classified as border trade. As for "transit trade," the DFT defines it as trade with third countries through land borders with neighboring countries based on the Border Transport Agreement (Department of Foreign Trade 2020).

Despite the lack of a clear-cut definition of border trade, close analysis of monthly trade data suggests that transit trade is excluded from border trade.[1]

[1] According to the figures released by the DFT, the volume of border trade with Laos was 260 million baht, while that of transit trade was 351 million baht in 2022 (DFT 2023). This implies that the trade the DFT regards as transit trade is not included in border trade, though their definition suggests otherwise. A confusing definition by the DFT was used without any modification in a report

Table 5.1 Thailand's border trade with its neighboring countries: 2018–2022

Unit: amount—million Baht, change—%

	Malaysia				Myanmar				Laos				Cambodia			
	Export		Import		Export		Import		Export		Import		Export		Import	
Year	Amount	Change	Amount	Change	Amount	Change	Amount	Change	Amount	Change	Amount	Change	Amount	Change	Amount	Change
2018	150,938	–	157,310	–	105,212	–	88,114	–	128,867	–	84,752	–	122,576	–	22,780	–
2019	126,763	−16.0	147,728	−6.1	99,392	−5.5	93,871	6.5	117,891	−8.5	79,555	−6.1	140,034	14.2	21,178	−7.0
2020	124,194	−2.0	125,308	−15.2	87,080	−12.4	77,706	−17.2	103,608	−12.1	86,214	8.4	133,046	−5.0	23,001	8.6
2021	182,464	46.9	153,532	22.5	119,655	37.4	84,512	8.8	124,769	20.4	90,045	4.4	143,115	7.6	25,989	13.0
2022	183,523	0.6	152,596	−0.6	143,582	20.0	120,056	42.1	156,738	25.6	103,343	14.8	164,186	14.7	34,129	31.3

Source: Department of Foreign Trade (2021, 2022, 2023)

However, not all goods that go to or come from third countries through neighboring countries are classified as transit trade; rather, transit trade only includes goods being traded under border transport agreements. The proportion of land trade with non-bordering countries such as China, Vietnam, and Singapore that falls under border transport agreements is unknown. Furthermore, there is no way to figure out how much trade classified as border trade with neighboring countries by the DFT is actually trade with third countries.

Table 5.2 shows the amount of transit trade with third countries through Thailand's four bordering countries, published by the DFT.

As shown in Table 5.2, the transit to border trade ratio differs considerably among Thailand's four neighboring countries. The vast majority of goods traded through the Thai–Lao border go to or come from third countries. According to DFT figures, 45.5% of Thailand's transit exports through Laos in 2021 went to China, 15.0% to Vietnam, and 39.5% to other countries such as the United States and European countries (transit exports to Hong Kong come under "other countries" in the DFT data). As for transit imports through Laos in 2021, 83.8% came from China, 13.4% from Vietnam, and 2.8% from other countries.

As for trade through the Thai–Malaysian border in 2021, about half of goods went to and came from third countries. According to the DFT, 37.5% of Thailand's transit exports through Malaysia went to China, 23.1% to Singapore, and 39.4% to other countries such as Taiwan, Japan, South Korea, and India in 2021, while 52.5% of Thailand's transit imports through the Thai–Malaysian border came from Singapore, 8.1% from China, and 39.4% from other countries (Department of Foreign Trade 2023).

Despite its high trade dependency, Thailand only has two deep-sea ports, both of which are located in the eastern part of the country; the south has none. Many agricultural products produced in southern Thailand are thus exported from deep-sea ports in Malaysia and Singapore. The distance between Hat Yai (one of the largest cities in southern Thailand) and Singapore is shorter than that between Hat Yai and Laem Chabang, the closest deep-sea port in Thailand.

Transit trade, as defined by the Thai government, occupies a much smaller share of goods traded through the Thai–Cambodian and Thai–Myanmar borders compared to the Thai–Lao and Thai–Malaysian border. Its share is especially small over the Thai–Myanmar border, partly because the Myanmar government is not yet ready to implement border transport agreements. This is partly because such agreements require a number of trade procedure reforms, but mainly because the roads and

submitted to the Senate Standing Committee on Commerce and Industry as well (Senate Standing Committee on Commerce and Industry 2000: 6). The National Economic and Social Development Council used a more simple definition without any mention to the Border Transport Agreement. It defines border trade as trade with Thailand's four bordering countries via border trading points, and transit trade as trade with non-bordering countries via one of the four bordering countries. It does not explicitly explain whether transit trade can include commodities sent to or from one of the four bordering countries via maritime route or not. (Office of the National Economic and Social Development Council 2016: 1). As this study uses the data compiled by the DFT, we exclude commodities sent to or from the bordering countries via maritime routes from transit trade.

Table 5.2 Thailand's border and transit trade with and through its neighboring countries

Unit: amount—million Baht, share—%

	Malaysia				Myanmar				Laos				Cambodia			
	Export		Import		Export		Import		Export		Import		Export		Import	
2021	Amount	Share	Amount	Share	Amount	Share	Amount	Share	Amount	Share	Amount	Share	Amount	Share	Amount	Share
T.Trade	164,139	47.4	127,613	45.4	2,431	2.0	4,539	5.1	292,962	70.1	192,419	68.1	1,795	1.2	5,366	17.1
B.Trade	182,464	52.6	153,532	54.6	119,655	98.0	84,512	94.9	124,769	29.9	90,045	31.9	143,115	98.8	25,989	82.9
Total	346,603	100.0	281,145	100.0	122,086	100.0	89,051	100.0	417,731	100.0	282,464	100.0	144,910	100.0	31,355	100.0

railways in Myanmar are underdeveloped and poorly maintained. It is time-consuming and costly to transport commodities from the Thai–Myanmar border to Myanmar's border with other countries, such as China, Bangladesh, and India. Furthermore, intensifying armed conflict between the Min Aung Hlaing government and ethnic minorities in the border areas in recent years made transit trade through Myanmar even more unfeasible.

As pointed out earlier, not all goods that go to or come from the third countries are classified by the DFT as transit trade. Only those traded in the framework of cross-border transport agreements such as the Greater Mekong Subregion Cross-Border Transport Agreement (GMS CBTA) and ASEAN Framework Agreement for the Facilitation of Goods in Transit (AFAFGIT) are included in the DFT's classification. Notably, a report submitted to the Department of Import and Export, Ministry of Industry and Commerce, Laos, in 2019 by an international consulting company based in Bulgaria wrote that many Lao traders prefer not to utilize cross-border transport agreements even when they are dealing in commodities that go to or come from third countries (Emerging Markets Consulting 2019: 8–11).

Our interviews with customs officers on the Thai side of the border also confirm that many commodities that go to and come from third countries are traded outside cross-border transport agreements and are thus classified as border trade. Though transit trade occupies a large portion of goods traded through the Thai–Lao and Thai–Malaysian borders (even in the DFT's official figures), the real shares of the goods that go to or come from the third countries are very likely to be much higher.

When we analyze the DFT's border trade data, we need to consider the often-neglected fact that the DFT's distinction between border and transit trade is so unclear. If we look only at the official border trade statistics, we overlook a large volume of transit trade, especially in Thai–Lao and Thai–Malaysian land trade. That is, we cannot assume that all commodities classified as border trade exports will actually be consumed in neighboring countries; some may end up being re-exported to third countries. Similarly, we cannot assume all commodities classified as border trade imports have been produced in neighboring countries; some may have been produced in third countries.

Yet another source of unreliability of Thailand's border trade data is the corruption of customs officers on the both sides of the borders and rule-breaking by traders. Notably, although all of Thailand's four bordering countries are members of the Association of Southeast Asian Nations (ASEAN), whose member countries signed the ASEAN Free Trade Area Agreement in 1992, not all trade among member countries is exempted from customs duties.

Table 5.3 shows the volume of imports from Myanmar to Thailand through the customs office at Maesot (by far the largest border trading town along the Thai–Myanmar border) as well as the customs duty collected on the Thai side of the border. The rate of customs duty varies depending on the type of commodity imported. For example, it is 10% for nylon fishing net and around 15% for livestock (based on interviews at the customs duty office in Maesot). Traders often under-declare the value of commodities at the customs office to reduce the amounts of

Table 5.3 Imports from Myanmar to Thailand and customs duty gathered at Maesot

Unit: million Baht, %

Fiscal year	Import	Custom duty	Average rate
2016	4,179	184	4.4
2017	5,302	122	2.3
2018	6,489	117	1.8
2019	9,668	127	1.3
2020	11,197	149	1.3
2021	20,032	105	0.5
2022	28,091	204	0.7

Source: Maesot Customs House (2024)

duties they are obliged to pay. Furthermore, it is not uncommon to bribe customs officers to make them turn a blind eye to the under-declaration.

In the following sections, we utilize statistical data compiled and published by Thailand's customs office and the DFT, keeping the abovementioned flaws, biases, and limitations of the data always in mind. In order to at least partially alleviate the deficiency of the statistical data, we also rely on findings from field research we conducted in Thailand's border areas over the past several years.

In order to conduct an in-depth analysis, we focus on border trade between Thailand and Myanmar in the following sections. Though border trade with Myanmar is not the largest among Thailand's four bordering countries, the Thai–Myanmar border is by far the longest (see exact figures above) and Myanmar's population is much larger than that of Thailand's other three neighbors. We also focus on Thai–Myanmar trade because transit trade occupies only a small fraction of the total trade volume. Thus, we can avoid the problems caused by the DFT's unclear distinction between border and transit trade.

5.2 Covid-19 in Thailand and Myanmar

Figure 5.1 shows the number of deaths caused by Covid-19 in Thailand. As the figure shows, Thailand managed to prevent the spread of Covid-19 until mid-2021. Though the Thai economy heavily relies on tourism and foreign investment, the Thai government strictly restricted the inflow of foreigners from mid-March 2020. Border crossings with its neighboring countries were also heavily restricted.

Although these severe restrictions prevented the spread of Covid-19 in 2020, they badly damaged the Thai economy. The Thai economy grew by 4.2% in 2017, 4.2% in 2018, and 2.1% in 2019, but plummeted –6.1% in 2020 (Bank of Thailand 2024, Table 5.2). Given this serious retraction of the economy and a rapid decline in its popularity, the Thai government gradually loosened restrictions in 2021. As a result, the economy started growing again but Covid-19 deaths spiked in mid-2021. This number decreased in late 2021, and the Thai government eventually lifted most restrictions in 2022.

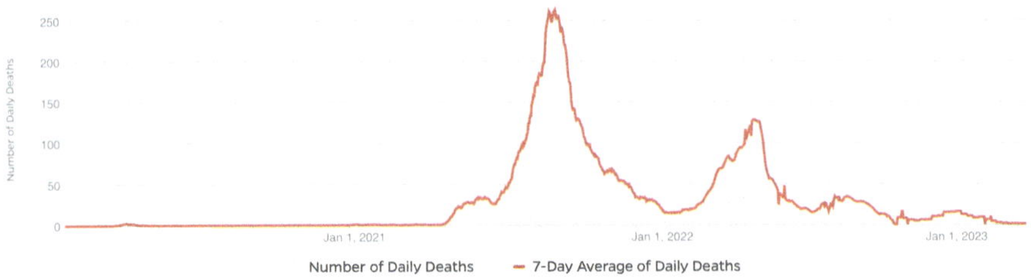

Fig. 5.1 Covid-19 deaths in Thailand (Coronavirus Resource Center, Johns Hopkins University 2023a)

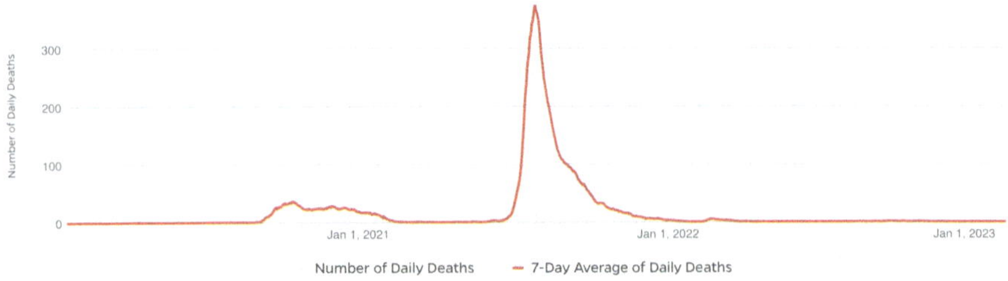

Fig. 5.2 Covid-19 deaths in Myanmar (Corona Virus Resource Center, Johns Hopkins University 2023b)

Figure 5.2 shows the number of deaths caused by Covid-19 in Myanmar. Notably, the public health service in Myanmar, especially in rural areas, is not well-managed. Political unrest after the coup in February 2021 worsened these issues and the dictatorial nature of the post-coup government led by Gen. Min Aung Hlaing restricted the free flow of information about the number of human casualties from Covid-19. Hence, it is widely believed that the real death toll is much larger than the official figures, on which Fig. 5.2 is based. Despite probably being inaccurate, Fig. 5.2 roughly reflects the general trend of the spread of Covid-19 in Myanmar; it suggests that, like in Thailand, Covid-19 did not spread extensively until mid-2021. Though the rapid spread of Covid-19 in the latter half of 2021 caused social havoc in Myanmar, it was somewhat overshadowed by increasingly intense conflict between the Min Aung Hlaing administration and the alliance of pro-democracy groups and armed ethnic minority organizations.

The Myanmar economy grew by 5.8% in 2017, 6.4% in 2018, and 6.8% in 2019, but shrank by −1.2% in 2020, nosedived −10.5% in 2021, and continued to decline by −4.0% in 2022 (International Monetary Fund 2024). It was not until 2023 that the Myanmar economy started to grow again (if official economic data released by the Min Aung Hlaing administration is to be believed). Armed conflict between the Min Aung Hlaing administration and anti-government forces has continued to intensify, and many border areas are now under the control of armed ethnic groups. Some of the routes that connect large cities such as Yangon, Naypyidaw, and Mandalay with border trading points are frequently disrupted by armed conflict.

5.3 The Impact of Covid-19 on Thai–Myanmar Trade and Substitutional Relations Between Land and Sea Trade

Thailand's GDP per capita stood at US$7336 at the end of 2023, while that of Myanmar was US$1190 (International Monetary Fund 2024). This huge gap in average income levels between the two countries, coupled with political instability in Myanmar, has resulted in a massive flow of migrant workers from Myanmar to Thailand in the past three decades. According to Thailand's Labor Ministry, 1,198,920 Myanmar nationals are working legally in Thailand as of February 2024 (Foreign Workers Administration Office 2024); it is widely believed that a much larger number of unregistered Myanmar nationals are working in Thailand. Most of those who work without proper documents sneak into Thailand through "natural border paths" between the two countries.[2]

The Myanmar economy relies heavily on remittance from undocumented migrant workers in Thailand, while the Thai economy also relies on these undocumented workers as an indispensable source of inexpensive and easily exploitable labor. The massive flow of undocumented migrant workers from Myanmar also gives corrupt members of the Thai police force an opportunity to extort bribes. Rampant corruption among police and military personnel in border areas has facilitated not only the flow of undocumented migrant workers but also the smuggling of commodities including narcotics.

Thailand and Myanmar have a similar area and population size. Thailand's land territory is 510,890 km^2, whereas that of Myanmar is 652,670 km^2. Thailand's population was estimated at 71.7 million as of 2023, while that of Myanmar was said to be 54.1 million. This population difference is expected to decrease; Thailand's population is projected to decline 7.4% to 66.4 million by 2050, while Myanmar's population is projected to grow 8.3% to 58.6 million over the same period (World Health Organization 2024a, b).

Table 5.4 compares Thai–Myanmar sea and land trade. Notably, Covid-19 had complex impacts on both forms of trade between the two countries. In 2020, both sea and land border trade between Thailand and Myanmar (except for sea imports from Myanmar to Thailand) declined due to strict restrictions on cross-border traffic and shrinking demand caused by economic recession. The increase in Thailand's sea imports from Myanmar can be explained as a response to prolonged closure of

[2] The National Economic and Social Development Council defines "natural border path" as an officially unapproved path used by local residents to visit their relatives on the other side of the border (Office of the National Economic and Social Development Council 2016: 2). Though it is called "natural," many of them are evidently man-made. In reality, not only local residents but also many types of people, such as undocumented migrant workers, members of armed ethnic groups who seek medical treatment in Thailand for their injury, political activists who need a hiding place on the other side of the border, criminals, and petty smugglers, have been using these natural border path to sneak in and out without going through formal immigration procedures. Goods transported through these natural border paths are not recorded in the official border trade statistics.

Table 5.4 Thailand's sea and land border trade with Myanmar: 2018–2022

Unit: million Baht, %

Year	Export to Myanmar						Import from Myanmar						Trade balance	
	T.Trade	S. Trade	Change	L. Trade	Change	L/T	T.Trade	S. Trade	Change	L. Trade	Change	L/T	T.Trade	L. Trade
2018	148,186	42,974	–	105,212	–	71.0	97,953	9,839	–	88,114	–	90.0	33,135	17,098
2019	135,140	35,748	−16.8	99,392	−5.5	73.5	101,917	8,046	−18.2	93,871	6.5	92.1	27,702	5,521
2020	117,554	30,474	−14.8	87,080	−12.4	74.1	88,077	10,371	28.9	77,706	−17.2	88.2	20,103	9,374
2021	136,247	16,592	−45.6	119,655	37.4	87.8	89,925	5,413	−47.8	84,512	8.8	94.0	11,179	35,143
2022	162,681	19,099	15.1	143,582	20.0	88.3	123,873	3,817	−29.5	120,056	42.1	96.9	15,282	23,526

Source: The Department of Foreign Trade, Thailand

Note: T. Trade = Total Trade (both land and sea trade); S. Trade = Sea Trade; L. Trade = Land Trade; L/T = the share of Land (Border) Trade in Total Trade

land-border crossings. Some commodities that used to be exported to Thailand by land in the pre-Covid-19 era were diverted to marine trading routes. The increase in Myanmar's sea exports to Thailand, however, was not large enough to offset the decline in its land exports. Thus, Myanmar's total exports to Thailand decreased in 2020, as shown in Table 5.4.

In 2021, quite different changes occurred in Thai–Myanmar trade. Myanmar's sea exports to Thailand declined significantly; however, this decline was offset by a significant increase in land exports. Thus Myanmar's total exports to Thailand increased slightly in 2021, despite the severe impacts of Covid-19 (the number of deaths caused by Covid-19 in 2021 was larger than in 2020 in the both countries as shown in Figs. 5.1 and 5.2 in the previous section). Similar trends can be observed in Thai exports to Myanmar in 2021. While Thailand's sea exports to Myanmar declined, this was offset by increased land exports. This shift from sea to land trade in 2021 can be explained as a response to increasing difficulties in transporting commodities from inland Myanmar to Yangon Ports.

Just after the Myanmar coup in February 2021, a large-scale civil disobedience movement broke out. It weakened the administrative capability of the government in many parts of the country. An increasing area of land and number of roads came under the control of armed ethnic groups. Insufficient vaccination and a lack of qualified medical personnel made Covid-19's fatality rate in Myanmar much higher than that in Thailand. As Covid-19 spread all over the country in the latter half of 2021, the Myanmar government locked-down many local towns and rural communities. These factors made domestic land transportation between many parts of the country and Yangon Ports much more time-consuming and costly.

Conversely, the Thai government gradually started loosening many restrictions in 2021. The Thai economy slowly started recovering, while the Myanmar economy continued to deteriorate (as outlined above). There was a resurgence in the inflow of undocumented migrant workers from Myanmar to Thailand as well as traffic through some of the trading gates on the Thai–Myanmar border. These factors caused the shift from sea to land trade routes.

It should also be noted that, as discussed above, there are no deep-sea ports in the Thai provinces facing the Indian Ocean. All the deep-sea ports in Thailand are located in the provinces that face the Gulf of Thailand, which is adjacent to South China Sea. Therefore, cargo ships that directly connect Myanmar and Thailand need to go through the Strait of Malacca. The land route between Yangon and Bangkok is about 900 km, while the maritime route stretches about 4400 km. Therefore, even a small change in transportation cost can cause massive shift from one route to the other.

Although Myanmar's sea imports from Thailand rebounded slightly in 2023, they are still at a much lower level than in the pre-Covid-19 era, as shown in Table 5.4. Myanmar's sea exports to Thailand continued to plunge in 2023. Land trade now accounts for about 97% of Myanmar's exports to Thailand.

These findings suggest that there are substitutional relations between land and sea trade in the case of Thailand and Myanmar. Covid-19-related disruption resulted in a shift from land to sea trade in the early stage, though this shift reversed in the later stage, as neighboring Thailand started lifting some of the restrictions it had imposed earlier in the pandemic. Intensified political tensions and the Myanmar government's loss of control in some of the border areas accelerated this reversal.

5.4 Semi-Illegal Nature of Border Trade Between Thailand and Myanmar

Akkanut (2012: 127–128) investigated Thai–Myanmar border trade between 1990 and 2010; by studying discrepancies between Thai and Myanmar customs records, he pointed out that most commodities smuggled across the Thai–Myanmar border go through export but not import customs clearance. Table 5.5 shows export and import figures for Thai–Myanmar border trade compiled by the customs offices on both sides of the border in recent years. Discrepancies in the figures recorded by importing and exporting countries inevitably occur even if there is no smuggling, because transportation and insurance costs are usually added to the import but not the export values. Furthermore, fluctuation in exchange rates and different timings of currency conversion may also cause discrepancies. Finally, the different treatment of transit trade in the compilation of trade data in each country can also cause discrepancies.

Table 5.5 Thai–Myanmar border trade: comparison of customs office records on both sides of the borders

Unit: Baht

	From Myanmar to Thailand		From Thailand to Myanmar	
Year	Thai import records	Myanmar export records	Thai export records	Myanmar import records
2015	121,185,577,583	120,573,890,580	140,535,867,709	70,548,829,740
2016	83,604,499,987	80,357,667,450	146,405,379,513	71,194,801,800
2017	84,348,956,701	87,868,271,920	146,094,908,771	70,547,003,120
2018	97,953,320,097	98,868,004,620	147,662,710,215	84,093,863,700
2019	101,916,642,656	96, 922,159,680	135,056,301,697	65,349,805,440
2020	88,077,227,123	90,373,477,520	117,365,460,633	57,876,926,480
2021	89,925,355,967	116,067,471,960	136,110,151,284	68,723,793,750

Source: Ministry of Commerce (2022), World Bank (2024)

Note: Year-end exchange rates were used to convert US$ in the Myanmar official statistics into Thai Baht

However, the size of these discrepancies, especially in the flow of goods from Thailand to Myanmar, is too large to be explained by these factors. Our interviews with Thai customs officers as well as both Thai and Myanmar businesspeople involved in the border trade suggested that a sizable portion of the commodities that go through customs procedures on the Thai side do not go through any official procedure on the Myanmar side.

One of the main reasons for the rampant avoidance of official customs procedures on the Myanmar side is the higher duty rates the Myanmar government imposes on imports compared with the Thai side. Notably, some commodities also fail to go through customs procedures on the Thai side. Although we cannot accurately estimate the amount of commodities that do not go through official customs procedures on both sides of the border, our field interviews suggest that, except for narcotics and illegal weapons, commodities that go through official customs procedures on the Thai side far outnumbers those which do not.[3]

Smuggling across the small and shallow river on the Thai–Myanmar border is a common sight and often gives casual observers the strong impression that the vast majority of goods that cross the Thai–Myanmar border is smuggled. Small-scale smuggling, however, is often not cost-effective. Transporting a large number of commodities in a large 10-wheel truck that can cross the two-lane concrete bridge over the river is often more cost-effective than carrying a small amount in a small boat or a small pick-up truck either on a barge or across small make-shift bridges.

Thai customs seldom collect export duties on the commodities that cross the border from Thailand to Myanmar. If the bribe demanded by officers or anyone else in control of border areas on the Myanmar side is smaller than the difference in transportation costs between the formal and illegal routes, it is economically rational to go through official customs procedures on the Thai side and evade formal procedures on the Myanmar side, rather than avoiding official procedures on the Thai side.

Overall, judging from the discrepancies shown in Table 5.6, about half of the commodities Thailand exports to Myanmar across the border through formal channels do not go through official procedures on the Myanmar side.

5.5 Composition of Thai–Myanmar Border Trade

According to statistics released by Thailand's DFT (relating to 2021), diesel oil (6.8%), non-alcoholic beverages (5.1%), cooking oil (4.5%), electric wire (4.3%), and spices and herbs (3.8%) are the main products Thailand exports to Myanmar via

[3] Some informants gave us a very rough estimate of the amount of the commodities that failed to go through official customs procedures on the Thai side (equivalent to about 30% of the commodities that go through official procedures). Further research is needed to confirm the accuracy of this estimate.

Table 5.6 Thai–Myanmar border trade: discrepancies in customs office records on both sides of the borders

Unit: Baht, %

Year	Thai Records – Myanmarese Records		(Thai Record – Myanmares Record) × 100/ Thai Records	
	Myanmar to Thailand	Thailand to Myanmar	Myanmar to Thailand	Thailand to Myanmar
2015	611,687,003	69,987,037,969	0.5	49.8
2016	3,246,832,537	75,210,577,713	3.9	51.4
2017	−3,519,315,219	75,547,905,651	−4.2	51.7
2018	−914,684,523	63,568,846,515	−0.9	43.1
2019	4,994,482,976	69,706,496,257	4.9	51.6
2020	−2,296,250,397	59,488,534,153	−2.6	50.7
2021	−26,142,115,993	67,386,357,534	−29.1	49.5

Source: Calculated from Table 5.5

land. As for Thailand's land imports from Myanmar, natural gas (65.1%), cereal crops (14.8%), aquatic animals (3.8%), iron (2.0%), and vegetables (1.8%) were the top five categories in 2021.

Aside from natural gas, which is sent from Myanmar to Thailand through the cross-border pipeline, cereal crops, especially maize, came to occupy a sizable portion of Thai–Myanmar border trade. Thailand started importing maize from Myanmar under the Special Economic Zone Development Policy in 2015. Under this pilot scheme, no import tax is levied on the import of maize at Maesot Customs House. This pilot program was implemented in order to solve the problem of illegal smuggling of agricultural products from neighboring countries into Thailand. In 2015, Thailand's imports of maize from Myanmar by land amounted to about 16.2 million baht (Office of Agricultural Economics 2017). Maize imports have continued to increase since then. Thailand's maize imports from Myanmar through the Customs Office at Maesot jumped to 4239 million baht in 2019, 5603 million baht in 2020, and 10,958 million baht in 2021 (Maesot Customs House 2024). In February 2020, Thailand also started importing maize at the customs office in Maesai (Maesai Customs House 2024).

These figures on Thailand's land imports of maize clearly show that Covid-19 did not significantly affect trade volumes. One of the explanations for this robustness against Covid-19 lies in the way that commodities are transported. Unlike in Europe, a truck driver carrying commodities destined to cross the border does not usually go further than a border town in the importing country, unless they are carrying frozen products. On the Thai side, this is because the Thai government is reluctant to allow foreign drivers who do not speak or understand the Thai language very well to drive large trucks beyond border towns. It is partly also because they want to protect jobs for Thai drivers. Hence, the trucks that carry maize from Myanmar to Thailand unload the maize at a warehouse in the suburbs of a border town in most cases. Similarly, Thai drivers transporting commodities from Thailand to Myanmar do not usually go beyond a border town on the Myanmar side; transportation within Myanmar is carried out by the locals. Since this has been an established practice since well before Covid-19, strict restrictions on the cross-border movement of people did not affect the volume of border trade between Thailand and Myanmar too severely.[4]

5.6 Conclusion

The paucity of reliable data on Thailand's border trade continues to make in-depth analysis challenging. This study tried to alleviate the problems caused by the lack of data and the questionable data compilation methods used by some government agencies through conducting field research. However, there are still many issues on which this study could not shed much light, such as trade settlement mechanism and roles played by drug dealers and human traffickers in border trade. Despite these limitations, this study offers original analysis on some of the intriguing but understudied issues regarding the impact of Covid-19 on Thailand's border trade.

Covid-19 undoubtedly affected Thailand's border trade. Its impacts, however, were not straightforward; some aspects of border trade declined while others increased. Its impacts even changed direction over time. In the case of Thai–Myanmar trade, the spread of Covid-19 (and anticipatory fear of its spread) caused a sharp decline in Myanmar's land exports to Thailand and the rapid growth of sea exports to Thailand in 2020; however, in the following years, Covid-19 caused an increase in land exports and a decrease in sea exports. Such fluctuations in the trade route imply that there are substitutional relations between land and sea trade. External shocks, such as the spread of Covid-19 and resultant restrictions on the flow of people, affect traders' choice between different trade routes.

This study also analyzed why regional border trade showed robustness against Covid-19 and pointed out the role of regional transportation methods that discourage truck drivers from going further than border towns in neighboring countries. The institutionalization of these transportation methods, which avoid long-distance cross-border driving, alleviated the potentially much more severe adverse impact of Covid-19 on regional border trade.

[4] Another primary reason for the robustness of Thai–Myanmar border trade against Covid-19 is that natural gas exports from Myanmar to Thailand go through a cross-border pipeline; this trade occupies a considerable portion of total border trade.

References

Akkanut W (2012) Thailand-Myanmar border trade. PSAKU Int J Interdiscip Res 1(1):124–143. https://papers.ssrn.com/sol3/papers.cfm?abstract_id=3042186. Accessed 11 Dec 2024

Bank of Thailand (2024) Key economic indicators. https://www.bot.or.th/en/statistics/economic-and-financial-index-and-indicators.html. Accessed 11 Dec 2024

Coronavirus Resource Center, Johns Hopkins University (2023a) Thailand: number of daily deaths (data timeline). https://coronavirus.jhu.edu/region/thailand. Accessed 11 Dec 2024

Coronavirus Resource Center, Johns Hopkins University (2023b) Myanmar: number of daily deaths (data timeline). https://coronavirus.jhu.edu/region/myanmar. Accessed 11 Dec 2024

Department of Foreign Trade (2020) คำนิยามการค้าชายแดน/ผ่านแดน (Definitions related to border/transit trade). https://www.dft.go.th/bts/bts-trader. Accessed 11 Dec 2024

Department of Foreign Trade (2021) ภาพรวมการค้าชายแดนและการค้าผ่านแดนของไทย (Overview of border trade and transit trade in Thailand). https://www.dft.go.th/Portals/3/ภาพรวม ม.ค-ธค.63.pdf. Accessed 11 Dec 2024

Department of Foreign Trade (2022) ภาพรวมการค้าชายแดนและการค้าผ่านแดนของไทย (Overview of border trade and transit trade in Thailand). https://www.dft.go.th/Portals/3/1.%20ภาพรวม%20ธันวาคม%2064(%2028%20มค.65).pdf. Accessed 11 Dec 2024

Department of Foreign Trade (2023) ภาพรวมการค้าชายแดนและการค้าผ่านแดนของไทย (Overview of border trade and transit trade in Thailand). https://www.dft.go.th/Portals/3/1.1.4%20%20ชายแดนผ่านแดน%20%20มค.-ธค%202565.pdf. Accessed 11 Dec 2024

Department of Local Administration (2014) รายชื่อจังหวัดที่มีพรมแดนติดต่อกับประเทศเพื่อนบ้าน (List of provinces that have borders with neighboring countries). https://www.dla.go.th/upload/asean/2014/6/1402286830288.pdf. Accessed 11 Dec 2024

Department of Treaties and Legal Affairs (2022) ข้อมูลเขตแดน (Boundary information). https://treaties.mfa.go.th/th/content/ข้อมูลเขตแดน. Accessed 11 Dec 2024

Emerging Markets Consulting (2019) Study to address issues faced by Lao trade transiting through Thailand and Vietnam (for Department of Import and Export Ministry of Industry and Commerce). https://www.laotradeportal.gov.la/upload/files/Announcement_1556164655.pdf. Accessed 11 Dec 2024

Foreign Workers Administration Office (2024) สถิติจำนวนต่างด้าวที่ได้รับอนุญาตทำงานคงเหลือทั่วราชอาณาจักร กุมภาพันธ์ 67 (Statistics on the number of foreigners who work in Thailand with work permits). https://www.doe.go.th/prd/assets/upload/files/alien_th/c834a1efb9b72c77bd3fffed4b8c44cd.pdf. Accessed 11 Dec 2024

International Monetary Fund (2024) World economic outlook database. https://www.imf.org/en/Publications/WEO/weo-database/2024/October/select-country-group. Accessed 11 Dec 2024

Maesai Customs House (2024) สถิติการนำเข้า-ส่งออก (Import-export statistics). https://maesai.customs.go.th/list_strc_download.php?ini_content=statistic_and_report_180205_01. Accessed 11 Dec 2024

Maesot Customs House (2024) สถิติสินค้านำเข้า 10 อันดับ ณ ด่านศุลกากรแม่สอด (Top 10 import-export products with the highest value). https://maesot.customs.go.th/data_files/182e9c0187fda529b2a1f88c0c8f0919.pdf. Accessed 11 Dec 2024

Ministry of Commerce (2022) Foreign trade statistics of Thailand. https://tradereport.moc.go.th/th/documentyear. Accessed 11 Dec 2024

Office of Agricultural Economics (2017) การศึกษาการค้าข้าวโพดเลี้ยงสัตว์ผ่านด่านชายแดน (Study of trade in animal feed corn through border checkpoints). https://คิดค้า.com/wp-content/uploads/2021/08/1.-งานวิจัย-สศก-การศึกษาการค้าข้าวโพดเลี้ยงสัตว์ผ่านด่านชายแดน.pdf. Accessed 11 Dec 2024

Office of the National Economic and Social Development Council (2016) นิยามที่เกี่ยวข้องกับการค้าชายแดน (Definitions related to border trade). https://www.nesdc.go.th/ewt_dl_link.php?nid=6211. Accessed 11 Dec 2024

Senate Standing Committee on Commerce and Industry (2000) รายงานการพิจารณาศึกษาเรื่องการส่งเสริมการค้าชายแดน (Study report on the promotion of border trade). https://prt.parliament.go.th/bitstreams/da858e88-1ceb-4749-a4d8-8c03b84f6366/download. Accessed 11 Dec 2024

World Bank (2024) World Integrated Trade Solution. https://wits.worldbank.org. Accessed 11 Dec 2024

World Health Organization (2024a) Health data overview for the Kingdom of Thailand. https://data.who.int/countries/764. Accessed 11 Dec 2024

World Health Organization (2024b) Health data overview for the Republic of the Union of Myanmar. https://data.who.int/countries/104. Accessed 11 Dec 2024

Chapter 6
Changes in Thailand's Poverty and Income Inequality Caused by COVID-19: Assessment Using Normative Measures

Akio Egawa

Abstract Although the COVID-19 pandemic negatively affected lower-income Thai households, the poverty ratio rose only slightly in 2020 and fell well below the pre-COVID-19 level by 2022; the Gini coefficient remained flat in 2020 and 2021, then fell in 2022. The Thai government attributes these outcomes to government support measures, particularly for low-income households. A more detailed analysis of changes in income distribution over time should be used to judge the improvement or worsening of income inequality. In conditions where classical theorems of welfare economics hold, a comparison of Lorenz curves (LCs) and Generalized Lorenz curves (GLCs, i.e. normative measures) provides an unambiguous conclusion on the improvement or worsening of income inequality and social welfare, regardless of social preference. I aimed to grasp the change in Thailand's state of income (in)equality and social welfare during the pandemic based on normative measures by deriving LCs and GLCs for each year and checking whether there is a relationship between Lorenz dominance and Generalized Lorenz dominance. Neither Lorenz dominance nor Generalized Lorenz dominance held between 2019 and 2022. The decrease in Thailand's Gini coefficient in 2022 does not necessarily indicate that income distribution was better than before the pandemic. In addition, it cannot be unambiguously concluded that government policy measures improved social welfare by 2022 compared with 2019.

Keywords COVID-19 · Poverty · Thailand · Income inequality · Lorenz dominance · Social welfare · Generalized Lorenz dominance

A. Egawa (✉)
Faculty of Economics, Momoyama Gakuin University, Izumi, Osaka, Japan
e-mail: aegawa@andrew.ac.jp

© The Author(s), under exclusive license to Springer Nature Singapore Pte Ltd. 2025

H. Taguchi (ed.), *Sustainability of Economic Growth in East Asia*,
New Frontiers in Regional Science: Asian Perspectives 82,
https://doi.org/10.1007/978-981-96-3731-7_6

6.1 Introduction

Thailand's poverty rate and Gini coefficient[1] declined from their peak in 2000 until 2019. However, in early 2020, concerns arose that the COVID-19 pandemic would have a greater impact on lower-income people, leading to a sharp increase in the number of poor and a significant worsening of income inequality. In practice, the domestic poverty rate[2] rose from 6.23% in 2019 to 6.83% in 2020 but fell to a slightly higher level than the pre-COVID-19 period at 6.32% in 2021; it further fell to 5.43% and 3.41% in 2022 and 2023, respectively, well below the pre-COVID-19 levels. In addition, the Gini coefficient barely rose to 0.350 in 2020 and 2021; from 0.348 in 2019, it fell to 0.343 in 2022 and 0.335 in 2023.

The Thai government noted that neither the poverty rate nor the Gini coefficient worsened significantly due to government support measures, particularly for low-income households. However, the fact that the poverty rate rose while the Gini coefficient remained unchanged from 2019 to 2021 suggests that the income distribution structure may have changed in a more disadvantageous way for the poor. This shows that the impact of COVID-19 on poverty and income inequality should not be judged solely by a descriptive approach (such as the Gini coefficient scores) but also by a more detailed analysis of changes in income distribution over time. The situation of poverty should also be assessed not only by numerical values (e.g., the poverty rate) but also by considering the changes in low-income people's living standards (e.g., amount of income and ways of spending) as well as changes in (the amount of) social welfare.[3] When conducting such an assessment, it is necessary to know the shape of the income distribution and social welfare functions (SWFs) for each year; however, it is very difficult to identify the latter. Notwithstanding, under conditions in which some classical theorems of welfare economics hold, it is possible to understand the improvement or worsening of income inequality and social welfare through normative measures, i.e., without the need to identify the shape of SWFs. This involves plotting Lorenz curves (LCs) and Generalized Lorenz curves

[1] The Gini coefficient is a scalar representation of the degree of income inequality, taking values between 0 and 1; the higher the value, the worse the income inequality (see, e.g., Barr 1998 and Lambert 2001 for a textbook explanation).

[2] In international comparisons, the "poverty line"—which is the standard for determining whether someone is poor—is the amount of spending at 1.90 purchasing power parity (PPP) dollars per day. Thailand's poverty rate, measured based on this global poverty line, is zero already. Thailand set its domestic poverty line at 2997 baht per person per month on average in 2022. This is equivalent to 8.51 PPP dollars of spending per day for the same year (the data used were derived from the International Monetary Fund [IMF]).

[3] In addition, the spending structure of each household was forced to change in response to COVID-19. For low-income earners, even if they could afford expenses higher than the poverty line, unavoidable spending related to COVID-19 increased. As a reaction to this, spending on daily living expenses may have declined. From this perspective, the living conditions of low-income households worsened, even though the Gini coefficient has not risen significantly and is now on a downward trend again. However, I will include the analysis of this point in a future study.

(GLCs) for each year in Thailand and checking whether there is a relationship called Lorenz dominance or Generalized Lorenz (GL) dominance.

In the above context, I aimed to understand the changes in Thailand's income distribution and social welfare during the COVID-19 pandemic by estimating income distribution functions for each year and comparing the derived LCs and GLCs from the perspective of whether Lorenz dominance or GL dominance holds between the corresponding years. This will help obtain suggestions on the effectiveness of poverty reduction measures and income redistribution policies implemented during that period.

6.2 Pitfalls of the Descriptive Approach (Scalar Representation) to Income Inequality

According to data, the Thai government's policy response during the COVID-19 pandemic halted worsening poverty and income inequality. The World Bank (2021) estimated that Thailand's domestic poverty rate would have risen to approximately 7.4% (6.23% in 2019) during the pandemic if it had not been for government support measures for low-income households (the actual poverty rate in 2020 was 6.83%). The Organization for Economic Co-operation and Development (OECD 2020) determined that the Thai economy was able to quickly adapt to the economic downturn caused by the COVID-19 pandemic; this suggests that the increase in the low-income population was mitigated by the government's support measures meant to aid the economy as a whole. In addition, the Office of the National Economic and Social Development Council (NESDC), Thailand's government agency responsible for promoting economic and social policies, estimated that the Gini coefficient would have risen to 0.383 (0.348 in 2019) without government policies to halt the worsening of income inequality (NESDC 2021). I agree with their assertion that the Thai government's policy measures were implemented promptly and mitigated a potential increase in poverty and the worsening of income inequality to some extent, although the size of the policy measures was not adequate (Egawa 2021, 2022). Furthermore, the use of the descriptive approach or a scalar representation (such as poverty rates and the Gini coefficient) to evaluate the effect of policies is a common practice among governments in many countries and is not unique to Thailand.

However, if policies are evaluated based only on the trends in these figures, the changes in the income distribution of society as a whole and the living conditions of the poor cannot be fully captured, and the conclusions will be insufficient. For example, when the income gap between people in the middle- and higher-income groups narrows and low-income earners fail to increase their income, income distribution becomes less advantageous for low-income earners. This situation was also observed in Thailand during the COVID-19 pandemic. Figure 6.1 shows the income growth rate by income decile group from 2019 to 2021, indicating that the income growth rates for the second through fourth income deciles were higher than the total

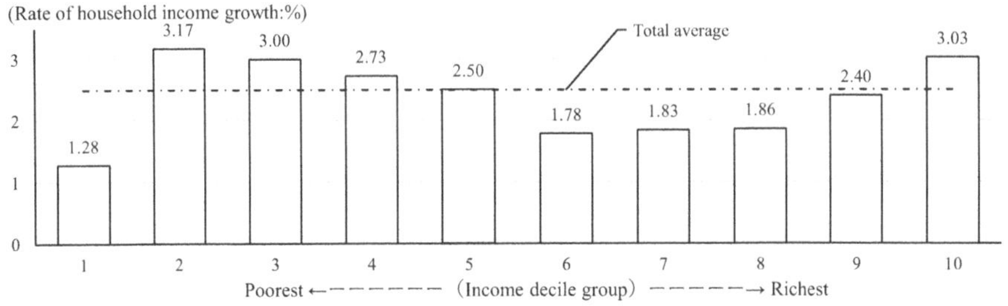

Fig. 6.1 Household income growth rate by income decile groups from 2019 to 2021 (NESDC 2022)

income growth rate (causing the Gini coefficient to decline), while at the same time, the income gap between the richest and poorest widened (raising the Gini coefficient). There is room to conclude that income distribution worsened during this period, even though the Gini coefficient remained almost unchanged. In addition, the income growth rate of the poor (which is below the total average) may be considered insufficient to improve society's satisfaction (or social welfare). In other words, the evaluation of poverty and income inequality can lead to different conclusions depending on the income distribution structure and shape of social preferences (i.e., SWFs). As SWFs are usually defined as the sum of individual utilities (i.e., the Benthamian assumption), it is necessary to know the shape of the von Neuman Morgenstern (vNM) utility function of assumed identical individuals in Thailand, the derivation of which is extremely difficult.

However, cases exist in which it is possible to assess changes in income distribution and social welfare without specifying a utility function. When the classical theorems of welfare economics hold, a normative measure—a simple visual comparison of the LCs of different years[4]—can lead to a solid conclusion regarding the change in the state of income inequality. When the two LCs do not intersect, one can unambiguously infer that the income distribution for a year whose LC is located above is more equal than that of the corresponding year, regardless of the shape of the SWF (or the shape of the vNM utility function); this situation is called Lorenz dominance. In a situation where Lorenz dominance does not hold (i.e., when the LCs intersect), it is not possible to unambiguously establish the rank of income inequality between the two states. Notwithstanding, even in such a case, it is possible to find a situation where the two GLCs (which are the LCs multiplied by the average income) do not intersect (a situation called Generalized Lorenz (GL) dominance). Shorrocks (1983) proved that, when GL dominance is observed, conclusions can be drawn unambiguously about changes in social welfare without having to specify individual utility functions; the social state in a year whose GLC is located above has greater social welfare than that in the corresponding year (the so-called Shorrocks theorem). Finding a GL dominance relationship, although telling nothing

[4]The LC shows the share of total income received by the lowest $100p\%$ (p assumes a value between 0 and 1) of individuals when all individuals are arranged in order from the poorest upward.

about the state of poverty itself, is sufficiently persuasive to assess the improvement of the conditions of poor and low-income earners from the perspective of whether society (or the country) succeeds in improving their state enough to increase their social welfare.

Both Lorenz dominance and GL dominance are basic theories of welfare economics introduced in textbooks such as that of Lambert (2001, p. 49). Previous studies utilizing the concept of GL dominance include Kakwani (1984), who found that the Philippines (which was Lorenz dominated by in India) had higher social welfare than India in 1970 because the GLC for the Philippines was located above that for India. Regarding the analysis of changes in social welfare and income inequality (or GLCs and LCs, respectively) over time in the same country, Jenkins (1991) deduced that, during Thatcher's years in the UK, the poorest took less and inequality increased, but, metaphorically speaking, the cake became larger and, as a result, overall well-being rose. At a more practical level, the Food Agricultural Organization (FAO) recommends, through its training program with Bellù and Liberati's (2005) material, to utilize the idea of GL dominance for policymaking and choosing the most efficient policy options to alleviate poverty and income inequality, which can maximize a country's social welfare. Nevertheless, as far as I have researched in English language publications, no previous studies focused on Thailand have conducted analyses based on normative measures.

6.3 Models, Data, and Methods for Deriving Income Distribution Functions

The analysis here includes the derivation of LCs and GLCs through the estimation of income distribution functions for Thailand for the relevant years and an examination of whether the classical theorem can be applied between two curves for the corresponding years. Considering the purpose of this analysis, I used the situation in 2019 (just before the outbreak of COVID-19) as the base year; all years thereafter until 2023 were covered because there may have been significant changes each year due to COVID-19 and the government's policy responses to it.

6.3.1 Models

To derive the LC for each year, it was necessary to specify the income distribution function for that year. Let x_i^t be the spending of individual i in year t and $f^t(x)$ be the income distribution function (the probability density function) for year t. Then, the cumulative density function (CDF) for year t is $F^t(x) = \int_0^x f^t(z)dz$. In this case, $\int_0^\infty f^t(x)dx = 1$, and $\int_0^\infty x \bullet f^t(x)dx = \mu^t$ (μ^t is the average income in year t). A Benthamian SWF in year t is formulated as $W^t = \int u(x) \bullet f^t(x)dx$, where $u(x)$ is the

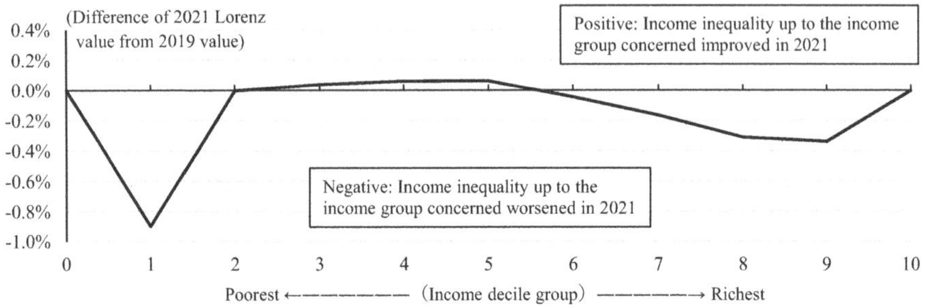

Fig. 6.2 Examples of situations where Lorenz dominance does not hold. The data were sourced from the NESDC (2022)

utility function for individuals (a vNM expected utility function, identical $\forall i$, strictly increasing, and concave $\forall x$).

If $p = F^t(y)$, then the LC is $L_{F^t}(p) = \int_0^y x \bullet f(x)dx / \mu^t$. When—and only when—there is a state of Lorenz dominance (expressed as $L_{F^t}(p) \geq L_{F^s}(p)$ for all $p \in (0, 1)$), we can unambiguously conclude that the income distribution in year t has a lower degree of income inequality than that in year s, regardless of social preference. Based on the situation in Fig. 6.1, we cannot firmly state that the income distribution remains equal and unchanged, even if the Gini coefficients are almost equal. Figure 6.2, which is the interpretation of Fig. 6.1 into a difference in Lorenz values at each decile, shows that the negative and positive values were switched twice. If the income distribution in 2021 Lorenz dominated that in 2019, the values on the graph would not have been negative. The judgment of the level of income inequality in the country will differ depending on which income class in Thailand we look at the most (i.e., the shape of the SWFs).

The GLC is $GL_{F^t}(p) = \int_0^y x \bullet f(x)dx$. Shorrocks' theorem can be expressed mathematically as $W^t \geq W^s \forall u(x) \Leftrightarrow GL_{F^t}(p) \geq GL_{F^s}(p) \forall p$. This can be interpreted as follows: When the GLCs between two points in time do not intersect (i.e., a state of GL dominance), we can draw an unambiguous conclusion about the level of social welfare without specifying the SWF (although we cannot make an unambiguous conclusion on the degree of income inequality). In this case, we can unambiguously conclude that year t (whose GLC is located above) realizes higher social welfare than year s, regardless of social preference.

6.3.2 Data Used

The data used to estimate the income distribution functions are "average consumption expenditure per person per month by decile groups" available from NESDC (2024). The basis for these statistical data comes from Thailand's Household Socio-Economic Survey (HSES). The reasons for using expenditure instead of income are twofold: Income data are available from the HSES only every 2 years, whereas

Table 6.1 Average expenditures by decile and Gini coefficient (official values by NESDC)

Year		2019	2020	2021	2022	2023
Decile by expenditures	1st (poorest)	2194	2161	2233	2461	2696
	2	3010	2998	3101	3391	3653
	3	3615	3649	3764	4113	4406
	4	4248	4319	4435	4867	5169
	5	4972	5068	5194	5675	6045
	6	5846	5969	6144	6658	7064
	7	6932	7070	7324	7883	8340
	8	8392	8561	8844	9476	9946
	9	10,623	10,896	11,184	12,024	12,394
	10th (richest)	18,464	18,612	19,227	20,288	21,003
Total average		6830	6930	7145	7684	8072
Gini coefficient by NESDC		0.3481	0.3495	0.3499	0.3428	0.3348

expenditure data are available annually, and the poverty line is based on expenditure. As the NESDC estimates the Gini coefficient based on expenditure per person, I used the same statistical data to estimate the income distribution function and analyze the income distribution structure.

For expenditure per person, it is necessary to use the average (statistical value) for each expenditure decile instead of the individual raw sample data. The sample size of the HSES is large at 57,600, and it would be ideal if individual raw sample data were used. However, the expenditure obtained from the raw sample data consists of "household expenditure" only, obtained through interviews with the head of the household every month (from January to December of the year).[5] Thus, there are no individual data for expenditure per person, and only statistical values in decile units based on estimates by the NESDC are available. Table 6.1 summarizes the average expenditure for each decile for the years analyzed. Thus, even from the limited number of values in Table 6.1, it is possible to derive the income distribution function using the following procedure.

6.3.3 *Method of Estimating the Income Distribution Functions*

In deriving $f(x)$, I did not specify the shape of the income distribution function in advance but specified it based on the goodness-of-fit test for each CDF. The software used in the estimation and test was EasyFit version 5.6, which is simple to use and suitable for calculating the goodness of fit and specifying CDFs. Although the statistical figures are "expenditure," for simplicity's sake, I employed the term of "income" decile in this study.

[5] See the National Statical Office (2024, p. 109).

[i] First, using the statistical data of the average income of each decile, I specified the CDF using EasyFit. The candidates of the CDF to be identified are all continuous functions with closed lower bounds and open upper bounds offered by the software, as the purpose of the specification is to generate random numbers, as described in [ii]. The Kolmogorov–Smirnov (KS) and Anderson–Darling tests are typical tests for specification, and in this analysis, the goodness of fit from the low-income to average-income part is important. Hence, I used the KS test results to specify CDF. I generated 5000 random numbers[6] from the specified CDF; they were sorted in ascending order. I conducted this random number generation 10 times and calculated the average value of the numbers with the same rank to minimize the influence of outliers on the high-income side of the random numbers on the estimate of the income distribution function in the process [iii].

[ii] Of the 5000 data created in process [i], the first (poorest) decile group is considered to consist of the first 500 data points (from the smallest upward). Likewise, I generated 10 income decile groups and multiplied each data point in the k-th decile group by the average expenditure of the k-th decile group published by the NESDC. I then divided each data point by the average of 500 data points within the k-th income decile group.

[iii] With 5000 data created in process [ii], I again specified the CDFs. The CDF candidates covered here are limited to those mentioned by McDonald (1984) and their special types: Singh–Maddala (Burr), Generalized-Gamma, Log-Logistic, Gamma, Inverse-Gamma, Log-Gamma, Inverse-Gaussian, Lognormal, and Pearson (types 5 and 6).[7]

[iv] The specified CDF in the process [iii] is mathematically "folded" at $0.1k$ $(k = 1, 2, \cdots, 10)$ points in order to make the average income of each decile equal to the mean of each decile estimated by the NESDC. If $p = F^t(m)$ and the average income of the k-th decile published by the NESDC, and that calculated from the model, are denoted as μ_k and $\tilde{\mu}_k = \int_{0.1(k-1)}^{0.1k} F^{t-1}(m)dm / 0.1$, respectively, then the expenditure of individual i at the smallest $0.1k$ income point is $F^{t-1}(0.1k) \bullet (1 + \tau_k)$, where $\tau_0 = 0$ and $\tau_k = 2 \bullet \left(\sum_{j=1}^{k} (-1)^{k-j} \bullet (\mu_j - \tilde{\mu}_j) \right) / F^{t-1}(0.1k)$. Using this, the expenditure of a person at point p in the k-th decile (i.e., the folded income distribution function), after folding, can be expressed as follows:

$$\hat{x}(p) = \left[1 + \left((k - 10p) \bullet \tau_{k-1} + (10p - (k-1)) \bullet \tau_k \right) \right] \bullet F^{t-1}(p) k = (1, 2, \cdots, 10)$$

The LC is derived using this income distribution function. **...[Curve L_A].**

---

[6] This is because EasyFit can generate a maximum of 5000 random numbers at once.

[7] However, McDonald did not suggest the CDF for estimation in general, but simply claimed that in many applications, Singh–Maddala provides a better fit than Generalized-Gamma or Lognormal and their special and limiting cases. I excluded Dagum (Inverse-Burr), Chi-squared, Pareto, Exponential, and Weibull here because the KS test statistics for these distributions in process [i] were too high for all years.

[v] Separate from process [iv], I specified another CDF for each year. First, I generated 5000 random numbers 10 times from the CDF specified by process [iii]. Then, I conducted the same procedure as in process [ii]. Next, I estimated the CDFs with EasyFit again and specified the CDF as the actual income distribution function for Thailand and used it without folding. I plotted the LCs using these functions. **... [Curve L_B].**

Table 6.2 shows the CDFs (and their parameters) estimated in processes [ii], [iii], and [v], as well as the functions whose KS test statistics ranked second and third lowest. The reasons for deriving two types of curves, L_A and L_B, are as follows. As individual raw data are not available and the process of calculating the Gini coefficients by NESDC is unknown, it is desirable to use continuous LCs without folds (i.e., curves L_B), which are not arbitrary in their manipulation and make

Table 6.2 Results of goodness-of-fit tests and the coefficients of the identified CDF

Year	Process	Results and coefficients
2019	[ii]	1. Pearson 6 [0.0640] (α1 = 115.93, α2 = 3.2654, β = 136.21, γ = 0) 2. Pearson 5 [0.0651] 3. Inverse-Gaussian [0.0710]
	[iv] L_A	**1. Lognormal [0.01567] (σ = 0.72152, μ = 8.4324, γ = 816.18) 2. Pearson 6 [0.01609] 3. Pearson 5 [0.01609]**
	[v] L_B	1. Lognormal [0.00841] (σ = 0.73743, μ = 8.4175, γ = 882.68) 2. Inverse-Gaussian [0.01160] 3. Pearson 6 [0.01462]
2020	[ii]	1. Log-gamma [0.0664] (α = 183.25, β = 0.04722) 2. Inverse-Gaussian [0.0674] 3. Pearson 6 [0.0678]
	[iv] L_A	**1. Pearson type 5 [0.01263] (α = 3.7612, β = 21054.0, γ = −645.0) 2. Lognormal [0.01571] 3. Log-gamma [0.01730]**
	[v] L_B	1. Pearson 6 [0.01249] (α1 = 61.539, α2 = 3.7549, β = 332.1, γ = −454.52) 2. Pearson 5 [0.01251] 3. Lognormal [0.01393]
2021	[ii]	1. Inverse-Gaussian [0.0687] (λ = 14319.0, μ = 7145, γ = 0) 2. Log-gamma [0.0701] 3. Pearson 5 [0.0707]
	[iv] L_A	**1. Pearson type 5 [0.01547] (α = 3.6886, β = 21066.0 γ = −612.57) 2.Pearson 6 [0.01551] 3. Lognormal [0.01594]**
	[v] L_B	1. Lognormal [0.01473] (σ = 0.68852, μ = 8.5481, γ = 561.04) 2. Pearson 5 [0.01557] 3. Pearson 6 [0.01565]
2022	[ii]	1. Log-gamma [0.0670] (α = 195.84, β = 0.04475) 2. Inverse-Gaussian [0.0673] 3. Pearson 6 [0.0678]
	[iv] L_A	**1. Pearson type 6 [0.01223] (α1 = 19.357, α2 = 3.9591, β = 1213.7 γ = −210.74) 2.Pearson 5 [0.01238] 3. Lognormal [0.01691]**
	[v] L_B	1. Lognormal [0.01232] (σ = 0.6829, μ = 8.6174, γ = 665.17) 2. Pearson 6 [0.01303] 3. Pearson 5 [0.01303]
2023	[ii]	1. Log-gamma [0.06644] (α = 209.77, β = 0.04206) 2. Inverse-Gaussian [0.0681] 3. Pearson 6 [0.06969]
	[iv] L_A	**1. Pearson type 6 [0.01532] (α1 = 988.62, α2 = 4.0531, β = 27.248 γ = −711.4) 2. Pearson 5 [0.01546] 3. Lognormal [0.01993]**
	[v] L_B	1. Lognormal [0.01296] (σ = 0.67244, μ = 8.6623, γ = 779.81) 2. Inverse-Gaussian [0.01642] 3. Pearson 6 [0.01645]

Table 6.3 Gini coefficient (official figure, estimated values from curves L_A and L_B. NESDC website and author's estimates)

Year	Gini coefficient				
		Curve L_A		Curve L_B	
	NESDC	Gini	(deviation)	Gini	(deviation)
2019	0.3481	0.3478	−0.00032	0.3444	−0.00370
2020	0.3495	0.3491	−0.00041	0.3511	+0.00162
2021	0.3499	0.3494	−0.00050	0.3414	−0.00847
2022	0.3428	0.3423	−0.00044	0.3339	−0.00883
2023	0.3348	0.3342	−0.00057	0.3258	−0.00895

mathematical processing easier. However, as shown in Table 6.3, the Gini coefficients calculated from curves L_B deviate significantly from the NESDC figures (depending on the year).[8] Given the actual range of change in the Gini coefficient over time, it is inappropriate to use curves L_B that produce Gini coefficients greater or smaller by 0.001 or more than the NESDC figures. Thus, I derived and used curves L_A for the analysis instead of curves L_B. Curves L_A can generate, by definition, the average expenditure values of each decile and total average expenditure which are fully consistent with the NESDC figures and are mathematically treatable (although much more complex). In addition, the Gini coefficients calculated from curves L_A deviated[9] from those of NESDC by less than 0.001. As long as $u(x)$ remains continuous and its shape remains unchanged regardless of the year, the small bending of the LC does not affect the conclusions reached through the analysis of Lorenz dominance or GL dominance.

6.4 Changes in Income Distribution after COVID-19 Based on Normative Measures

Regarding the examination of changes in the LCs during the COVID-19 pandemic (i.e., visually comparing the shape of the LC from 2019 to 2023), the difference of LCs in a single year was too small to be visually discernible. Figure 6.3 shows the

[8] In deriving L_B as well as L_A, I used the average expenditure spending figures from the NESDC. Although it is possible to use the average expenditure figures produced in the CDF estimations, employing these figures in practice results in a larger deviation in most cases, especially for the LC on the high-income side.

[9] In calculating the Gini coefficient for L_A, since it would be extremely complicated to calculate from the formula for the LC of L_A, I used the calculated Lorenz values for each percentile based on the formula for the LC of L_A. Then, I multiplied those Lorenz values by the income of the percentile and added them up and calculated the Gini coefficient. Hence, there may be an error between the value calculated only from the formula of L_A, but the error is negligibly small.

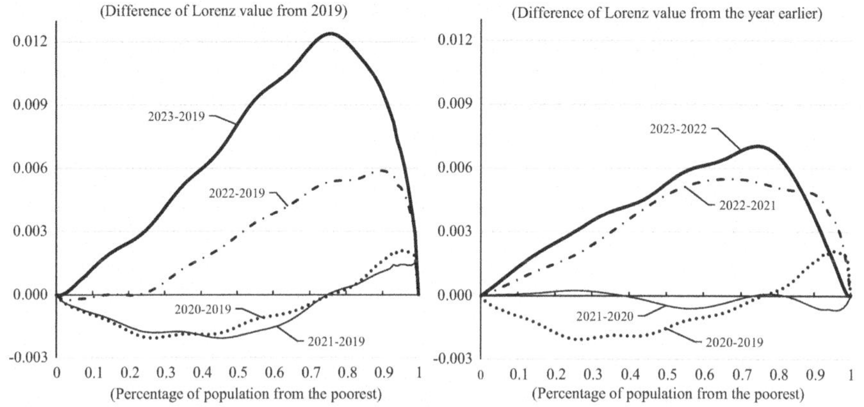

Fig. 6.3 Differences in Lorenz values between the two different years during COVID-19

difference in the Lorenz value at each percentile of the income rankings of the two groups to confirm whether the Lorenz dominance relationship was detected.[10]

First, the thick line on the left-hand side of Fig. 6.3 compares the LCs for the latest survey year, 2023 (the Gini coefficient calculated from the model is 0.3342), with 2019 indicating the pre-COVID situation (0.3478). The LC for 2023 is higher than that for 2019, except for the first two percentiles. That is, the LC for 2023 does not Lorenz dominate that for 2019, and we cannot unambiguously conclude that income inequality has improved over the past 4 years, although the Gini coefficient in 2023 is much lower than that in 2019. Comparing the income distributions in 2019 and 2022 (the thick dotted line on the left-hand side of Fig. 6.3), the LC for 2022 is lower than that for 2019 at the first two income deciles; the gap becomes positive from the third to the seventh income deciles and widens at almost the same pace, decelerates from the eighth to the ninth deciles, and shrinks at the tenth decile. This means that the middle- and high-income classes (excluding the super-rich) were able to increase their expenditure during the COVID-19 pandemic for 3 years, but the poor and low-income earners were unable to increase it (or even reduce it) compared to other income classes, and the gap in expenditure with other income deciles widened.

When and how this situation arose can be analyzed from the right-hand side of Fig. 6.3 by examining the annual changes. In 2020 (the Gini coefficient is 0.3491), when the COVID-19 outbreak caused economic activity to stagnate, the downward deviation of the LC for 2020 from that for 2019 widened for low-income groups (the first- and second-income deciles). As pointed out by the World Bank and NESDC, this suggests that the COVID-19 pandemic had a greater negative impact

[10] Because the difference between the two L_A curves is small, the graph of the difference appears to have many large waves, which makes it visually difficult to understand the conclusion of the comparison. Thus, here, I applied a moving average of 13 percentiles in Fig. 6.3 in order to minimize the waves as much as possible without losing consistency when no moving average was applied.

on poor and low-income earners. Furthermore, the Lorenz value for 2020 was lower than that for 2019, up to the 74th percentile of the income ranking. In 2021 (the Gini coefficient is 0.3494), as stated by the NESDC (2021), the Thai government implemented income support measures for low-income earners. However, as seen from the thin solid line on the right-hand side of Fig. 6.3, the Lorenz value for 2021 is greater than that for 2020 up to the fourth income decile group, but only marginally. This means that the effect of policy measures for boosting spending for low-income earners did not improve income inequality, regardless of social preference, even though they might alleviate the further worsening of the income gap of the first through third income deciles against the richest only marginally. On the other hand, the two valleys on the negative side of the thin solid line imply income transfers from the middle-income class to the low-income deciles and from high-income earners to the super-rich group, the latter of which had a negative impact on the Gini coefficient. Between the LCs for 2022 and 2021 (the thick dotted line on the right-hand side of the figure), the income distribution in 2022 dominates that of 2021. However, although expenditure from the first through third income deciles grew in 2022, this increase was not sufficient to offset the decline in the past 2 years for these income groups. In addition, the gap in the Lorenz values widened from the fourth to the sixth income deciles at an accelerated pace. As a result, while income inequality appears to have improved in Thailand by 2022 compared to the pre-COVID period (the dotted line on the left-hand side of Fig. 6.3), low-income earners might not be able to feel an improvement in income equality. In 2023, judging from the bold solid line on the right-hand side of Fig. 6.3, poor and low-income earners (the first through fourth income deciles) could receive more from the previous year (year 2022); however, because the income distribution in 2023 does not Lorenz dominate that in 2019, it could not have succeeded in offsetting the loss of the Lorenz value since the outbreak of the pandemic.

6.5 Existence of GL Dominance after COVID-19

Changes in the situation of poverty should be examined regarding the COVID-19 pandemic. However, the official poverty-related statistics published by the Thai government are not consistent with this study because the number of poor people is calculated for each prefecture using their own poverty lines, which vary by prefecture. The Thai government summed the number of poor people reported from all prefectures and divided it by the national population to calculate the country's poverty ratio. The domestic poverty line for the whole country is merely a reference value and will mask the true situation if this figure is directly used to calculate the extent of poverty. In fact, when the derived income distribution function is used, the proportion of individuals below the national average poverty line (2997 baht/month) in 2022 is approximately 9%, deviating significantly from the NESDC figure of 5.43%. Notwithstanding, because data on income (expenditure) deciles are provided only at the national average level, it is not possible to derive income distribution functions at the provincial and prefectural levels.

Therefore, an analysis of poverty in Thailand using CDFs and poverty rates at the national level would not be consistent. However, it is still possible to infer changes in circumstances from changes in income distribution among poor- and low-income earners after the COVID-19 pandemic using the income distribution function derived so far. Furthermore, normative measures (i.e., a comparison of GLCs over time) will lead to policy implications for how the government and civil society can improve social welfare through more assistance for poor and low-income earners.

6.5.1 Annual Changes in Income Distribution for Low-Income Earners

Figure 6.4 shows the income distribution function (in CDF form) from 2019 to 2023 for the three lowest income deciles. These income distribution functions are the same as those used to derive L_A curves, but income (in practice, expenditure) is divided by the consumer price index (left-hand figure) and the national poverty line (right-hand figure) to remove the effects of fluctuations in price and living conditions (i.e., the income distribution functions in real terms). In addition, since we should grasp visually the rate of change—rather than the amount of change—here, income (expenditure) is expressed as a natural logarithm. The reason for employing the poverty line as well as the consumer price index is that for those whose income is slightly above the poverty line, if an increase in expenditure in nominal terms is not enough to cover the increase in the costs of necessities to avoid falling into poverty, this implies a deterioration in living standards (and some households would fall into poverty).

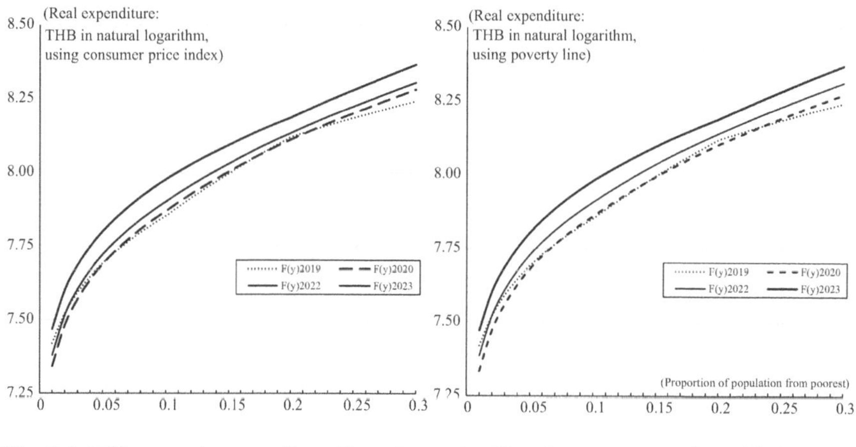

Fig. 6.4 Differences in expenditure (in real terms) of low-income earners from 2019 through 2023, depicted in estimated income distribution functions

Figure 6.4 (both parts) indicates the following:

1. As the expenditure of low-income earners in 2023 is greater than that of other years at all points (not only for those in the first three income deciles but also for other groups), it is clear that the GLC for 2023 is dominant against those for other years (the GL value at the 100p percentile point is equal to the cumulative income of the 100p percentile point of the poorest sector of the population). Thus, we can unambiguously conclude that social welfare was greater in 2023 than in other years.
2. From 2019 to 2020, COVID-19 had a more serious impact on those with lower incomes, leading to a decline in expenditure in real terms. We can see this trend for those in the poorest fifth percentile and between the 18th and 21st percentiles when income is divided by the consumer price index, and for those in the poorest seventh percentile and between the 17th and 23rd percentiles when income is divided by the poverty line. For those higher than these thresholds, expenditures in 2020 exceeded those in 2019 in real terms.
3. The income distribution for 2021 is almost unchanged from that of 2020 at all points until the 30th percentile of the low-income population (thus, the graph for 2021 is omitted from Fig. 6.4 to maintain its visibility). This means that the fruit of economic recovery from 2020 to 2021 is—contrary to the government's intention of regressive redistribution—uniform among the first 30 percentiles. The government's uniform support for low-income earners resulted in a uniform income increase for the poorest 30 percentiles, which continued until 2022. However, the GLC for 2022 dominated that for 2020 (and 2021). Since the outbreak and spread of COVID-19 in 2020, the government has implemented various policies for low-income earners, including emergency cashflow measures for households and flat-amount benefit payments. However, the policy did not significantly affect the restoration of income distribution. Even so, the economic recovery succeeded in raising the expenditure of the first 30 percentiles.
4. For the poorest 1% of the population, real expenditure is lower in 2022 than in 2019. Hence, we cannot unambiguously conclude that social welfare is greater in 2022 than in 2019. The COVID-19 pandemic made the extremely poor more unequal, and the government failed to restore them to the state they had been in before COVID-19[11] (as of 2022). Various consumption-stimulating measures were taken, and their utilization rate was high, but the benefit for low-income earners was considered small for reasons discussed later on.
5. The fact that the income of those in the third decile increased in 2020 indicates that the policy prevented those close to poverty from falling into poverty. This outcome is consistent with the Thai government's basic policies on poverty. The Thai government has long paid close attention to the increase in the number of people who are not poor but close to poverty, defined as those whose expenditures

[11] Of course, it is possible that income distribution may have been more unequal, even among the lowest 30% of individuals without this.

are between 100% and 120% of the poverty line.[12] This is because the population of this group has not decreased much over the long term and because they are at higher risk of falling (back) into poverty if there is an economic shock. Although we cannot calculate this from the income distribution function derived in this study, the Thai government published statistics on the number of people in this income group, which was 5.4 million (7.8% of the population) in 2019. Since the total population ratio of the poor and those close to poverty is 14.0%, the fact that the policy effect reached those in the poorest three income deciles means that even if the number of poor people increased due to the COVID-19 pandemic, the number of people at risk of falling into poverty was likely to decline. In fact, in 2020, the year of the COVID-19 pandemic, the number of people close to poverty fell to 5.14 million (7.4% of the population).

The fact that the income distribution function for 2019 crosses that for 2020 onward (except for 2023) at the low-income percentile points implies that GL dominance did not hold between 2019 and the corresponding years during the COVID-19 pandemic. I verified this by drawing the GLCs for 2019 and 2022. As the difference in the GL values at the lower percentile points was small between 2019 and 2022 and average expenditure was growing, it is possible that the situation in 2022 GL dominates that in 2019, and we may reach some conclusions about the social states of these two points of time (there is no Lorenz dominance relationship between them) without specifying SWFs. Figure 6.5 depicts whether GL dominance is present (I employed real average expenditure to calculate the GLCs using the consumer price index) between the 2 years. The GLC for 2019 is higher up to the second percentile point (considered to be people in extreme poverty), but from the third percentile point onward, the GLC for 2022 is higher. In other words, GL dominance does not hold. On the other hand, as examined above, GLC for 2023 is dominant

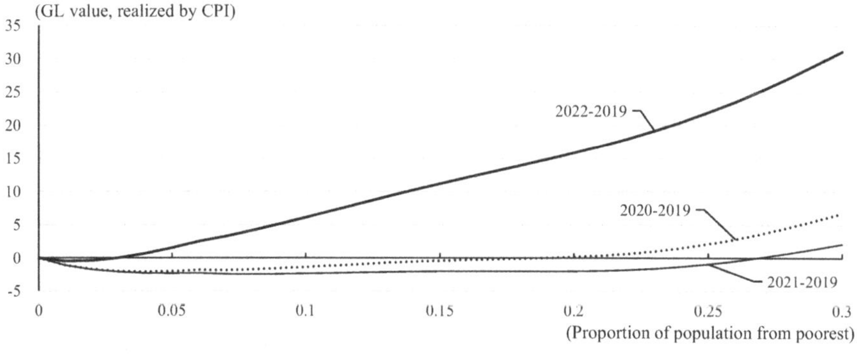

Fig. 6.5 The GL dominance of each year during COVID-19 over the base year (2019)

[12] For example, in discussions on the United Nations Sustainable Development Goals (SDGs), the Thai government has stated the importance of improving the living standards of those who are not in poor but close to poverty (Ministry of Foreign Affairs 2017, p. 8).

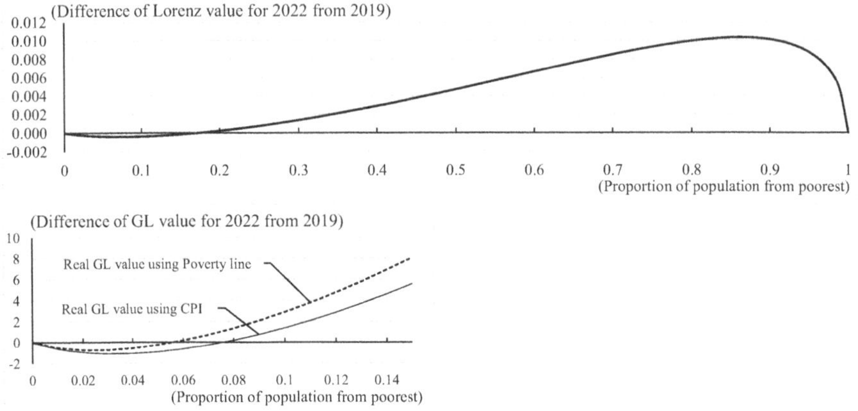

Fig. 6.6 Checking the existence of Lorenz dominance and GL dominance of 2022 over 2019 (using curves L_B)

over that for 2019. This means that the Thai government spent 4 years recovering a social welfare level that was unambiguously above the pre-COVID level.

In the analysis, I used curve L_A, generated from a folded income distribution function. Consequently, the graphs (lines) in each figure are not smooth. If they are not smooth and have fluctuations near the horizontal axis, the observations detecting Lorenz and GL dominance are affected by fluctuations. Hence, I also employed curve L_B, which is not folded, to check the consistency of the above findings. Checking the relationship linking Lorenz dominance and GL dominance between 2019 and 2022 (Fig. 6.6) with curves L_B, the results based on curves L_A are supported.

6.6 Discussion and Policy Implications

I assessed Thailand's policy response to the COVID-19 pandemic for the first year of its occurrence, especially in terms of efforts to identify the policies needed for each stage of the response and the prompt implementation of projects; however, the scale was too small for low-income earners to become better off (Egawa 2021). The lack of a Lorenz dominance relationship between 2019 and 2022 and between 2019 and 2023 suggests that the government was still unable to (relatively) increase the size of support schemes for the extremely poor and, as a result, could not realize a more equal income distribution, regardless of social preferences. Moreover, the World Bank (2022) pointed out that the new and temporary support measures introduced in Thailand during the COVID-19 pandemic may not have had a significant effect on reducing poverty, even though they had an impact on the overall economy. In order to be able to confidently and unambiguously conclude that social welfare has increased in the 3 years since COVID-19 compared to before COVID-19, the government should have implemented more policies focusing on those in extreme poverty in terms of the size of policy delivery to realize GL dominance in 2022 over 2019.[13] Because the GL value for the poor can be raised by increasing the average receipt of benefits from the government, the government should have adopted the following two policy options:

First, considering the World Bank's (2021) survey results, the government should have improved the eligibility and access of the extremely poor to the government's consumption support schemes. According to the results of a telephone survey of Thai people conducted by the World Bank, 46% of households were not satisfied with the Thai government's COVID-19 measures, and 26% of low-income households were unable to access government consumption support-related programs. In other words, a shortage of policy delivery may be caused by low-income earners' inability to access the programs. As a result, support measures for low-income earners (e.g., to purchase daily necessities) have not sufficiently reached this population, but they have reached middle- and high-income earners well. This has resulted in a greater income gap between low- and middle-income earners and a narrower gap between middle- and high-income earners. Guaranteeing 26% of low-income earners' access to government schemes would increase average expenditure on their strata.

Second, the government should have limited access to schemes and increase the amount of support for the poor and those at risk of falling into poverty. According to the NESDC (2023), the poverty rate and ratio of those at risk of falling into poverty to the total population are 5.43% and 6.64% in 2022, respectively. In contrast, the number of State Welfare Card holders (cards issued to low-income earners allowing holders to receive government subsidies for the purchase of daily necessities) amounted to almost a quarter of the total population over 18 years of age. Then, if the government had increased subsidies for the holders who were in poverty and reduced them for the remaining holders in 2022, GL dominance would have held owing to the increase in GL value for the poor.[14]

---

[13] Here, the Dardanoni and Lambert (1988) theorem can be employed to consider a situation where GL dominance does not hold. If the individual's utility function—although required to specify its shape—satisfies $u' > 0$, $u'' < 0$, $u''' > 0$ at all income points and GLCs cross only once, we could unambiguously say that the situation, like Thailand after COVID-19, is a socially less desirable one than pre-COVID-19 in light of social welfare. This corresponds to the case where Thai society has a Rawlsian social preference that prioritizes increasing the income of low-income earners in improving income distribution and thus social welfare. Hence, in order to draw firm conclusions about the situation of the poor and social welfare in 2019 and 2022, it is necessary to specify the utility function. Since I focused on whether income inequality improved or worsened unambiguously using a normative approach, I did not derive the specific shape of the utility function or conduct analysis using it.

[14] This change might not be supported if the government's aim of the State Welfare Card project was to realize a Lorenz-dominance situation in 2022 over 2019, because, according to Fig. 6.3 (the bold dotted line in the lefthand figure), more than 20% of the population faced worsening income inequality, even with the project.

6.7 Conclusions

The Thai government has stated that the number of poor in Thailand only increased slightly, and income inequality did not worsen after the outbreak and spread of COVID-19 due to the effectiveness of successive government support measures geared toward low-income earners. Many of the government's COVID-19 countermeasures were aimed at the immediate plight of low-income earners (such as assistance in purchasing daily necessities and financial support for small- and medium-sized enterprises and tourism businesses), and the timeliness of the policy implementation should be positively assessed given the economic environment at the time. Government policies during the COVID-19 pandemic certainly prevented an increase in the number of the poor. However, the government's self-assessment is based solely on a descriptive approach or scalar representation of the situation, such as the poverty rate and Gini coefficient. The assessment of policy effects should be conducted by examining changes in income distribution and the improvement of social welfare through support for the poor.

I have attempted to highlight these points by deriving the income distribution functions for relevant years and calculating the Lorenz value and GL value to visually compare social situations (i.e., using normative measures), ultimately aiming to determine whether Lorenz dominance and GL dominance held. My findings are as follows: First, to analyze the situation during the COVID-19 pandemic, support measures were designed to prevent those at risk of falling into poverty from actually becoming poor, rather than direct support for those who were already poor at the time. It is possible that income inequality for low-income earners worsened, even though the Gini coefficient remained almost unchanged. Since then, contrary to their supposed purpose, measures for low-income earners have had an equal impact regardless of income class, and their income-raising effect was weak throughout the COVID-19 pandemic until 2022. The Gini coefficient has improved, but it is still unclear whether income distribution has become more favorable for society than it was in 2019, as Lorenz dominance did not hold between 2022 and 2019. Moreover, as a result of insufficient measures (in size) being taken for the extremely poor, we cannot unambiguously infer that the government's policy delivery improved social welfare by 2022 over 2019 because GL dominance did not hold.

The success of the mission of a government democratically elected by citizens with Bentham standards of behavior should be measured by the improvement of social welfare. The fact that the poverty rate declined and that the Gini coefficient began to decline to a record-low level in 2022 does not equate to an improvement in social welfare or the equalization of income distribution. In Thailand, we cannot unambiguously state that social welfare has improved compared to the pre-COVID-19 situation, nor can we unambiguously deduce that income distribution has become more equal. For the government and politicians, "unambiguity" in policy assessment has the same meaning as "confidence." To ensure that the government's efforts do not end up as mere self-praise but as praise with confidence,

Lorenz dominance and GL dominance should be observed in the assessment, and more policies targeting the extreme poor should be implemented with sufficient size to assure GL dominance (and even Lorenz dominance).

References

Barr N (1998) The economics of the welfare state, 3rd edn. Oxford University Press, Oxford

Bellù LG and Liberati P (2005) Social welfare analysis of income distributions: ranking income distributions with generalised Lorenz curves. EASYPol Module 002, FAO. https://www.fao.org/3/a-am389e.pdf

Dardanoni V, Lambert PJ (1988) Welfare ranking of income distributions: a rôle for the variance and some insights for tax reform. Soc Choice Welf 5:1–17. https://doi.org/10.1007/BF00435494

Egawa A (2021) Impact of the resurgence of COVID-19 on the Thai economy and responses (tentative assessment). Japan Thailand Association Thai-koku Joho 55-5:21–31. (in Japanese)

Egawa A (2022) The situation of the Thai economy and its outlook. Japan-Thailand association. Thai-koku Joho 56-4:14–27. (in Japanese)

Jenkins SP (1991) Income inequality and living standards: changes in the 1970s and 1980s. Fisc Stud 12(1):1–28

Kakwani NC (1984) Welfare ranking of income distributions. Adv Econom 3:191–213

Lambert PJ (2001) The distribution and redistribution of income, 3rd edn. Manchester University Press, Manchester

McDonald JB (1984) Some generalized functions for the size distribution of income. Econometrica 52:647–663. https://doi.org/10.2307/1913469

Ministry of Foreign Affairs, Thailand (2017) Thailand's voluntary national review on the implementation of the 2030 Agenda for sustainable development. https://sustainabledevelopment.un.org/content/documents/16147Thailand.pdf

National Statistical Office (2024) The 2023 household socio-economic survey: whole kingdom. Bangkok. https://www.nso.go.th/nsoweb/storage/survey_detail/2024/20240702120458_75928.pdf

NESDC (2021) Poverty and inequality report 2020 (ความยากจนและความเหลื่อมล้ำของประเทศไทย ปี 2563). (in Thai). https://www.nesdc.go.th/ewt_dl_link.php?nid=11972&filename=Social_Poverty

NESDC (2022) Poverty and inequality report 2021 (ความยากจนและความเหลื่อมล้ำของประเทศไทย ปี 2564). (in Thai). https://www.nesdc.go.th/ewt_dl_link.php?nid=13081&filename=Social_Poverty

NESDC (2023) Poverty and inequality report 2022 (ความยากจนและความเหลื่อมล้ำของประเทศไทย ปี 2565). (in Thai). https://www.nesdc.go.th/ewt_dl_link.php?nid=14557&filename=Social_Poverty

NESDC (2024) Poverty and inequality report 2023 (ความยากจนและความเหลื่อมล้ำของประเทศไทย ปี 2566). (in Thai). https://www.nesdc.go.th/ewt_dl_link.php?nid=15744&filename=Social_Poverty

OECD (2020) OECD economic surveys: Thailand 2020 economic assessment. OECD Publishing, Paris. https://doi.org/10.1787/ad2e50fa-en

Shorrocks AF (1983) Ranking income distributions. Economica 50:1–17. https://doi.org/10.2307/2554117

World Bank (2021) Thailand poverty brief. https://documents1.worldbank.org/curated/en/780771636649923876/pdf/Thailand-Poverty-Brief.pdf

World Bank (2022) East Asia and Pacific economic update April 2022—braving the storms, Washington D.C.. https://www.worldbank.org/en/region/eap/publication/braving-the-storms-global-launch-of-the-east-asia-and-pacific-economic-update-april-2022

Chapter 7
Future of the South Korean Economy After COVID-19: Focusing on the Semiconductor Industry

Yuichi Takayasu

Abstract The COVID-19 pandemic led to an economic recession in many countries around the world. While the South Korean economy experienced a temporary slowdown, it quickly recovered and expanded at a time when COVID-19 was spreading and infection numbers were at their highest. However, the economy reversed course and entered a recession when the COVID-19 pandemic ended. This paper first analyzed the factors that contributed to the expansion of the South Korean economy during the COVID-19 pandemic. We also examined the reasons for the recession after the pandemic ended. The results revealed that sluggish exports, especially semiconductor exports, caused the South Korean economy to expand despite the spread and severity of COVID-19, which also triggered a recession once the COVID-19 pandemic ended.

The South Korean semiconductor industry is characterized by a focus on producing memory semiconductors, the demand for which is extremely volatile. Demand increases significantly when the economy is strong and declines sharply during slumps. During the COVID-19 pandemic, semiconductor production was high because of special demand. The large increase in demand for memory semiconductors also helped curb the recession. Without this special demand, the economy would have slowed significantly and could have fallen into a serious recession. Demand for memory semiconductors declined sharply once the COVID-19 pandemic ended, leading to an economic recession.

In the post-pandemic era, the South Korean industry must break away from its excessive dependence on semiconductors by fostering new industries. However, it will be difficult to break away from this semiconductor-centric structure in the near future, because it will take time to foster new industries. Therefore, we believe that South Korea's semiconductor industry needs to shift its focus from memory semiconductors, for which demand and prices are highly volatile because they are general-purpose products, to logic semiconductors, for which stable growth is

Y. Takayasu (✉)
Faculty of Economics, Daito Bunka University, Itabashi-ku, Tokyo, Japan
e-mail: y-takayasu@ic.daito.ac.jp

© The Author(s), under exclusive license to Springer Nature Singapore Pte Ltd. 2025

H. Taguchi (ed.), *Sustainability of Economic Growth in East Asia*,
New Frontiers in Regional Science: Asian Perspectives 82,
https://doi.org/10.1007/978-981-96-3731-7_7

expected primarily due to their made-to-order characteristics, leading to moderate demand and price fluctuations. South Korea's economy will become more stable if the semiconductor industry can be restructured in this manner. One option for the South Korean economy could be to increase the weighting of non-memory semiconductors within the semiconductor industry.

7.1 Introduction

The outbreak of COVID-19 in Wuhan City, China, in December 2019 and its subsequent spread worldwide in 2020 affected global economies in the succeeding years. The first case of infection in South Korea was reported on January 20, 2020. The Disease Control and Prevention Agency (2022) reported 705,900 cases in South Korea (an average of 965.7 cases per day) in 2 years, starting from the first confirmed case on January 20, 2020 to January 19, 2022. The incidence rate per 100,000 cases was 1.367, while 6480 deaths occurred among the infected, resulting in a fatality rate of 0.92%.

Instead of taking hardline migration control measures such as lockouts, South Korea took steps to minimize the economic impact as much as possible, focusing on small, medium, and micro businesses. Furthermore, IT-based infection prevention measures were taken to reduce the number of cases while simultaneously ensuring minimal impact on economic activities.

The South Korean economy experienced a significant downturn following the outbreak but began to recover in early 2020. One reason the South Korean economy recovered early from recession amid the continuing spread of COVID-19 was the strong performance of semiconductor businesses, which comprise the most important industry in South Korea. A factor behind the strong performance of the global semiconductor industry was the spread of COVID-19 and the restrictions imposed in its wake, which severely changed the digital behavior of the world's population, in turn, boosting global demand for semiconductors. This special demand for semiconductors helped the South Korean economy recover quickly, and the country's economy showed strong performance despite several subsequent waves of the spread of COVID-19 infections.

However, in 2023, when the pandemic subsided, the South Korean economy went into recession. This is because the South Korean semiconductor industry stagnated as a result of the shrinking of the global semiconductor market. Furthermore, because of structural factors, the South Korean semiconductor industry was strongly affected by the contraction of the global semiconductor market. The negative effects of the COVID-19 pandemic were offset by an increase in special demand for semiconductors worldwide, and the economy expanded as a result. When the spread of COVID-19 ceased, the economy went into a full recession.

The South Korean economy was not negatively affected by the pandemic, which had incidentally led to a special boom in semiconductors. Conversely, if the special demand for semiconductors had shrunk during the pandemic, causing demand for semiconductors to shrink, the South Korean economy would have been negatively affected. The South Korean economy is heavily influenced structurally by trends in the semiconductor industry. The long-term challenge for the South Korean economy after the COVID-19 pandemic has been to move away from an economic structure that is overly dependent on semiconductors and to support itself through various industries. However, developing an industry to replace the semiconductor industry will take time. Therefore, the next best policy is to transform the South Korean semiconductor industry such that it ceases to swing between favorable and unfavorable conditions and experiences relatively small swings and stable growth prospects. It is realistic to proceed with this transformation first.

This study presents the factors that contributed to the expansion of the South Korean economy during the COVID-19 pandemic and the reasons for the recession after the outbreak ended. It explains the need for structural reform in the South Korean semiconductor industry after the spread of the COVID-19 infection.

The rest of this paper is structured as follows. In Sect. 7.2, we discuss the economic trends during the period of the COVID-19 outbreak in South Korea. In Sect. 7.3, we show that, based on the government's economic assessment, the South Korean economy expanded for most of the period, driven by strong exports, despite the spread of COVID-19. Furthermore, we show that semiconductors were the main contributor to the country's strong export performance. In Sect. 7.4, we reveal that the South Korean semiconductor industry experienced significant upswings and downswings because this industry's structure is dependent on digital memory. We also suggest that the direction the Korean economy should aim for after the spread of COVID-19 is to change the semiconductor industry's structure that is currently concentrated on memory and increase the proportion of non-memory production.

Before we get into the main topic, we summarize the spread of COVID-19 based on reports by the Disease Control and Prevention Agency (2022), Ha et al. (2023), and the Ministry of Health and Welfare (2023). The first COVID-19 cases were confirmed on January 20, 2020, and the spread of COVID-19 largely ended on January 19, 2023. These 3 years can be divided into six periods. We classified the first through the third periods based on the Disease Control and Prevention Agency's (2022) report, while the fourth through the sixth periods were classified based on Ha et al.'s (2023) work, with additional data from the Ministry of Health and Welfare (2023). The duration, total number of infected people, number of infected people per day, and characteristics for each period are shown in Table 7.1.

7.2 Economic Trends after the COVID-19 Pandemic Outbreak

Here, we discuss the business climate before and after the spread of COVID-19. We examine economic trends based on the Composite Index of Business Indicators. Considering the Composite Index of Business Indicators, Statistics Korea

Table 7.1 Summary of the six periods of the spread of COVID-19

	Period	Total infected people (person)	Infected people per day (person)	Characteristics
First period	January 20, 2020 ~ august 11, 2020	14,660	72	Infection rates were high in rural areas (within certain communities, etc.)
Second period	August 12, 2020 ~ November 12, 2020	13,280	143	Most infections occurred in the capital region
Third period	November 13, 2020 ~ July 6, 2021	133,600	560	Group infections were at their highest, and infections through contact were also on the rise
Fourth period	July 7, 2021 ~ January29, 2022	544,360	2764	Increasing number of cases with unknown infection routes
Fifth period	January 30, 2022 ~ June 25, 2022	17,490 Thousand	119 Thousand	The omicron variant became mainstream Nationwide infection
Sixth Period	June 26, 2022 ~ October 2022	4900 thousand	72 Thousand	–

Sources: Disease Control and Prevention Agency (2022), Ha et al. (2023), and the Ministry of Health and Welfare (2023)

emphasizes the role of the Cyclical Component of Coincident Index in determining the peaks and bottoms of the business cycle, which is usually used to determine the business climate. First, we examine the changes in the Cyclical Component of Coincident Index. The Cyclical Component of Coincident Index fell sharply in 2018 and turned upward at one point in 2019. However, it fell rapidly beginning in February 2020, the month after the first confirmed cases of COVID-19 (Fig. 7.1).

The Cyclical Component of Coincident Index was 100.3 in January 2020, then fell to 96.4 in May 2020. However, from June onward, it gradually rose, and the upward trend continued until February 2022. The Cyclical Component of Coincident Index began to decline after August 2022. The downward trend then continued into 2024. Furthermore, Statistics Korea announced that South Korea had been in recession since 2017, with May 2020 being the economic trough. The report also states that the economic recession that had continued since September 2017 ended and that the economy has entered a period of expansion since May 2020.

The sharp drop in the Cyclical Component of the Coincident Index from February to May 2020 can be attributed to the COVID-19 pandemic, as Statistics Korea (2023) reported. However, the Cyclical Component of the Coincident Index rose after June 2020, and no significant declines occurred after that. It then remained flat from March 2022 onward and began to decline from November 2022. In other words, as far as the Cyclical Component of Coincident Index is concerned, the economy expanded for most of the period when the spread of COVID-19 continued, while the recession accelerated only briefly in the early stages of the outbreak. The

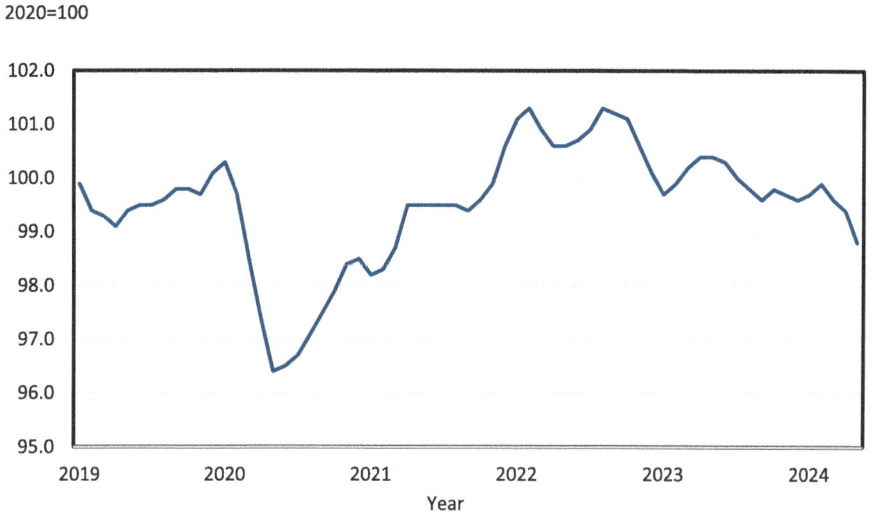

Fig. 7.1 Composite index of business indicator cyclical component of coincident index. Source: Compiled by the Statistics Korea database

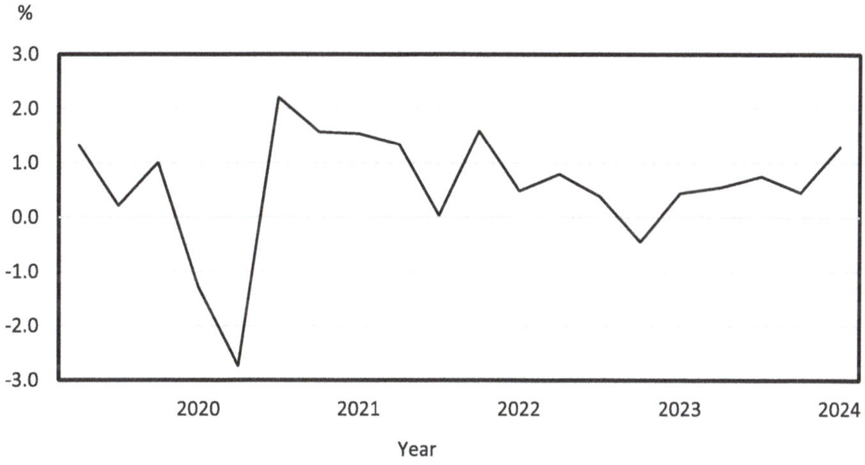

Fig. 7.2 Seasonally adjusted quarterly GDP (QoQ). Source: Compiled by the Bank of Korea database

economic recession is then confirmed to have begun at approximately the same time when the spread of COVID-19 ceased.

Looking at the seasonally adjusted quarterly gross domestic product (GDP) quarter-on-quarter (QoQ) (Fig. 7.2), January to March 2020 fell by −1.3% (−5.0% on an annualized basis), and April to June 2020 fell by −2.7% (−10.5% on an annualized basis), presenting a significant decline. However, from July to September, the growth rate turned sharply positive at 2.2% (9.1% annually) and remained relatively high. From late 2022 to 2023, although positive growth was generally maintained, the growth rate remained relatively low. In other words, with regard to quarterly GDP movements, growth was significantly negative in the first 6 months, during which the spread of COVID-19 continued. Since then, growth has remained relatively high. Furthermore, it is confirmed that the growth rate declined at about the same time the spread of COVID-19 ended.

The number of infected cases indicates that the spread of COVID-19 gradually increased in severity since the first cases were confirmed on January 20, 2020, reaching a peak in the first half of 2022. It then slowed in the second half of 2022. Conversely, according to the Cyclical Component of Coincident Index and quarterly GDP trends, the economy rapidly deteriorated in the first half of 2020, and GDP growth was significantly negative. However, as the spread of COVID-19 became increasingly serious, the economy entered an expansionary phase and quarterly GDP growth was relatively high. As the spread of COVID-19 declined, the economy entered a recessionary phase, and quarterly GDP growth remained relatively low. The above implies that the spread of COVID-19 had little impact on the South Korean economy.

7.3 Key Drivers of Economic Trends as Seen in Government Economic Assessment and Data

First, we examine changes in the government's economic assessment (Ministry of Economy and Finance, "Current Economic Situation," a monthly report) to clarify why exports were the main factor behind the expansion of the South Korean economy for most of the period despite the spread of COVID-19. The government's economic assessment is made mainly by referring to economic indicators 2 months prior to the month of the announcement, so it is necessary to pay attention to a time lag of about 2 months between changes in economic assessments.

The first mention of the novel coronavirus appeared in March 2020. The March 2020 economic assessment stated that the spread of COVID-19 "appears to have increased uncertainty in the real economy."[1] From March 2020 to April 2022, most economic assessments mentioned COVID-19.

Since March 2020, the assessment that "uncertainty in the real economy is increasing" has continued, and shrinking domestic demand has been cited as the cause of this. In July 2020, there was no change in the assessment of "increasing uncertainty in the real economy," but there were indications of improvement in domestic demand. A decrease in exports was cited as the cause, changing the reasons previously cited. However, the decline in exports was considered to have eased by August. Furthermore, the recovery trend in exports continued in October. Despite this recovery, it was stated that "real economic uncertainty persists" because of the

[1] Economic assessments are described in summary form, not in full text.

spread of COVID-19 infection again. From December 2020 to February 2021, the export assessment was further revised upward, indicating that the recovery is expanding. However, the economic assessment maintained a bearish level.

In addition, the Composite Index of Business Indicator of the Cyclical Component of the Coincident Index and quarterly GDP trends confirm that the economy was recovering in the first half of 2020. However, it is conceivable that the government was concerned about COVID-19 and continued to make cautious decisions.

Finally in March 2021, the phrase "uncertainty in the real economy" was removed and was replaced with the phrase "exports continue to improve while domestic demand remains sluggish due to the spread of COVID-19." The overall economic assessment changed with this statement. Then, in April, it was determined that sluggish domestic demand had eased, which was, in effect, a sign of economic expansion. Thereafter, a statement was added that "there is uncertainty in domestic demand, mainly due to the slump in face-to-face services, partly because of the re-spread of COVID-19 infection." However, the assessment remained unchanged, suggesting that the economy was expanding.

From the government's view, the economic assessment from 2020 to 2021 can be summarized as follows: (1) The government was cautious and pointed out uncertainties for a long period. However, the view was removed, and it was suggested that the economy was expanding even during the spread of COVID-19. (2) Domestic demand consistently expanded and drove the economy during COVID-19, while personal consumption, mainly face-to-face services, repeatedly improved and deteriorated due to the spread of COVID-19.

In May 2022, the assessment of exports, which had been the economy's driving force, changed. Specifically, it was pointed out that export recovery may come to a halt. Then, in June, the economic assessment was revised downward with the addition of the phrase "concern about recession," based on the assessment stating "although domestic demand is improving, the momentum of export growth has weakened." Furthermore, the slumping exports in November made the severity of the situation even clearer. Then, in December, the rising rate of price increases weakened domestic demand, which had been strong. Combined with sluggish exports, this rise accelerated the economic slowdown.

In February 2023, the economic assessment was revised to "the economy is in recession, mainly due to sluggish exports, although the speed of domestic demand recovery is slowing amid rising prices." This redefinition means that the economic situation changed from a potential recession to an actual recession; therefore, the economic assessment was further revised downward. Moreover, the assessment that "the economy is in recession" continued until July 2023. The time of the government's determination that the economy is "in recession" generally coincides with the time when, with regard to the Composite Index of Business Indicator, the Cyclical Component of the Coincident Index and the quarterly GDP figures deteriorated.

In August 2023, the assessment that "the economy is in a recession" changed. The assessment of the economy for this month was that "export volumes of semiconductors and other products are recovering, and some signs of recession are becoming milder." Furthermore, in November, the economic assessment was further revised to "Production and exports of semiconductors and other manufacturing industries are recovering, and signs of economic recovery are gradually emerging."

Based on the government's view so far, the economic assessment from 2022 to 2023 can be summarized as follows. (1) The economic assessment was revised downward from expansion to recession when the spread of COVID-19 was nearing its end, and the recession continued until the second half of 2023. (2) Sluggish exports were the primary contributor to the recession, and the recovery of exports such as semiconductors brought signs of economic recovery.

Given the government's economic assessment above, strong exports explain the economic expansion during the spread of COVID-19, and sluggish exports explain why the economy receded when the pandemic was nearing its end. Furthermore, the economic assessment since August 2023 indicates that semiconductors were leading the export movement.

Therefore, we examine overall export movements and semiconductor exports. Since seasonally adjusted export statistics have not been published, we examine the comparison with the same month last year. First, we examine overall exports. Figures from the Korea International Trade Association database show that the year 2019 remained weak, with more than half of the months in negative double-digits. In 2020, the negative trend narrowed significantly, but increased again from April to August, with the negative trend exceeding 20% in April and May (Fig. 7.3).

The negative trend then turned positive in November 2020, followed by double-digit growth in 2021, with May and June recording increases of more than 40%. The double-digit increase continued until May 2022; since then, the positive trend narrowed and turned downward in October 2022. While double-digit negative growth

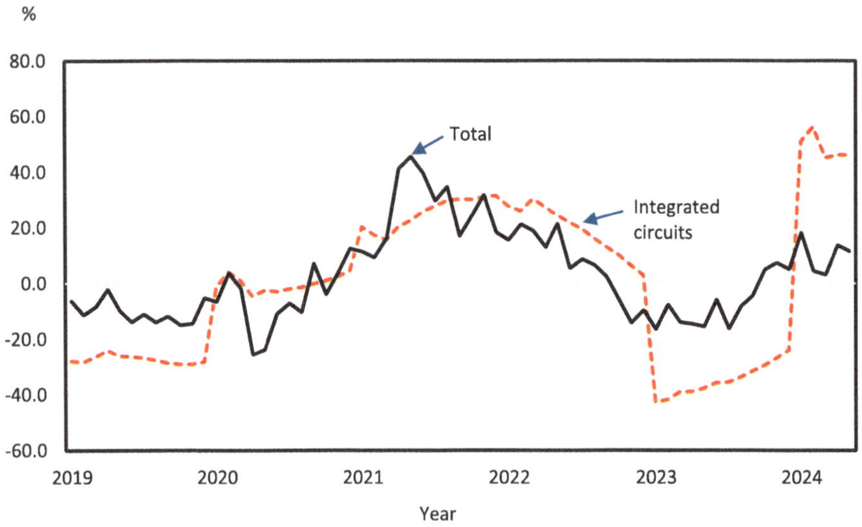

Fig. 7.3 Exports of semiconductors and integrated circuits (YoY). Source: Korean International Trade Association database

generally continued through the first half of 2023, it turned upward in October. It has been doing well since the beginning of 2024, recording double-digit increases.

So far, we have examined overall export movements, which generally align with the government's assessment. Next, we examine the semiconductor trend. The HS code 8542 (integrated circuits) was used for semiconductors. The export value of semiconductors in 2023 comprised 16.5% of total export values, the highest export value among the HS code 4-digit items. Semiconductor exports YoY were weak in 2019 and consistently lower than 20% (Fig. 7.3). However, the decline narrowed significantly in 2020, with a mix of positive and negative numbers. Semiconductor exports began to recover noticeably in 2021, generally increasing by more than 20% in the first half and more than 30% in the second half. This situation continued for some time in 2022, maintaining an increase of more than 20% in the first half of the year. However, the growth rate began to decline in the second half of the year, with only a single-digit increase in November and December.

A noticeable change in the semiconductor export trend occurred in 2023. The months of January and February 2023 recorded declines exceeding 40% and exceeding 30%, respectively, through September. After October, semiconductor exports remained negative by more than 20% until December 2023. However, exports showed a significant increase in 2024 and continued to increase by more than 40% after increasing by more than 50% in January and February 2024.

Semiconductor trends generally follow those of overall exports. However, especially after 2019 and 2023, the decrease and increase in semiconductor sales exceeded the figures of overall exports. Thus, although the government's economic assessment excluded semiconductors as a factor in export trends until August 2023, semiconductor trends significantly impacted overall export trends even before that time. In light of the above analysis, it is summarized that the main reason for economic expansion despite the spread of COVID-19 infections was the strong performance of exports, especially semiconductor exports. Furthermore, the main reason for the economic recession after the COVID-19 pandemic had mostly subsided was the sluggish performance of exports, especially semiconductor exports.

7.4 Vulnerability of the South Korean Semiconductor Industry Concentrating on Digital Memory[2]

One of the main reasons the economy expanded despite the spread of COVID-19 was the strong performance of semiconductor exports. The reason for the strong performance of semiconductor exports was the change in people's behavior due to the spread of COVID-19.

The World Semiconductor Trade Statistics (WSTS): The Japan Council edits and publishes semiconductor market forecasts published semi-annually by the WSTS

[2] Most of Sect. 7.4 is quoted from Takayasu (2024).

for the Japanese market. According to this document, the WSTS's Fall 2020 forecast indicates that lifestyle changes due to the spread of COVID-19 increased demand for semiconductors. Furthermore, the Spring 2021 forecast indicates that since the spread of COVID-19, more time was spent at home, and demand for PCs and tablet terminals had increased. These factors dramatically increased Internet data transmissions and demand for capital investment in infrastructure, such as cloud computing services, significantly impacting the semiconductor market. The Fall 2021 forecast also indicated that following the spread of COVID-19, demand for PCs, tablets, Wi-Fi devices, and other equipment required for working from home, classes, and other activities increased. Furthermore, demand for video distribution and game consoles for home entertainment also grew, dramatically increasing data traffic over the Internet. Additionally, the semiconductor market had many positive factors due to higher investment in infrastructure equipment such as cloud services.

When the spread of COVID-19 had generally ended, the slump in semiconductor exports occurred for several reasons, including the end of the so-called special demand at home, global inflation, and the stalling of semiconductor demand due to heightened geopolitical risks represented by Russia's prolonged invasion of Ukraine. The WSTS Japan Council made this point in its Spring 2023 forecast.

The two main types of semiconductors are logic semiconductors, which control electronic devices, and memory semiconductors, which store data. Therefore, we examine the trends of these two types of semiconductor markets using the WSTS data. To clarify the differences by semiconductor type, we look at the trends from 2012. First, the long-term trend of logic semiconductors (value basis, YoY) is characterized by a relatively stable growth trend, with single-digit growth in most cases, even during strong periods (Fig. 7.4). However, memory semiconductors are extremely volatile, with large increases during strong periods and significant decreases during slumps. For example, the trend increased by 61.5% in 2017 and decreased by 32.6% in 2019.

The growth rates were generally the same when the COVID-19 infection was spreading, 11.1% for logic semiconductors and 10.4% for memory semiconductors in 2020, whereas in 2021, the rates were 30.8% for logic semiconductors and 30.9% for memory semiconductors. However, as the COVID-19 pandemic subsided in 2022 and 2023, logic semiconductors maintained a relatively strong performance, increasing by 14.0% in 2022. Conversely, memory semiconductors slumped with a 15.6% decrease. In 2023, although logic semiconductors saw a significant slowdown in growth, they still maintained an increase of 1.1%, while memory semiconductors saw a larger decline of 28.9%, further exacerbating the sluggish situation.

The South Korean semiconductor industry is focusing on producing memory semiconductors. Samsung Electronics and SK Hynix are the two major semiconductor manufacturers in South Korea. In 2022, Samsung Electronics and SK Hynix were at first and fourth place, respectively, in profit ranking. However, according to Gartner (2024), Samsung Electronics dropped to second place (behind Intel) and SK Hynix to sixth place in 2023 due to poor performance in the semiconductor field.

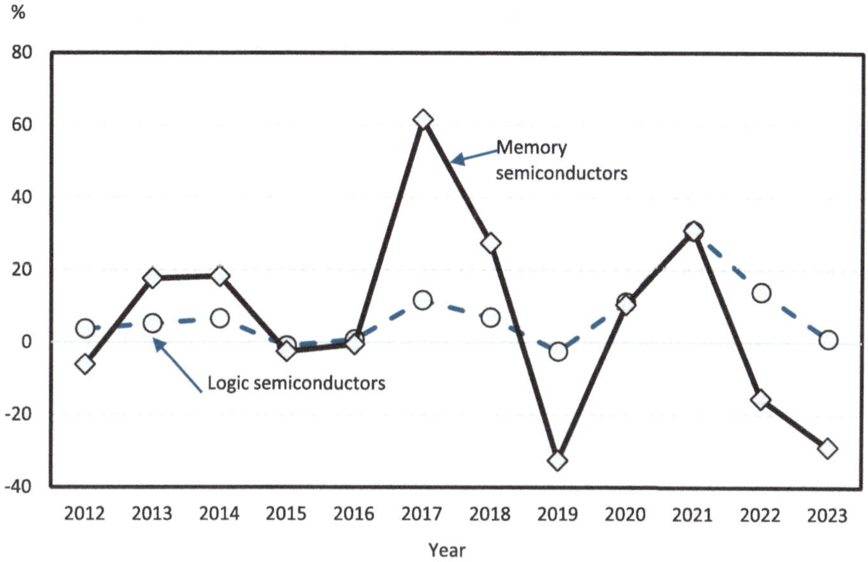

Fig. 7.4 Global logic and memory semiconductor markets (YoY). Source: Created based on the reports of WSTS Japan Council

Dynamic random-access memory (DRAM) and NAND are the main memory semiconductor products. DRAM can record data only when electricity is present, temporarily storing data and providing a working space for applications and other operations. NAND is a recording medium because data is not erased even when the device is not energized. According to Masumori (2024), Samsung Electronics and SK Hynix accounted for 38.9% and 34.3% of the global DRAM market from July to September 2023, respectively. South Korean companies alone comprised about three-quarters of the global share. Regarding NAND, Samsung Electronics and SK Hynix remain in first and second place, accounting for 31.4% and 20.2% of the market, respectively. Samsung Electronics also produces logic semiconductors. However, they are not a mainstay compared to memory semiconductors, indicating that South Korean semiconductor companies are concentrating on them.

The South Korean semiconductor industry is focusing on producing memory semiconductors. Memory semiconductors fluctuate widely between good and bad periods. The South Korean economy has also been affected by these fluctuations, overworking during strong memory semiconductor demand periods and slowing during slumps. At the time of the COVID-19 pandemic, the semiconductor industry was strong because of special demand. Moreover, a significant increase in memory semiconductors also prevented the economy from going into recession. However, without this special demand, the economy would have slowed significantly and could have experienced a serious recession. Furthermore, demand for memory semiconductors dropped sharply when the COVID-19 pandemic ended, leading to an economic recession.

Therefore, to make the South Korean economy more stable, the South Korean semiconductor industry must make a full-scale entry into non-memory semiconductors. According to the Industrial Research Institute (2023), the global semiconductor market in 2022 was valued at USD600 billion, with memory semiconductors comprising 23.9% and non-memory semiconductors 76.1%. Furthermore, South Korea's share of non-memory semiconductor sales was only 3.3%, which was far lower than that of the United States at 54.5%. South Korea ranked sixth behind Europe, Taiwan, Japan, and China.

There are many types of non-memory semiconductors. The ones that South Korean companies manufacture full-scale are cutting-edge logic semiconductors. South Korean companies are involved in the entire memory semiconductor manufacturing process, from design to manufacturing and sales. When South Korean companies manufacture cutting-edge semiconductors, they use the foundry business model, in which they manufacture the front-end processes of semiconductors designed by other companies, that is, making and inspecting IC chips on a silicon wafer. Semiconductor manufacturing can be largely divided into front-end and back-end processes. The front-end process is explained above, while the back-end process involves cutting out the finished silicon wafers to make IC chips and fixing them to frames.

Samsung Electronics instituted its foundry division in 2017 and began full operations in 2019. According to Trend Force (2023), Samsung Electronics reached the second-largest global market share in the July to September period of 2023, behind Taiwan's TSMC. However, TSMC had a 56.4% market share, while Samsung Electronics only had 11.7% and would not easily surpass TSMC. In any case, Samsung Electronics has obtained the world's second-largest market share in less than 5 years since it began full-scale operations. Therefore, the South Korean semiconductor industry has taken the first step toward a balanced industrial structure by increasing the production weight of non-memory semiconductors, especially cutting-edge logic semiconductors. It is thought that, once the industry gets on track, South Korea's economy will become more stable, and the improvement in technological capabilities will contribute to raising productivity.

7.5 Conclusion

This study first analyzed the factors that contributed to the expansion of the South Korean economy during the spread of COVID-19. We also examined the reasons for the recession after the infections ceased. The results reveal that sluggish exports, especially semiconductor exports, caused the economy to expand despite the spread and severity of COVID-19 and caused the economy to recede when the COVID-19 pandemic ended.

The South Korean semiconductor industry is characterized by its concentration on producing memory semiconductors, which are incredibly volatile, increasing significantly during strong periods but declining sharply during slumps. When COVID-19 spread, semiconductors were strong because of the special demand for them. A large boost in memory semiconductors also helped keep the economy from recession. However, without this special demand, the economy would have slowed significantly and could have fallen into a serious recession. Furthermore, demand for memory semiconductors dropped sharply when the COVID-19 pandemic ended, leading to an economic recession.

After COVID-19, the South Korean semiconductor industry must increase its production weight of non-memory semiconductors, especially cutting-edge logic semiconductors. The South Korean economy will become more stable if these structural changes in the semiconductor industry can be accomplished. One direction the South Korean economy should take is to increase the weight of non-memory semiconductors in the semiconductor industry.

References

English References

Gartner (2024) "Gartner says worldwide semiconductor revenue declined 11% in 2023." Press Release (January 16, 2024). (English references)

Trend Force (2023) "Top ten semiconductor foundries report a 1.1% quarterly revenue decline in 2Q23, Anticipated to Rebound in 3Q23, Says Trend Force"

Japanese References

Masumori Ayumi (2024) "The current status and strategy of the South Korean semiconductor industry standing between the U.S.-China conflict," Regional and Analytical Report, Japan External Trade Organization

Korean references

Disease Control and Prevention Agency (2022) 2-year report of domestic confirmed COVID-19 (1.20.2020–1.19.2022). Weekly Health and Disease 15:7

Ha J-H et al. (2023) Current status and characteristics of COVID-19 outbreaks in metropolitan area. (2020.1.20.–2022.8.31)

Korea Institute for Industrial Economics and Trade (2023) Topography and policy implications of the global non-memory semiconductor market. KIET Industrial Economics Industrial Focus. (Korean references).

Ministry of Health and Welfare (2023) COVID-19, Changes in infectious disease response in the last three years (Press release, January 20, 2023)

Statistics Korea (2023) Base cycle date setting for recent business cycle periods (Press release, March 2, 2023)

Takayasu Y (2024) The evolving South Korean economy?–cutting-edge logic semiconductors, biotechnology, and AI. In: Asaba Y (ed) Facing South Korea for the first time. Horitsu Bunka Sha

Chapter 8
Air Pollution and its Control Governance in Chinese Provinces in the Post-COVID-19 Era: Panel Estimations of Provincial Environmental Kuznets Curves

Hiroyuki Taguchi and Takeshi Fujino

Abstract China's rapid industrialization and urbanization have deteriorated its environmental air quality. This study focuses on air pollution in terms of CO, NO_2, O_3, $PM_{2.5}$, PM_{10}, and SO_2 in Chinese provinces. Although the heterogeneity of environmental Kuznets curves (EKCs) from Chinese provinces has been studied, the positions of provincial EKCs (which reflect the province-specific pollution impact not affected by provincial income levels) have not been investigated to date. Therefore, through factor analysis of the heterogeneity of provincial pollution under the EKC framework, we investigate how governance shortages for pollution control contribute to provincial pollution levels. We found that the governance shortage for pollution control accounted for about 50–70% of the province-specific air pollution levels. Our results indicate that China still has a significant policy space to mitigate air pollution. In the post-COVID-19 era, when industrial activities have recovered, pollution-control governance is vital for making China's economic growth sustainable.

Keywords Air pollution · Pollution-control governance · Chinese provinces · Environmental Kuznets curve

H. Taguchi (✉)
Strategic Research Center, Saitama University, Saitama, Japan
e-mail: htaguchi@mail.saitama-u.ac.jp

T. Fujino
Graduate School of Science and Engineering, Saitama University, Saitama, Japan

© The Author(s), under exclusive license to Springer Nature Singapore Pte Ltd. 2025
H. Taguchi (ed.), *Sustainability of Economic Growth in East Asia*,
New Frontiers in Regional Science: Asian Perspectives 82,
https://doi.org/10.1007/978-981-96-3731-7_8

8.1 Introduction

China's living standards have significantly improved since the implementation of the Open Door Policy and Reform Policy in 1978. Based on the World Bank income classification, China's economic status was promoted from the low-income category to the lower-middle-income category in 1997 and then to the upper-middle-income category in 2010.[1] However, the industrialization and urbanization accompanying this rapid economic development have resulted in serious damage to China's environment. Recognizing the environmental challenges confronting the country, China's government has worked over the past decade to establish environmental authorities and introduce a comprehensive legal framework for environmental protection measures. The government has also set numerical targets to reduce the main pollutants and invested considerable resources in working toward national targets. These efforts have shown some success; however, much more work must be done.

Air pollution is a vital issue that affects both human survival and socioeconomic development. Two forces are responsible for much of China's air pollution. The first is China's extreme dependence on coal. In 2023, coal satisfied 55% of China's energy demand,[2] making China the world's largest coal consumer. The second factor is China's booming cities. Increasing urbanization, accompanied by increased automobile use and largely untreated municipal waste emissions, has increased the proportion of the population exposed to the greater pollution levels found in urban areas. The World Bank (2022) demonstrated that 42%of China's population still lives in areas that do not meet the World Health Organization air quality guidelines, and almost all Chinese cities have particulate matter 2.5 ($PM_{2.5}$) concentrations above the guidelines' recommended thresholds. It estimates that direct economic losses amount to approximately 0.5% of the annual gross domestic product. According to the Environmental Performance Index,[3] China ranks 168th out of 180 countries in terms of air quality.

In addition to the nationwide air pollution issue, another vital concern in China is the regional heterogeneity of pollution levels and the factors influencing them. Air pollution levels largely vary by province, as do the income levels and pollution-control governance that affect them (Table 8.1). The gaps in provincial pollution levels are as follows: 33.0 times between Guangdong (the lowest) and Qinghai (the highest) in carbon monoxide (CO), 25.5 times between Guangdong and Qinghai in nitrogen dioxide (NO_2), 39.9 times between Guangdong and Tibet in ozone (O_3), 26.3 times between Guangdong and Qinghai in fine particulate matter ($PM_{2.5}$), 29.4 times between Guangdong and Ningxia in particulate matter (PM_{10}), and 42.6 times between Guangdong and Qinghai in Sulfur dioxide (SO_2). Gaps have also been noted in the factors affecting pollution levels: 4.5 times between Beijing (the

[1] See the website: https://datahelpdesk.worldbank.org/knowledgebase/articles/906519

[2] See the website of National Bureau of Statistics of China: https://www.stats.gov.cn/english/

[3] See the website: https://epi.yale.edu/

Table 8.1 Air pollution and its influential variables in Chinese provinces, 2019

	CO	NO_2	O_3	$PM_{2.5}$	PM_{10}	SO_2	*ypc*	*gov*
Beijing	3.2	161.8	316.4	189.4	305.3	20.2	127,816	13.149
Tianjin	7.0	303.8	537.2	373.0	579.7	79.1	79,377	13.019
Hebei	1.3	52.0	96.9	67.2	127.1	20.9	37,909	10.855
Shanxi	3.2	110.2	208.4	141.3	274.9	67.9	40,851	8.440
Inner Mongolia	3.4	123.0	287.4	129.9	291.7	70.3	56,765	5.289
Liaoning	2.1	67.4	165.0	94.7	166.6	42.8	46,399	10.178
Jilin	3.1	103.6	257.6	144.2	253.5	45.2	39,585	9.286
Heilongjiang	1.8	62.3	177.5	92.6	165.1	32.8	33,595	8.848
Shanghai	2.7	165.9	309.9	143.7	194.2	27.5	121,299	14.297
Jiangsu	0.9	41.8	89.0	51.2	86.1	10.5	93,882	13.424
Zhejiang	1.1	51.3	105.2	49.4	84.7	10.8	78,860	13.134
Anhui	1.2	53.2	123.9	75.4	122.3	16.0	49,455	11.515
Fujian	1.6	47.7	160.4	58.1	98.6	16.0	83,630	12.344
Jiangxi	1.8	51.5	144.8	75.8	128.3	27.4	44,234	10.927
Shandong	0.8	35.5	79.9	50.7	96.5	13.5	56,397	11.349
Henan	0.9	35.1	76.3	61.7	103.5	11.1	42,522	9.708
Hubei	1.5	51.3	118.6	76.3	122.5	15.6	56,788	10.842
Hunan	1.3	37.7	97.8	64.5	91.6	13.6	49,459	9.748
Guangdong	0.6	21.7	53.9	21.8	36.9	6.5	68,259	13.669
Guangxi	1.7	42.3	112.8	61.7	101.7	21.5	33,915	9.033
Hainan	5.6	114.2	668.9	158.5	302.3	45.6	41,565	6.475
Chongqing	2.7	122.2	154.5	118.5	184.1	23.5	62,176	12.586
Sichuan	0.9	34.6	66.1	45.3	69.3	10.7	45,290	11.041
Guizhou	1.6	48.2	154.7	63.0	103.1	28.4	36,729	8.981
Yunnan	1.5	41.4	139.4	46.8	81.9	19.5	40,611	8.685
Tibet	15.1	397.1	2150.2	290.7	741.6	158.5	39,917	5.454
Shaanxi	2.1	95.3	144.2	124.7	221.3	24.9	51,742	10.398
Gansu	2.7	103.9	292.2	114.1	273.2	55.8	28,171	9.640
Qinghai	19.8	553.4	1215.5	573.0	1105.0	276.9	38,082	7.412
Ningxia	11.0	413.3	1021.2	444.1	1086.3	234.0	43,180	9.320
Xinjiang	3.6	138.3	253.1	163.2	302.1	28.4	41,769	7.830

Notes: For the variable descriptions, see Table 2

highest) and Gansu (the lowest) in gross regional product (GRP) per capita (*ypc*), and 2.6 times between Shanghai and Tibet for the provincial governance indicator (*gov*).

The reason for picking up the provincial governance indicator is that provincial pollution levels depend on local governments' capacities for implementing environmental regulations. MacBean (2007) argued that despite the mass of laws and policy tools in place in China and the widespread use of environmental officials throughout the country, compliance with regulations appears to be poor. The main reasons for this were identified as the higher value placed on conventionally measured economic growth and job maintenance or expansion by other departments in local governments. Thus, China's environmental prospects appear to depend strongly on how each province addresses the problems associated with the implementation of environmental protection regulations.

Environmental issues are often studied using the analytical framework of the environmental Kuznets curve (EKC), including research conducted in China. However, EKC analyses conducted to date have concentrated on EKC modalities depending on pollutants and provinces, and there have been no empirical studies explicitly uncovering the nexus between provincial pollution levels and pollution-control governance. Thus, the motivation for the present study is to fill this gap in the research on EKC governance links in Chinese provinces.

This study focuses on air pollution measures to address CO, NO_2, O_3, $PM_{2.5}$, PM_{10}, and SO_2 in Chinese provinces, aiming to investigate the contributions of pollution-control governance shortages to provincial pollution levels based on a factor analysis of the heterogeneity of provincial pollution under the EKC's analytical framework. To achieve these goals, this study takes the following steps. First, based on provincial panel data, the EKC is estimated econometrically using a fixed-effect model. Second, the province-specific pollution effect is extracted from the fixed effect, which is not affected by provincial income level, on the EKC. Third, the alternative EKC is re-estimated by replacing the fixed-effect model with pollution-control governance. Fourth, the governance shortage contributing to the province-specific pollution level is quantified through a factor analysis. The main finding of this study is that the governance shortage in pollution control accounts for approximately 50–70% of provincial air pollution levels. Therefore, China has the capacity to mitigate air pollution through improvements in policy implementation. Moreover, in the post-COVID-19 era, when industrial activities have recovered, pollution-control governance is vital for ensuring the sustainability of China's economic growth.

The remainder of this paper is organized as follows. Section 8.2 reviews the literature related to the EKC, including air pollution in China, and clarifies the contributions of this study. Section 8.3 presents the materials and methods used in the empirical study. Section 8.4 presents and discusses the estimation results. Finally, section 8.5 summarizes and concludes the paper.

8.2 Literature Review and Contributions

This section reviews the literature related to EKC issues, including the air pollution EKC in China, and clarifies the contributions of this study.

The EKC provides an analytical framework for examining how economies deal with environmental issues. This framework proposes an inverted U-shaped relationship between pollution and economic development. Kuznets's name was attached to the curve by Grossman and Krueger (1995), who noted its resemblance to the inverted U-shaped relationship Kuznets identified between income inequality and development. According to Dasgupta et al. (2002), in the EKC dynamic process, during the first stage of industrialization, pollution worsens rapidly because people are more interested in employment and income than in clean air and water, and environmental regulation is correspondingly weak. In wealthy societies, pollution decreases along this curve because the leading industrial sectors become cleaner, people value the environment, and regulatory institutions become more effective.

Since the World Bank (1992) initially discussed EKC issues, empirical tests and theoretical debates have intensified, supporting the applicability of the EKC to certain regions and environmental problems (e.g., Grossman and Krueger 1995; Lopez 1994; Selden and Song 1994; Stokey 1998). At the initial stage up to the 1990s, most of the empirical research focused on validating the EKC hypothesis and its requirements using cross-sectional data. However, since the late 1990s, EKC studies have shifted from cross-sectional to time-series analyses and have examined the heterogeneity of EKCs from individual economies in terms of curve shapes and positions. In this context, Dasgupta et al. (2002) presented three different EKC scenarios from the conventional inverted-U EKC: race to the bottom (pessimistic, with a continuation of the highest level of pollution), new toxics (pessimistic with a higher curve, owing to newly emerging pollutants), and the revised EKC (optimistic with a lower and flatter curve, owing to better pollution management). These scenarios have been subjected to empirical analyses (e.g., Dinda 2004; Mukhopadhyay and Chakraborty 2005; Taguchi 2012; Taguchi and Murofushi 2010). Sarkodie and Strezov (2019) comprehensively reviewed the heterogeneity of the EKC modalities in terms of curve shapes and positions.

A large body of literature examines the EKC in several countries and at several levels of environmental quality. However, the number of studies on the EKC in China has increased since the 2000s. Therefore, the number of EKC studies that cover total provinces or specific areas is relatively limited in China, particularly for air pollution (Table 8.2). The estimations show ambiguous and mixed outcomes: some studies identify the validity of the inverted U-shaped EKC (e.g., Chang et al. 2021; Chen and Chen 2015; Jayanthakumaran and Liu 2012; Moriwaki and Shimizu 2023; Song et al. 2008; Wang et al. 2016; Xu et al. 2021; Yan et al. 2023), whereas the others demonstrate that the EKC modality is dependent on regions (e.g., Song et al. 2021; Song et al. 2013) and pollutants (e.g., Brajer et al. 2011; Cui et al. 2021; Li et al. 2016; Liu et al. 2007), and invalid (e.g., Shen 2006).

This study makes several contributions to the literature. First, this study covers all air pollutants (CO, NO_2, O_3, $PM_{2.5}$, PM_{10}, and SO_2) in Chinese provinces, whereas previous studies targeted selected air pollutants. Thus, this study's outcomes are comprehensively generalized to the issue of air pollution in China. Second, this study elucidates the nexus between provincial pollution levels and pollution-control governance. Previous studies have concentrated on the EKC's "shapes" depending on pollutants and provinces. This study focuses on analyzing the heterogeneity of

Table 8.2 Literature review of the EKC on water pollution in China

	Sample areas	Air pollutants	Summary
Yan et al. (2023)	30 provinces	SO_2, soot, and dust	Inverted-U shaped EKC
Moriwaki and Shimizu (2023)	291 cities	SO_2	Inverted-U shaped EKC
Xu et al. (2021)	30 provinces	NO_X	Inverted-U shaped EKC
Cui et al. (2021)	31 provinces	SO_2, CO_2, NO_X, and dust	EKC validity depends on pollutants
Song et al. (2021)	74 cities	Quality including atmosphere index	EKC shape depends on cities
Chang et al. (2021)	284 cities	$PM_{2.5}$	Inverted-U shaped EKC
Li et al. (2016)	30 provinces	CO_2, SO_2	EKC validity depends on pollutants
Wang et al. (2016)	31 provinces	SO_2	Inverted-U shaped EKC
Chen and Chen (2015)	31 provinces	CO_2	Inverted-U shaped EKC
Song et al. (2013)	31 provinces	Waste gas emission	EKC shape depends on provinces
Jayanthakumaran and Liu (2012)	30 provinces	SO_2	Inverted-U shaped EKC
Brajer et al. (2011)	139 cities	Composite indices	EKC shape depends on pollutants
Song et al. (2008)	29 provinces	Waste gas emission	Inverted-U shaped EKC
Liu et al. (2007)	Shenzhen	TSP, SO_2, and NO_X	EKC shape depends on pollutants
Shen (2006)	31 provinces	SO_2, dust	No existence of Inverted-U shaped EKC

Sources: Authors' description

EKCs in different Chinese provinces in terms of their "positions" that reflect the province-specific pollution effects not affected by the provincial income levels and investigates the contributions of pollution-control governance shortages to province-specific pollution levels.

8.3 Empirical Analyses

This section presents empirical analyses consisting of EKC econometric estimations using provincial panel data and a factor analysis of the heterogeneity of province-specific air pollution. This section begins with descriptions of the methodology and data.

8.3.1 Methodology and Data

This study generally follows the original form of the EKC: the standard nonlinear model, in which air pollution per capita is regressed on income per capita and its square. The first specification in Eq. (8.1) applies a fixed-effect model for provincial panel data estimation to explicitly demonstrate the province-specific pollution effects and runs the alternative models in Eq. (8.2) by replacing the fixed effect with a pollution-control governance indicator to elucidate the contribution of governance shortages to province-specific pollution levels. The equations used for the estimations are as follows:

$$\ln\left(aco_{it}, ano_{it}, ao3_{it}, ap1_{it}, ap2_{it}, aso_{it}\right)$$

$$= \alpha_0 + \alpha_1 \ln ypc_{it} + \alpha_2 \left(\ln ypc_{it}\right)^2 + f_i + f_t + \varepsilon_t \quad (8.1)$$

$$\ln\left(aco_{it}, ano_{it}, ao3_{it}, ap1_{it}, ap2_{it}, aso_{it}\right)$$

$$= \beta_0 + \beta_1 \ln ypc_{it} + \beta_2 \left(\ln ypc_{it}\right)^2 + \beta_3\, gov_{it} + f_t + \varepsilon_t \quad (8.2)$$

where the subscripts i and t denote a sample of 31 Chinese provinces and the years 2014–2019, respectively; *aco*, *ano*, *ao3*, *ap1*, *ap2*, and *aso* represent the air pollutants CO, NO_2, O_3, $PM_{2.5}$, PM_{10}, and SO_2, expressed as per 100 million persons, respectively;[4] *ypc* shows the GRP per capita in terms of yuan at constant prices in 2010; *gov* denotes a governance indicator; f_i and f_t show a time-invariant country-specific fixed effect and a country-invariant time-specific fixed effect, respectively; ε denotes a residual error term; $\alpha_{0\ldots2}$, and $\beta_{0\ldots3}$ represent estimated coefficients; and "ln" shows a logarithm form, which is set to avoid scaling issues for the air pollutants and GRP per capita. The explanatory variables in Eqs. (8.1) and (8.3), *ypc* and *gov*, are lagged by 1 year to help avoid reverse causality in the model specifications, including the endogenous interaction between the dependent and independent variables.

Regarding the data sources, the data on air pollutants are retrieved from the National Climatic Data Center (NCDC);[5] data on GRP per capita are from the China Statistical Yearbook; and the governance indicator is from the index of "development of market intermediaries and legal environment" as one of five aspect indices

[4] In the case of CO, the value is processed ten times because the negative value should be avoided in the logarithm term.

[5] See the NCDC website: https://www.cnemc.cn/sssj/.The air pollutant data are collected from 2033 observation sites and compiled by averaging the data in each province.

Table 8.3 List of variables

Variables	Description
Dependent variable	
aco	*Carbon monoxide (CO), mg/m*^{3}*, per 100 million persons, logarithm*
ano	*Nitrogen dioxide (*NO_2*), μg/m*^{3}*, per 100 million persons, logarithm*
ao3	*Ozone (*O_3*), μg/m*^{3}*, per 100 million persons, logarithm*
ap1	*Fine particulate matter (*$PM_{2.5}$*), μg/m*^{3}*, per 100 million persons, logarithm*
ap2	*Particulate matter (*PM_{10}*), μg/m*^{3}*, per 100 million persons, logarithm*
aso	*Sulfur dioxide (*SO_2*), μg/m*^{3}*, per 100 million persons, logarithm*
Explanatory variables	
ypc	*Gross regional product (GRP)* per capita, *2010 prices, RMB, one-year lagged, logarithm*
gov	*Governance indicator, "Development of market intermediary organizations and legal environment" in the "China Marketization Index" by* Fan et al. (2019), *one-year lagged*

Sources: Authors' description

Table 8.4 Descriptive statistics

Variables	Obs.	Median	Std. Dev.	Min.	Max
Dependent variable					
aco	186	3.078	0.841	1.808	5.607
ano	186	4.297	0.809	3.079	6.574
ao3	186	5.203	0.860	3.980	8.080
ap1	186	4.717	0.776	3.080	6.871
ap2	186	5.214	0.854	3.607	7.641
aso	186	3.786	0.937	1.879	6.658
Explanatory variables					
ypc	186	10.542	0.392	9.901	11.714
gov	186	7.309	3.210	0.460	14.132

Sources: Authors' calculations

of the provincial-level "Index of Marketization" developed by the National Economic Research Institute of China Reform Foundation (NERI).[6] This index ranges from 0 (weak governance) to 10 (strong governance).

This study constructs a set of panel data for 31 provinces in the period of 2014–2019.[7] Tables 8.3 and 8.4 present the variable list and descriptive statistics for the variable data, respectively.

Notes on the specifications of the estimation models in Eqs. (8.1) and (8.2) are required for an additional description. Eq. (1) applies a fixed-effect model,

[6] See the website: https://cmi.ssap.com.cn/. Fan et al. (2019) have analyzed the effects of the index on economic growth and total factor productivity.

[7] This study excludes 2020 owing to the serious effects of COVID-19 on economic activities.

represented by f_i and f_t, for the provincial panel data estimation. The Hausman test is generally used to select between a fixed- and random-effects model (Hausman 1978). However, this study focuses on explicitly demonstrating province-specific pollution effects, and time-specific factors such as economic fluctuations due to external shocks should be considered. In addition, adopting the fixed-effects model helps alleviate the endogeneity problem by absorbing unobserved time-invariant heterogeneity among the sample provinces. The estimation sets Guangdong as the benchmark province for extracting province-specific pollution effects, because it shows the best performance for air pollution (Table 8.1). The significantly positive coefficient of the province-specific fixed effect suggests that the air pollution in a particular province is more serious than that in Guangdong. The ordinary hypothesis of the EKC postulating an inverted U-shaped path between air pollution and GRP per capita would be verified if α_1, $\beta_1 > 0$ and α_2, $\beta_2 < 0$ a are significant.

Equation (8.2) represents the alternative models, replacing the province-specific fixed effects with the pollution-control governance indicator. No multicollinearity exists in the regressor combinations in Eq. (8.2) (i.e., *ypc*, *gov*). This is because the variance inflation factors (VIFs) reflecting the level of collinearity between the regressors indicate a lower value than the criterion of collinearity (10 points). According to the authors' estimation, the VIF values of *ypc* and *gov* in Eq. (8.2) are 2.427. The governance indicator (*gov*) is expected to have a negative coefficient for air pollution because higher governance enables pollution mitigation.

This study applies the Poisson pseudo-maximum likelihood (PPML) estimator to the estimations. The PPML estimator was selected because sample data with heterogeneity in the provincial properties would be plagued by heteroskedasticity and autocorrelation, and in such cases, the ordinary least squares (OLS) estimator leads to bias and inconsistency in the estimates. The PPML estimator corrects for heteroscedastic error structures across panels and autocorrelation with panels, as suggested by Silva and Tenreyro (2006) and Kareem et al. (2016). We used EViews (version 12) (IHS Global Inc., CA, USA) to process the data and estimations.

8.3.2 Panel Unit Root and Co-integration Tests

For the subsequent estimation, we investigated the stationary property of the panel data by utilizing panel unit root tests and, if necessary, a panel co-integration test for a set of variable data. The panel unit root tests were first conducted on the null hypothesis, such that the level and/or the first difference of the individual data have a unit root. In cases where the unit root tests reveal that each variable's data are not stationary in the level, but are stationary in the first difference, the set of variable data corresponds to the case of $I(1)$. This can be further examined using a co-integration test for the "level" data. If the data for a set of variables are identified as having co-integration, the use of the "level" data is justified for model estimation.

For the panel unit root tests, this study applied the Levin et al. (2002) test as a common unit root test and the Im et al. (2003) test as an individual unit root test. The

Table 8.5 Panel unit root and co-integration tests

	Unit root test	
	Level	1st difference
Levin, Lin, and Chu		
aco	2.557	−15.368 ***
ano	−7.891 ***	−16.179 ***
ao3	−11.509 ***	−15.468 ***
ap1	1.213	−23.166 ***
ap2	0.549	−23.428 ***
aso	2.505	−18.957 ***
ypc	3.835	−8.925 ***
gov	−9.423 ***	−36.717 ***
Im, Pesaran, and Shin		
aco	4.986	−6.198 ***
ano	−0.851	−5.683 ***
ao3	−0.772	−4.398 ***
ap1	4.420	−8.412 ***
ap2	4.214	−6.340 ***
aso	6.815	−5.350 ***
ypc	8.363	−1.327 *
gov	−0.667	−14.838 ***
	Panel cointegration test	
	Panel ADF	Panel PP
group of		
aco	−4.085 ***	−4.819 ***
ano	−3.481 ***	−4.307 ***
ao3	−1.796 **	−2.911 ***
ap1	−6.050 ***	−7.801 ***
ap2	−5.649 ***	−4.971 ***
aso	−3.268 ***	−2.621 ***

Note: ***, **, and * denote statistical significance at the 99%, 95%, and 90% levels, respectively
Sources: Authors' estimations

common unit root test assumes a common unit root process across cross-sections, whereas the individual unit root test allows for individual unit root processes that vary across cross-sections. For the panel co-integration test, the study used the residual co-integration test developed by Pedroni (2004). All test equations contained an individual intercept, with the lag length being an automatic selection.

Table 8.5 presents the test results. The common unit root test does not reject the null hypothesis of a unit root on data for most variables, and the individual tests do not reject it on any of them at their levels. However, both tests reject this in their first differences at the conventional significance levels. Thus, the variables almost follow the case of $I(1)$. The panel co-integration test is conducted further on the combinations of variables in Eq. (8.2). The Pedroni residual co-integration test suggests that the level series of a set of variable data is co-integrated into the respective combinations. Thus, this study utilizes level data for the estimations.

8.4 Results and Discussion

Tables 8.6, 8.7, 8.8, 8.9, 8.10, and 8.11 present the estimation results in the form of a log link function for air pollutants: CO (*aco*), NO_2 (*ano*), O_3 (*ao3*), $PM_{2.5}$ (*ap1*), PM_{10} (*ap2*), and SO_2 (*aso*), respectively. Column (i) displays the outcomes of the fixed-effect models and column (ii) presents the results of the alternative models containing the pollution-control governance indicator (*gov*) instead of the fixed effects. The findings from the estimation results are summarized below.

8.4.1 EKC Identification by Fixed-Effect Model

First, the EKC hypothesis, which assumes an inverted U-shaped relationship between air pollution level and GRP per capita (where the coefficients of the GRP per capita are significantly positive and those of its square are significantly negative), is confirmed in limited cases: the estimation of column (i) for O_3, $PM_{2.5}$, PM_{10}, and SO_2. The reason why the EKC is not necessarily identified in all estimations appears to be that the sample period of 2014–2019 is too short to form an inverted U-shaped path. This does not lead to serious problems because the main research focus of this study is the positions of provincial EKCs rather than their shapes.

8.4.2 Extraction of Provincial-specific Pollution Effects

Second, the fixed-effect models in columns (i) identify the positive coefficients as the province-specific fixed effects at conventional significance levels for all pollutants (CO, NO_2, O_3, $PM_{2.5}$, PM_{10}, and SO_2) in all provinces except for O_3 in Sichuan. The positive provincial fixed effects indicate that provincial EKCs are located above Guangdong, which is the benchmark, suggesting that the province-specific pollution effects (not affected by provincial income level on the EKC) are larger than those in Guangdong. These results are in line with the simple observations on air pollution in all provinces (Table 8.1). The degree of air pollution is indicated by the magnitude of the coefficients of the provincial fixed-effects. For example, that of CO in Beijing (column (i) in Table 8.6 is exp. (1.752)), which is six times larger than that in Guangdong.

Table 8.6 Estimation results: CO (*aco*)

Estimation	(i)	(ii)
ypc	0.253	0.004
	(1.299)	(0.023)
ypc^2	−0.006	0.041 **
	(−0.018)	(2.397)
gov		−0.187 ***
		(−6.361)
Dummy for fixed effect		
Beijing	1.752 ***	
Tianjin	2.490 ***	
Hebei	0.954 ***	
Shanxi	1.855 ***	
Inner Mongolia	1.731 ***	
Liaoning	1.292 ***	
Jilin	1.658 ***	
Heilongjiang	1.161 ***	
Shanghai	1.384 ***	
Jiangsu	0.363 ***	
Zhejiang	0.581 ***	
Anhui	0.789 ***	
Fujian	0.891 ***	
Jiangxi	1.116 ***	
Shandong	0.410 ***	
Henan	0.652 ***	
Hubei	0.967 ***	
Hunan	0.833 ***	
Guangxi	1.103 ***	
Hainan	2.237 ***	
Chongqing	1.488 ***	
Sichuan	0.446 ***	
Guizhou	1.057 ***	
Yunnan	1.053 ***	
Tibet	3.414 ***	
Shaanxi	1.503 ***	
Gansu	1.726 ***	
Qinghai	3.523 ***	
Ningxia	2.928 ***	
Xinjiang	1.977 ***	
Cross-sections	31	31
Periods	2014–2019	2014–2019
Total observations	186	186

Note: *** and ** denote statistical significance at the 99% and 95% levels, respectively
Sources: Authors' estimation

Table 8.7 Estimation results: NO_2 (*ano*)

Estimation	(i)	(ii)
ypc	0.567 ***	0.030
	(2.726)	(0.177)
ypc^2	−0.024	0.048 ***
	(−1.275)	(2.761)
gov		−0.157 ***
		(−5.479)
Dummy for fixed effect		
Beijing	2.124 ***	
Tianjin	2.620 ***	
Hebei	0.957 ***	
Shanxi	1.520 ***	
Inner Mongolia	1.697 ***	
Liaoning	1.163 ***	
Jilin	1.659 ***	
Heilongjiang	1.174 ***	
Shanghai	1.993 ***	
Jiangsu	0.644 ***	
Zhejiang	0.899 ***	
Anhui	0.859 ***	
Fujian	0.850 ***	
Jiangxi	0.852 ***	
Shandong	0.494 ***	
Henan	0.561 ***	
Hubei	0.901 ***	
Hunan	0.549 ***	
Guangxi	0.707 ***	
Hainan	1.735 ***	
Chongqing	1.735 ***	
Sichuan	0.487 ***	
Guizhou	0.998 ***	
Yunnan	0.656 ***	
Tibet	3.078 ***	
Shaanxi	1.457 ***	
Gansu	1.626 ***	
Qinghai	3.245 ***	
Ningxia	2.894 ***	
Xinjiang	1.887 ***	
Cross-sections	31	31
Periods	2014–2019	2014–2019
Total observations	186	186

Note: *** denotes statistical significance at the 99% level
Sources: Authors' estimations

Table 8.8 Estimation results: O_3 (*ao3*)

Estimation	(i)	(ii)
ypc	5.196 ***	0.238
	(3.373)	(1.287)
ypc^2	−0.255 ***	0.038 **
	(−3.539)	(2.048)
gov		−0.197 ***
		(−6.315)
Dummy for fixed effect		
Beijing	2.103 ***	
Tianjin	2.266 ***	
Hebei	0.427 ***	
Shanxi	1.105 ***	
Inner Mongolia	1.588 ***	
Liaoning	1.005 ***	
Jilin	1.441 ***	
Heilongjiang	0.976 ***	
Shanghai	2.060 ***	
Jiangsu	0.646 ***	
Zhejiang	0.803 ***	
Anhui	0.535 ***	
Fujian	1.094 ***	
Jiangxi	0.785 ***	
Shandong	0.325 ***	
Henan	0.169 *	
Hubei	0.679 ***	
Hunan	0.423 ***	
Guangxi	0.662 ***	
Hainan	2.252 ***	
Chongqing	1.028 ***	
Sichuan	0.142	
Guizhou	0.888 ***	
Yunnan	0.709 ***	
Tibet	3.560 ***	
Shaanxi	0.954 ***	
Gansu	1.504 ***	
Qinghai	2.855 ***	
Ningxia	2.787 ***	
Xinjiang	1.334 ***	
Cross-sections	31	31
Periods	2014–2019	2014–2019
Total observations	186	186

Note: ***, **, and * denote statistical significance at the 99%, 95%, and 90% levels, respectively
Sources: Authors' estimations

Table 8.9 Estimation results: $PM_{2.5}$ (*ap1*)

Estimation	(i)	(ii)
ypc	0.967 ***	0.332 **
	(4.533)	(2.086)
ypc^2	−0.060 ***	0.021
	(−3.034)	(1.342)
gov		−0.141 ***
		(−5.100)
Dummy for fixed-effect		
Beijing	2.566 ***	
Tianjin	2.890 ***	
Hebei	1.022 ***	
Shanxi	1.619 ***	
Inner Mongolia	1.681 ***	
Liaoning	1.279 ***	
Jilin	1.720 ***	
Heilongjiang	1.225 ***	
Shanghai	2.079 ***	
Jiangsu	0.938 ***	
Zhejiang	0.949 ***	
Anhui	1.079 ***	
Fujian	0.951 ***	
Jiangxi	1.066 ***	
Shandong	0.765 ***	
Henan	0.823 ***	
Hubei	1.207 ***	
Hunan	0.886 ***	
Guangxi	0.841 ***	
Hainan	1.796 ***	
Chongqing	1.663 ***	
Sichuan	0.589 ***	
Guizhou	0.983 ***	
Yunnan	0.500 ***	
Tibet	2.757 ***	
Shaanxi	1.563 ***	
Gansu	1.454 ***	
Qinghai	3.138 ***	
Ningxia	2.943 ***	
Xinjiang	1.896 ***	
Cross-sections	31	31
Periods	2014–2019	2014–2019
Total observations	186	186

Note: *** and ** denote statistical significance at the 99% and 95% levels, respectively
Sources: Authors' estimations

Table 8.10 Estimation results: PM_{10} (*ap2*)

Estimation	(i)	(ii)
ypc	1.181 ***	0.448 ***
	(6.867)	(2.597)
ypc^2	−0.076 ***	0.017
	(−4.761)	(1.004)
gov		−0.173 ***
		(−5.836)
Dummy for fixed effect		
Beijing	2.570 ***	
Tianjin	2.924 ***	
Hebei	1.084 ***	
Shanxi	1.714 ***	
Inner Mongolia	2.040 ***	
Liaoning	1.315 ***	
Jilin	1.719 ***	
Heilongjiang	1.178 ***	
Shanghai	2.038 ***	
Jiangsu	1.025 ***	
Zhejiang	0.974 ***	
Anhui	0.988 ***	
Fujian	1.055 ***	
Jiangxi	1.031 ***	
Shandong	0.903 ***	
Henan	0.839 ***	
Hubei	1.173 ***	
Hunan	0.799 ***	
Guangxi	0.740 ***	
Hainan	1.894 ***	
Chongqing	1.604 ***	
Sichuan	0.523 ***	
Guizhou	0.910 ***	
Yunnan	0.566 ***	
Tibet	3.138 ***	
Shaanxi	1.691 ***	
Gansu	1.775 ***	
Qinghai	3.337 ***	
Ningxia	3.291 ***	
Xinjiang	2.032 ***	
Cross-sections	31	31
Periods	2014–2019	2014–2019
Total observations	186	186

Note: *** denotes statistical significance at the 99% level

Sources: Authors' estimations

Table 8.11 Estimation results: SO_2 (*aso*)

Estimation	(i)	(ii)
ypc	5.559 **	0.603 ***
	(2.248)	(3.703)
ypc^2	−0.251 **	−0.010)
	(−2.070)	(−0.607)
gov		−0.160 ***
		(−5.550)
Dummy for fixed effect		
Beijing	1.404 ***	
Tianjin	2.617 ***	
Hebei	1.491 ***	
Shanxi	2.712 ***	
Inner Mongolia	2.393 ***	
Liaoning	1.982 ***	
Jilin	2.167 ***	
Heilongjiang	1.794 ***	
Shanghai	1.690 ***	
Jiangsu	0.739 ***	
Zhejiang	0.692 ***	
Anhui	1.111 ***	
Fujian	0.826 ***	
Jiangxi	1.647 ***	
Shandong	1.029 ***	
Henan	0.989 ***	
Hubei	1.007 ***	
Hunan	0.986 ***	
Guangxi	1.320 ***	
Hainan	1.747 ***	
Chongqing	1.391 ***	
Sichuan	0.696 ***	
Guizhou	1.633 ***	
Yunnan	1.280 ***	
Tibet	3.298 ***	
Shaanxi	1.514 ***	
Gansu	2.439 ***	
Qinghai	3.838 ***	
Ningxia	3.969 ***	
Xinjiang	1.659 ***	
Cross-sections	31	31
Periods	2014–2019	2014–2019
Total observations	186	186

Note: *** and ** denote statistical significance at the 99% and 95% levels, respectively
Sources: Authors' estimations

8.4.3 Re-estimation Results of Alternative EKC Model

Third, in the alternative model containing the pollution-control governance indicator capacity (*gov*) in column (ii), the coefficients of *gov* are significantly negative for all pollutants, as shown in Tables 8.6, 8.7, 8.8, 8.9, 8.10, and 8.11. The negative coefficients of *gov* for all pollutants suggest that pollution-control governance affected provincial pollution levels and that the heterogeneity of provincial pollution could be explained by differences in provincial pollution-control governance. The joint estimation outcomes of province-specific pollution effects and the workability of pollution-control governance raise questions regarding the quantitative contributions of provincial governance shortages to provincial pollution levels.

8.4.4 Factor Analysis on Pollution-control Governance

We quantified the contributions of provincial pollution-control governance to province-specific pollution effects. Tables 8.12, 8.13, 8.14, 8.15, 8.16, and 8.17 present the analytical results for CO, NO_2, O_3, $PM_{2.5}$, PM_{10}, and SO_2, respectively. Columns (a) repeats the provincial fixed effects in Tables 8.6, 8.7, 8.8, 8.9, 8.10, and 8.11, representing the province-specific pollution effects, respectively; column (b) presents the period average of provincial pollution-control governance indicators (*gov*); column (c) computes the *gov* deviations from that of Guangdong (the benchmark), excluding the those in Beijing, Tianjin, Shanghai, and Zhejiang which have governance indicators higher than that of Guangdong; column (d) indicates the *gov* contributions to the provincial-specific pollution effects by multiplying the *gov* deviations with the estimated *gov* coefficients in Tables 8.6, 8.7, 8.8, 8.9, 8.10, and 8.11; and column (e) demonstrates the *gov* contribution ratios to provincial-specific pollution effects by dividing column (d) by column (a).

The first rows in column (e) of Tables 8.12, 8.13, 8.14, 8.15, 8.16, and 8.17 demonstrate that the average *gov* contribution ratios among the sample provinces are 0.724 for CO, 0.680 for NO_2, 1.226 for O_3, 0.560 for $PM_{2.5}$, 0.669 for PM_{10}, and 0.471 for SO_2. Thus, the governance shortage for pollution control accounts for approximately 50–70% of province-specific air pollution levels, except for O_3.

8.4.5 Discussion

The factor analysis in this study verifies that province-specific pollution is significantly affected by provincial pollution-control governance. This finding on the nexus between provincial pollution levels and pollution-control governance is in line with previous policy studies on Chinese provincial environmental performance, such as Zheng et al. (2015) and Wu and Gao (2021). Zheng et al. (2015) found

Table 8.12 Provincial pollution and pollution-control governance (CO)

CO	Fixed-effect (a)	*govg* (b)	(b) -Benchmark (c)	(c) × -0.187 (d)	(d) / (a) (e) av. 0.724
Beijing	1.752	11.684	–	–	–
Tianjin	2.490	11.870	–	–	–
Hebei	0.954	6.418	−4.551	0.851	0.891
Shanxi	1.855	5.098	−5.871	1.098	0.592
Inner Mongolia	1.731	2.785	−8.183	1.530	0.884
Liaoning	1.292	7.355	−3.614	0.676	0.523
Jilin	1.658	6.811	−4.157	0.777	0.469
Heilongjiang	1.161	7.797	−3.171	0.593	0.511
Shanghai	1.384	13.073	–	–	–
Jiangsu	0.363	9.192	−1.777	0.332	0.915
Zhejiang	0.581	12.444	–	–	–
Anhui	0.789	8.159	−2.809	0.525	0.665
Fujian	0.891	9.891	−1.078	0.201	0.226
Jiangxi	1.116	6.784	−4.184	0.782	0.701
Shandong	0.410	8.683	−2.286	0.427	1.042
Henan	0.652	6.882	−4.086	0.764	1.172
Hubei	0.967	6.565	−4.404	0.823	0.852
Hunan	0.833	7.304	−3.665	0.685	0.823
Guangxi	1.103	5.416	−5.552	1.038	0.941
Hainan	2.237	3.490	−7.478	1.398	0.625
Chongqing	1.488	9.109	−1.860	0.348	0.234
Sichuan	0.446	8.431	−2.538	0.474	1.064
Guizhou	1.057	3.664	−7.304	1.365	1.292
Yunnan	1.053	2.755	−8.213	1.535	1.458
Tibet	3.414	1.541	−9.428	1.763	0.516
Shaanxi	1.503	8.715	−2.253	0.421	0.280
Gansu	1.726	5.241	−5.728	1.071	0.620
Qinghai	3.523	2.473	−8.496	1.588	0.451
Ningxia	2.928	4.833	−6.135	1.147	0.392
Xinjiang	1.977	3.600	−7.368	1.378	0.697

Sources: Authors' estimations

empirical support for the positive effects of provincial energy-saving regulations and environmental standards on improving local air quality in China. Wu and Gao (2021) highlighted provincial differences in the efficiency of air pollution control arising from the heterogeneity of environmental regulations in Chinese provinces. Unlike previous policy studies, this study explicitly and quantitatively demonstrates the effects of governance on air pollution.

Table 8.13 Provincial pollution and pollution-control governance (NO_2)

	Fixed effect	*govg*	(b) -Benchmark	(c) × -0.157	(d) / (a) (e)
	(a)	(b)	(c)	(d)	av. 0.680
Beijing	2.124	11.684	–	–	–
Tianjin	2.620	11.870	–	–	–
Hebei	0.957	6.418	−4.551	0.716	0.748
Shanxi	1.520	5.098	−5.871	0.923	0.608
Inner Mongolia	1.697	2.785	−8.183	1.287	0.758
Liaoning	1.163	7.355	−3.614	0.568	0.489
Jilin	1.659	6.811	−4.157	0.654	0.394
Heilongjiang	1.174	7.797	−3.171	0.499	0.425
Shanghai	1.993	13.073	–	–	–
Jiangsu	0.644	9.192	−1.777	0.279	0.434
Zhejiang	0.899	12.444	–	–	–
Anhui	0.859	8.159	−2.809	0.442	0.514
Fujian	0.850	9.891	−1.078	0.169	0.199
Jiangxi	0.852	6.784	−4.184	0.658	0.773
Shandong	0.494	8.683	−2.286	0.359	0.727
Henan	0.561	6.882	−4.086	0.643	1.146
Hubei	0.901	6.565	−4.404	0.693	0.768
Hunan	0.549	7.304	−3.665	0.576	1.050
Guangxi	0.707	5.416	−5.552	0.873	1.234
Hainan	1.735	3.490	−7.478	1.176	0.678
Chongqing	1.735	9.109	−1.860	0.292	0.169
Sichuan	0.487	8.431	−2.538	0.399	0.819
Guizhou	0.998	3.664	−7.304	1.149	1.151
Yunnan	0.656	2.755	−8.213	1.292	1.968
Tibet	3.078	1.541	−9.428	1.483	0.482
Shaanxi	1.457	8.715	−2.253	0.354	0.243
Gansu	1.626	5.241	−5.728	0.901	0.554
Qinghai	3.245	2.473	−8.496	1.336	0.412
Ningxia	2.894	4.833	−6.135	0.965	0.333
Xinjiang	1.887	3.600	−7.368	1.159	0.614

Sources: Authors' estimations

8.5 Conclusions

This study focused on air pollution in terms of CO, NO_2, O_3, $PM_{2.5}$, PM_{10}, and SO_2 in Chinese provinces and investigated the contribution of pollution-control governance shortages to provincial pollution levels. Specifically, this study applies a factor analysis that evaluates the heterogeneity of provincial pollution under the EKC framework. The study's contribution to the literature lies in its framework for

Table 8.14 Provincial pollution and pollution-control governance (O_3)

	Fixed effect	*govg*	(b) -Benchmark	(c) × -0.197	(d) / (a) (e)
	(a)	(b)	(c)	(d)	av. 1.226
Beijing	2.103	11.684	–	–	–
Tianjin	2.266	11.870	–	–	–
Hebei	0.427	6.418	−4.551	0.895	2.097
Shanxi	1.105	5.098	−5.871	1.154	1.044
Inner Mongolia	1.588	2.785	−8.183	1.609	1.013
Liaoning	1.005	7.355	−3.614	0.710	0.707
Jilin	1.441	6.811	−4.157	0.817	0.567
Heilongjiang	0.976	7.797	−3.171	0.623	0.639
Shanghai	2.060	13.073	–	–	–
Jiangsu	0.646	9.192	−1.777	0.349	0.541
Zhejiang	0.803	12.444	–	–	–
Anhui	0.535	8.159	−2.809	0.552	1.033
Fujian	1.094	9.891	−1.078	0.212	0.194
Jiangxi	0.785	6.784	−4.184	0.823	1.048
Shandong	0.325	8.683	−2.286	0.449	1.383
Henan	0.169	6.882	−4.086	0.803	4.740
Hubei	0.679	6.565	−4.404	0.866	1.274
Hunan	0.423	7.304	−3.665	0.720	1.704
Guangxi	0.662	5.416	−5.552	1.091	1.648
Hainan	2.252	3.490	−7.478	1.470	0.653
Chongqing	1.028	9.109	−1.860	0.366	0.356
Sichuan	0.142	8.431	−2.538	0.499	3.510
Guizhou	0.888	3.664	−7.304	1.436	1.617
Yunnan	0.709	2.755	−8.213	1.614	2.277
Tibet	3.560	1.541	−9.428	1.853	0.521
Shaanxi	0.954	8.715	−2.253	0.443	0.464
Gansu	1.504	5.241	−5.728	1.126	0.749
Qinghai	2.855	2.473	−8.496	1.670	0.585
Ningxia	2.787	4.833	−6.135	1.206	0.433
Xinjiang	1.334	3.600	−7.368	1.448	1.086

Sources: Authors' estimations

analyzing the heterogeneity of Chinese provinces' EKCs in terms of their positions (not their shapes) using a fixed-effect model in the EKC panel estimation to extract the province-specific pollution effects and then conducting a factor analysis to uncover the contribution of provincial pollution-control governance to provincial pollution.

Table 8.15 Provincial pollution and pollution-control governance ($PM_{2.5}$)

	Fixed effect	*govg*	(b) -Benchmark	(c) × -0.141	(d) / (a) (e)
	(a)	(b)	(c)	(d)	av. 0.560
Beijing	2.566	11.684	–	–	–
Tianjin	2.890	11.870	–	–	–
Hebei	1.022	6.418	–4.551	0.639	0.626
Shanxi	1.619	5.098	–5.871	0.825	0.510
Inner Mongolia	1.681	2.785	–8.183	1.150	0.684
Liaoning	1.279	7.355	–3.614	0.508	0.397
Jilin	1.720	6.811	–4.157	0.584	0.340
Heilongjiang	1.225	7.797	–3.171	0.446	0.364
Shanghai	2.079	13.073	–	–	–
Jiangsu	0.938	9.192	–1.777	0.250	0.266
Zhejiang	0.949	12.444	–	–	–
Anhui	1.079	8.159	–2.809	0.395	0.366
Fujian	0.951	9.891	–1.078	0.151	0.159
Jiangxi	1.066	6.784	–4.184	0.588	0.551
Shandong	0.765	8.683	–2.286	0.321	0.420
Henan	0.823	6.882	–4.086	0.574	0.697
Hubei	1.207	6.565	–4.404	0.619	0.513
Hunan	0.886	7.304	–3.665	0.515	0.581
Guangxi	0.841	5.416	–5.552	0.780	0.927
Hainan	1.796	3.490	–7.478	1.051	0.585
Chongqing	1.663	9.109	–1.860	0.261	0.157
Sichuan	0.589	8.431	–2.538	0.357	0.606
Guizhou	0.983	3.664	–7.304	1.026	1.044
Yunnan	0.500	2.755	–8.213	1.154	2.307
Tibet	2.757	1.541	–9.428	1.325	0.481
Shaanxi	1.563	8.715	–2.253	0.317	0.203
Gansu	1.454	5.241	–5.728	0.805	0.553
Qinghai	3.138	2.473	–8.496	1.194	0.380
Ningxia	2.943	4.833	–6.135	0.862	0.293
Xinjiang	1.896	3.600	–7.368	1.035	0.546

Sources: Authors' estimations

The main findings of the empirical estimations are summarized as follows. First, the fixed-effect models verified that all provinces had more serious air pollution than Guangdong, as province-specific effects. Second, the alternative models revealed that province-specific air pollution was significantly affected by provincial pollution-control governance. Third, factor analysis demonstrated that the governance shortage for pollution control accounts for approximately 50–70% of the province-specific air pollution levels.

Table 8.16 Provincial pollution and pollution-control governance (PM_{10})

	Fixed-effect	*govg*	(b) -Benchmark	(c) × -0.173	(d) / (a) (e)
	(a)	(b)	(c)	(d)	av. 0.669
Beijing	2.570	11.684	–	–	–
Tianjin	2.924	11.870	–	–	–
Hebei	1.084	6.418	–4.551	0.788	0.727
Shanxi	1.714	5.098	–5.871	1.016	0.593
Inner Mongolia	2.040	2.785	–8.183	1.417	0.694
Liaoning	1.315	7.355	–3.614	0.626	0.476
Jilin	1.719	6.811	–4.157	0.720	0.419
Heilongjiang	1.178	7.797	–3.171	0.549	0.466
Shanghai	2.038	13.073	–	–	–
Jiangsu	1.025	9.192	–1.777	0.308	0.300
Zhejiang	0.974	12.444	–	–	–
Anhui	0.988	8.159	–2.809	0.486	0.492
Fujian	1.055	9.891	–1.078	0.187	0.177
Jiangxi	1.031	6.784	–4.184	0.724	0.703
Shandong	0.903	8.683	–2.286	0.396	0.438
Henan	0.839	6.882	–4.086	0.707	0.843
Hubei	1.173	6.565	–4.404	0.762	0.650
Hunan	0.799	7.304	–3.665	0.634	0.794
Guangxi	0.740	5.416	–5.552	0.961	1.299
Hainan	1.894	3.490	–7.478	1.295	0.684
Chongqing	1.604	9.109	–1.860	0.322	0.201
Sichuan	0.523	8.431	–2.538	0.439	0.840
Guizhou	0.910	3.664	–7.304	1.264	1.389
Yunnan	0.566	2.755	–8.213	1.422	2.510
Tibet	3.138	1.541	–9.428	1.632	0.520
Shaanxi	1.691	8.715	–2.253	0.390	0.231
Gansu	1.775	5.241	–5.728	0.992	0.559
Qinghai	3.337	2.473	–8.496	1.471	0.441
Ningxia	3.291	4.833	–6.135	1.062	0.323
Xinjiang	2.032	3.600	–7.368	1.276	0.628

Sources: Authors' estimations

Regarding this study's policy implications, the empirical results suggest that China has considerable policy space to mitigate air pollution by enhancing governance for pollution control, such as through the development and training of human resources. In the post-COVID-19 era, when industrial activities have recovered, pollution-control governance would be vital for sustainable economic growth in China.

Table 8.17 Provincial pollution and pollution-control governance (SO_2)

	Fixed-effect	*govg*	(b) -Benchmark	(c) × -0.160	(d) / (a) (e)
	(a)	(b)	(c)	(d)	av. 0.471
Beijing	1.404	11.684	–	–	–
Tianjin	2.617	11.870	–	–	–
Hebei	1.491	6.418	−4.551	0.728	0.488
Shanxi	2.712	5.098	−5.871	0.939	0.346
Inner Mongolia	2.393	2.785	−8.183	1.309	0.547
Liaoning	1.982	7.355	−3.614	0.578	0.292
Jilin	2.167	6.811	−4.157	0.665	0.307
Heilongjiang	1.794	7.797	−3.171	0.507	0.283
Shanghai	1.690	13.073	–	–	–
Jiangsu	0.739	9.192	−1.777	0.284	0.384
Zhejiang	0.692	12.444	–	–	–
Anhui	1.111	8.159	−2.809	0.449	0.404
Fujian	0.826	9.891	−1.078	0.172	0.209
Jiangxi	1.647	6.784	−4.184	0.669	0.406
Shandong	1.029	8.683	−2.286	0.366	0.355
Henan	0.989	6.882	−4.086	0.654	0.661
Hubei	1.007	6.565	−4.404	0.705	0.699
Hunan	0.986	7.304	−3.665	0.586	0.594
Guangxi	1.320	5.416	−5.552	0.888	0.673
Hainan	1.747	3.490	−7.478	1.196	0.685
Chongqing	1.391	9.109	−1.860	0.298	0.214
Sichuan	0.696	8.431	−2.538	0.406	0.583
Guizhou	1.633	3.664	−7.304	1.169	0.716
Yunnan	1.280	2.755	−8.213	1.314	1.027
Tibet	3.298	1.541	−9.428	1.508	0.457
Shaanxi	1.514	8.715	−2.253	0.361	0.238
Gansu	2.439	5.241	−5.728	0.916	0.376
Qinghai	3.838	2.473	−8.496	1.359	0.354
Ningxia	3.969	4.833	−6.135	0.982	0.247
Xinjiang	1.659	3.600	−7.368	1.179	0.710

Sources: Authors' estimations

The limitations of this study include a lack of detailed research on individual provinces and regions. China exhibits regional heterogeneity in terms of pollution levels and the factors affecting them. Examining the complexity of pollution mechanisms and policy performance in specific regions through detailed case studies would enable the development of region-specific recommendations and prescriptions for the management of air pollution in China.

Acknowledgment The authors would like to extend their gratitude to Mr. Jun-Jun Ma for his collaborative efforts in environmental data collection. His expertise has greatly benefited this study.

References

Brajer V, Mead RW, Xiao F (2011) Searching for an environmental Kuznets Curve in China's air pollution. China Econ Rev 22:383–397

Chang HY, Wang W, Yu J (2021) Revisiting the environmental Kuznets curve in China: A spatial dynamic panel data approach. Energy Econ 104:105600

Chen L, Chen S (2015) The estimation of environmental Kuznets Curve in China: Nonparametric panel approach. Comput Econ 46:405–420

Cui L, Hunt A, Morley B (2021) The effectiveness of environmental spending in China and the environmental Kuznets Curve. Sustainability 13:12141

Dasgupta S, Laplante B, Wang H, Wheeler D (2002) Confronting the environmental Kuznets Curve. J Econ Perspect 16(1):147–168

Dinda S (2004) Environmental Kuznets Curve hypothesis: a survey. Ecol Econ 49:431–455

Fan G, Ma G, Wang X (2019) Institutional reform and economic growth of China: 40-year progress toward marketization. Acta Oecon 69(s1):7–20

Grossman G, Krueger A (1995) Economic growth and the environment. Q J Econ 112:353–378

Hausman J (1978) Specification tests in econometrics. Econometrica 46:1251–1271

Im KS, Pesaran MH, Shin Y (2003) Testing for unit roots in heterogeneous panels. J Econom 115:53–74

Jayanthakumaran K, Liu Y (2012) Openness and the Environmental Kuznets Curve: Evidence from China. Econ Model 29:566–576

Kareem FO, Martinez-Zarzoso I, Brümmer B (2016) Fitting the gravity model when zero trade flows are frequent: a comparison of estimation techniques using Africa's trade data. Global Food Discussion Papers, No. 77

Levin A, Lin CF, Chu C (2002) Unit root tests in panel data: Asymptotic and finite-sample properties. J Econom 108:1–24

Li X, Yan X, An Q et al (2016) The coordination between China's economic growth and environmental emission from the Environmental Kuznets Curve viewpoint. Natu Hazards 83:233–252

Liu X, Heilig GK, Chen J, Mikko Heino M (2007) Interactions between economic growth and environmental quality in Shenzhen, China's first special economic zone. Ecol Econ 62:559–570

Lopez R (1994) The environment as a factor of production: the effects of economic growth and trade liberalization. J Environ Econ Manag 27(2):163–184

Pedroni P (2004) panel cointegration; asymptotic and finite sample properties of pooled time series tests with an application to the PPP hypothesis. Economic Theory 20:597–625

MacBean A (2007) China's environment: problems and policies. World Econ 30(2):195–362

Moriwaki S, Shimizu M (2023) A simultaneous investigation of the environmental Kuznets curve for the agricultural and industrial sectors in China. J Asia Pac Econ 28(1):133–155

Mukhopadhyay K, Chakraborty D (2005) Is liberalization of trade good for the environment? Evidence from India. Asia Pac Dev J 12(1):109–136

Sarkodie SA, Strezov V (2019) A review on Environmental Kuznets Curve hypothesis using bibliometric and meta-analysis. Sci Total Environ 649:128–145

Selden TM, Song D (1994) Environmental quality and development: is there a Kuznets Curve for air pollution emissions? J Environ Econ Manag 27:147–162

Shen J (2006) A simultaneous estimation of environmental Kuznets Curve: evidence from China. China Econ Rev 17:383–394

Silva JMCS, Tenreyro S (2006) The log of gravity. Rev Econ and Stat 88:641–658

Song ML, Zhang W, Wang SH (2013) Inflection point of environmental Kuznets curve in Mainland China. Energy Policy 57:14–20

Song T, Zheng T, Tong L (2008) An empirical test of the environmental Kuznets curve in China: A panel cointegration approach. China Econ Rev 19:381–392

Song W, Ye C, Liu Y, Cheng W (2021) Do China's urban–environmental quality and economic growth conform to the Environmental Kuznets Curve? Int J Environ Res Public Health 18:13420

Stokey NL (1998) Are there limits to growth? Int Econ Rev 39:1–31

Taguchi H, Murofushi H (2010) Evidence on the interjurisdictional competition for polluted industries within China. Environ Dev Econ 15(3):363–378

Taguchi H (2012) Environmental Kuznets Curve in Asia: the case of SO2 and CO2 emissions. Asia Pac Dev J 19(2):77–92

Wang Y, Han R, Kubota J (2016) Is there an environmental Kuznets Curve for SO2 emissions? A semi-parametric panel data analysis for China. Renew Sust Energ Rev 54:1182–1188

World Bank (1992) Development and the environment, world development report. Oxford University Press, Washington, DC

World Bank (2022) China: country climate and development report. World Development Report. World Bank, Washington, DC

Wu X, Gao M (2021) Effects of different environmental regulations and their heterogeneity on air pollution control in China. J Regul Econ 60:140–166

Xu B, Zhong R, Liu D, Liu Y (2021) Investigating the impact of energy consumption and nitrogen fertilizer on NOx emissions in China based on the environmental Kuznets curve. Environ Dev Sustain 23:17590–17605

Yan J, Lu W, Xu X, Lian J (2023) Empirical study of the environmental Kuznets Curve in China based on provincial panel data. Sustainability 15:5225

Zheng S, Yi H, Li H (2015) The impacts of provincial energy and environmental policies on air pollution control in China. Renew Sust Energ Rev 49:386–394

Chapter 9
Economic Functions of Foreign Aid Inflows in Thailand

Hiroaki Sakurai

Abstract This chapter summarizes the research on the effects of foreign aid inflows to Thailand using time series analysis. After World War II, Thailand received foreign aid, executed mainly during the 1980s, and experienced rapid economic growth. As both rapid economic growth in Thailand and foreign aid occurred simultaneously, this analysis can contribute to economic growth in other countries and areas. The main results of this study are as follows: First, the impact of foreign aid on economic growth is positively estimated using growth accounting. In contrast, the relationship between public investment and economic growth in Thailand is not necessarily estimated effectively, partly because public investment is also used for the rural area. Second, this impact is caused by investments stimulated by foreign aid, including inward foreign direct investments. Conversely, foreign aid itself does not directly effectuate poverty reduction. Finally, foreign aid inflows are considered to reduce fiscal debt in Thailand without currency appreciation; that is, neither the fungibility nor Dutch disease effect occurs in Thailand through aid inflows. These results indicate that foreign aid helps to strengthen the Thai economy and affects the economic growth to a certain extent. Although these fundamental functions of foreign aids are effective in maintaining sustainable growth in emerging market economies, Thailand has become less attractive for Japanese companies after COVID-19, which is a new research topic.

Keywords Foreign aid inflows · Economic Growth · Thailand

H. Sakurai (✉)
Department of International Communication, Gakushuin Women's College, Shinjuku-ku, Tokyo, Japan

© The Author(s), under exclusive license to Springer Nature Singapore Pte Ltd. 2025

H. Taguchi (ed.), *Sustainability of Economic Growth in East Asia*,
New Frontiers in Regional Science: Asian Perspectives 82,
https://doi.org/10.1007/978-981-96-3731-7_9

9.1 Introduction

One of the dreams for human being is removing poverty including famine and epidemic. However, foreign aid, expected to help poverty people at the first step, is still under discussion in its effectiveness. Although a two-gap model for foreign aid to compensate for capital accumulation was suggested during the 1960s as an effect of foreign aid, this effect was obscure regardless of the huge amount of foreign aid, especially in African countries. Reflecting on these elements, foreign aid is effective only if the government of the recipient country uses it efficiently (Burnside and Dollar 2000). In contrast, Easterly et al. (2004) show that foreign aid is ineffective. This discussion signifies that foreign aid does not necessarily contribute to economic growth without any conditions. Although the short-term effects of foreign aid can be determined, it is difficult to examine the long-term effects of foreign aid.

Moreover, the social infrastructure constructed by foreign aid provides an opportunity to establish private firms, including large factories. This effect is called the "vanguard effect" of foreign aid. Foreign direct investment contributes to the economic growth (Borensztein et al. 1998; Hsiao and Hsiao 2006); thus, inviting foreign companies through foreign direct investment is ideal for economic growth. As the relationship between economic growth and poverty reduction is robust (Dollar and Kraay 2002; Besley and Burgess 2003), this study underscores foreign aid to promote economic growth.

Thailand has experienced relatively stable economic growth for more than half a century (Fig. 9.1). During this process, the poverty ratio reduced (Fig. 9.2). Figure 9.1 shows that rapid growth is one of the sources for reducing the poverty ratio from the late 1980s to the beginning of the 1990s. One reason for this rapid

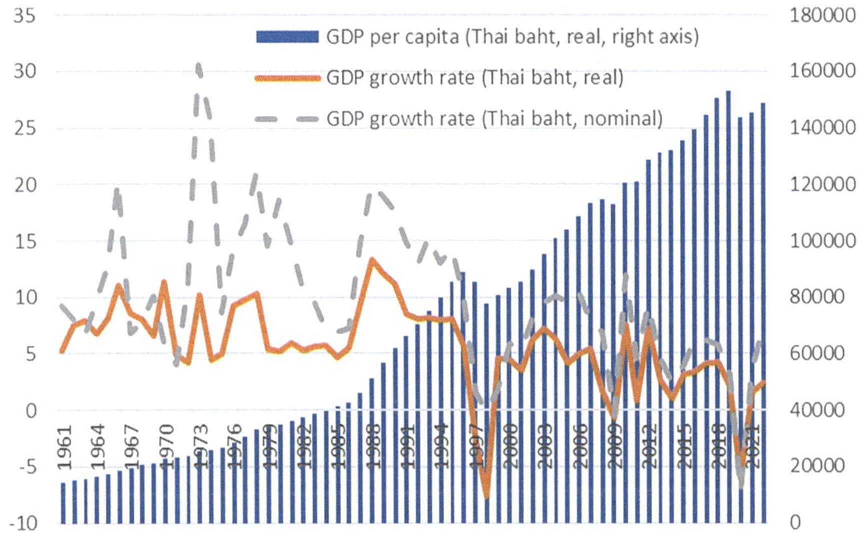

Fig. 9.1 Economic growth in Thailand. *Source*: World Development Indicators

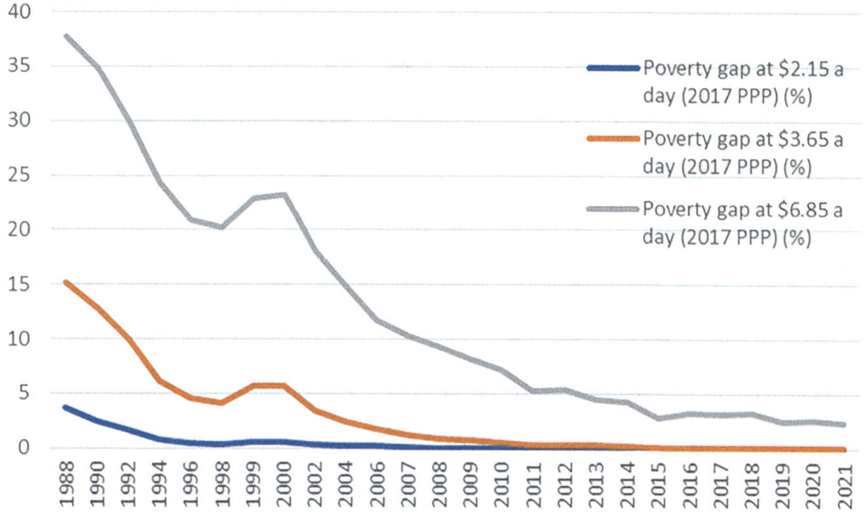

Fig. 9.2 Poverty ratio in Thailand. *Source*: World Development Indicators

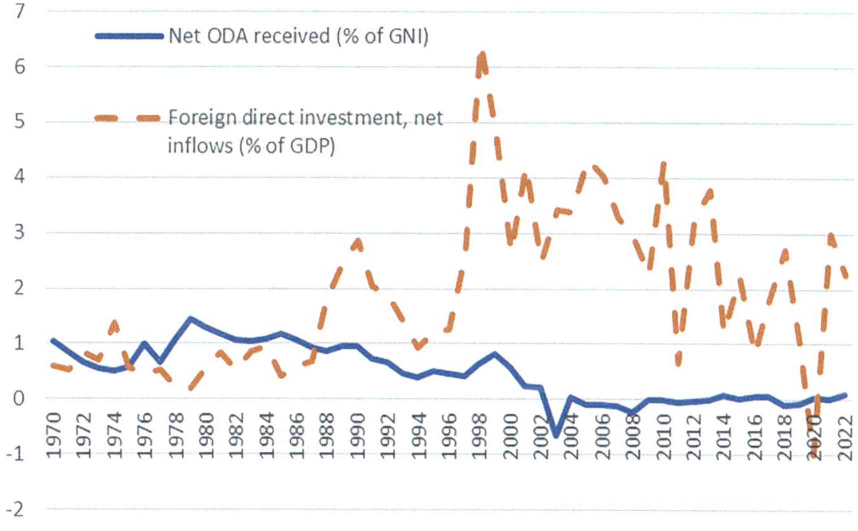

Fig. 9.3 Inflow of ODA and FDI toward Thailand. *Source*: World Development Indicators

growth is the policy change at the beginning of the 1980s that released restrictions on investment and trade. In addition, social infrastructure developed during the 1980s by foreign aid concentrated in the eastern area of Bangkok vicinity. Many Japanese companies are located in this area after the Plaza Agreement of 1985 (Fig. 9.3). The representative project is the Eastern Seaboard Development Plan for

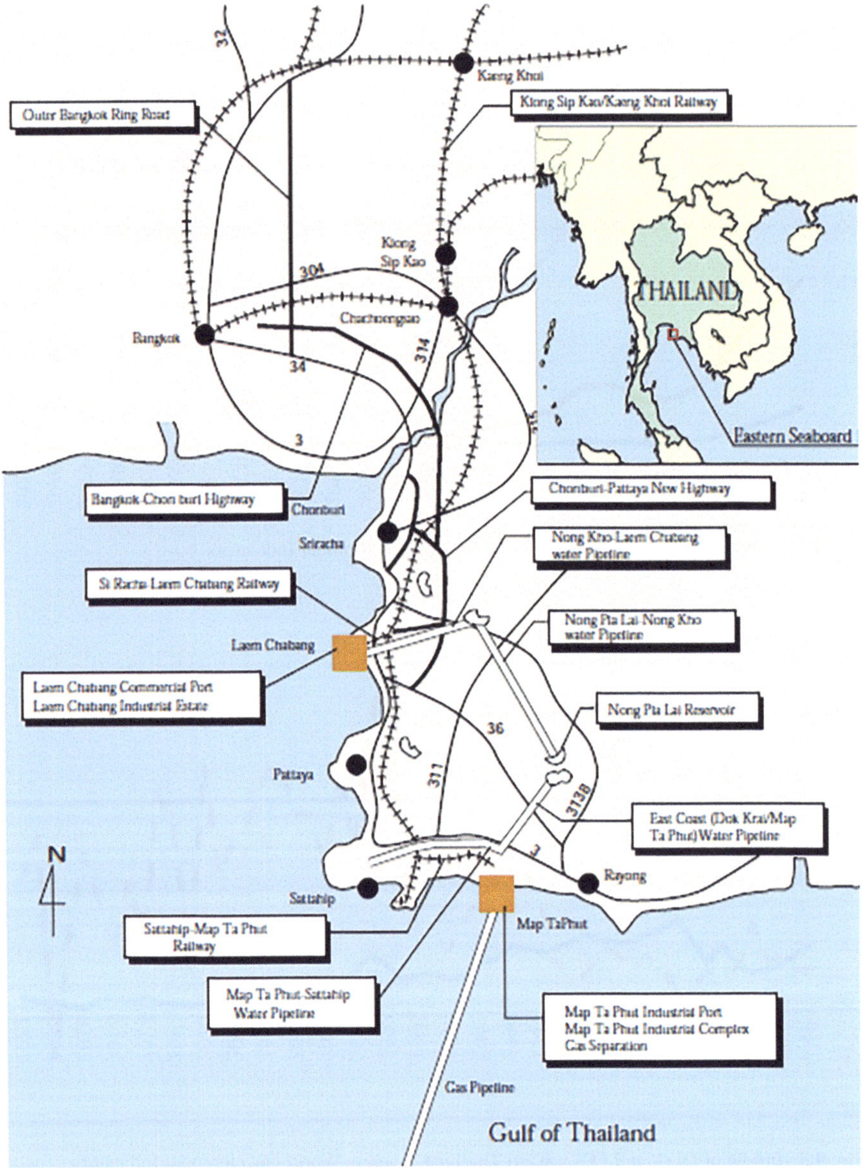

Fig. 9.4 Eastern Sea Board development. *Source*: JBIC 2000

industrialization, including the deep-sea port, highway, electricity, and water supply to industrial areas (Fig. 9.4).

The author was employed in the foreign aid department of the Government of Japan during the mid-2000s and experienced strong opposition against providing foreign aid. In contrast, members engaged in foreign aid believed that foreign aid contributed to the local economy and society. Many opportunities are provided for a good project to contribute to the local economy through foreign aid. Subsequently, the experience of working in Thailand prompted the author to demonstrate the effect of foreign aid in Thailand. Moreover, as economic growth reduces the poverty ratio in developing economics, it is important to promote economic growth. This study demonstrates the effects of foreign aid and extends it to other developing countries. Data restrictions are a major problem in proving this effect quantitatively. In Thailand, as most data are used after the 1997 financial crisis, the method of proving this is difficult. Additionally, this study analyzes the effect of foreign aid on the entire country, not on each project, which is its primary objective.

This chapter focuses on the effects of foreign aid in Thailand from the following perspectives: First, the relationship between foreign aid and economic growth. Considering that most foreign aid to Thailand involves the construction of social infrastructure, the productivity approach is adequate for measuring the effect on the country. The results show that foreign aid to Thailand contributes toward its economic growth to a certain extent. Second, it examines the mechanism of the effect of foreign aid on the Thai economy, which includes vanguard effect, sectoral approach, and direct effect. The results indicate that the main reason for the effect of foreign aid is an increase in productivity, mainly in the manufacturing sector. Finally, it explores the effect of fungibility and exchange rate on fiscal conditions as the Dutch disease effect. The recipient country may use another way to save money if foreign aid increases; this is called fungibility. Furthermore, aid inflows cause local currency appreciation, as experienced in the Netherlands in the 1960s owing to an increase in oil exports. Previous research shows that neither effect is observed in Thailand.

9.2 Previous Literature

9.2.1 Relationship Between Foreign Aid and Economic Growth

This subsection discusses the effect of foreign aid on economic growth and productivity of social infrastructure since this study integrates the third-generation model of measuring the effect of foreign aid with productivity model.

As the literature on the relationship between foreign aid and economic growth is complex, this discussion is divided into four generations (Arndt et al. 2016; Nowak-Lehmann and Gross 2021). The first generation examines the relationship between domestic savings as a financing investment and foreign aid as a complement to savings (Hansen and Tarp 2000). The second generation investigates the link between aid and investment using the Harrod–Domar model. In this model, savings and aid are used to finance investment, and also constant investment and productivity of capital determine economic growth. However, previous studies show that a substantial portion of aid is consumed rather than invested (Hansen and Tarp 2000;

Nowak-Lehmann et al. 2012). By contrast, in the third-generation model, the aggregate effect of aid directly impacts per capita income or economic growth using the Solow growth model. The results of the aid effectiveness are divided into positive and negative (Burnside and Dollar 2000; Easterly et al. 2004). The criterion for aid effectiveness is the governance of the recipient country (Burnside and Dollar 2000; Collier and Dollar 2002). Easterly et al. (2004) reports that Burnside and Dollar's (2000) results are unstable. Discussion using a third-generation model is ongoing; the short-term effects are easy to estimate, whereas the long-term effects are difficult to estimate (Nowak-Lehmann et al. 2012). Additionally, the industrial level is easier to estimate than the area within a country (Addison et al. 2017).

Social infrastructure contributes to economic growth. However, old or unused infrastructure weakens this function. From this perspective, Aschauer (1989) estimates the productivity of public social infrastructure in the United States since such fragile infrastructure cannot be used owing to its construction during the 1960s. In Japan, this approach was popular during the 1990s since the construction of social infrastructure ended after rapid economic growth (Iwamoto 1990; Mitsui and Inoue 1997). In addition, the infrastructure in urban area (Yoshino and Nakano 1994) and effect on the agricultural industry is relatively small (Yoshino et al. 1999). Miyagawa et al. (2013) revise this approach because Japan also faced the problem of deteriorating social infrastructure in the 2010s.

9.2.2 Source of Extending the Economic Growth

This subsection includes the mechanism or function of foreign aid toward the economic growth. This mechanism is divided into three parts: vanguard effect, sectoral approach, and direct effect.

First, the vanguard effect occurs when foreign aid effectuates foreign direct investment. Kimura and Todo (2010) examine foreign aid as a vanguard using a gravity model in the East Asian region and find positive results.

Second, a sectoral approach is used. This field includes "macro–micro problem." It is difficult to measure the impact of foreign aid on the entire country even when a huge amount of money is distributed. Mosley (1987) introduces this difficulty, and Arndt et al. (2010) extend it. However, it is difficult to extend this further because of data restrictions in areas such as cities or provinces and other effects such as spillover effects. Thus, the effect of foreign aid is relatively easier to grasp for each industry in a country because obtaining industrial data of entire country is easier than acquiring semi-macro data. Selaya and Thiele (2010) examine the relationship between foreign aid and sectoral growth using panel data from Burnside and Dollar (2000) and show that foreign aid affects secondary and tertiary industries.

Finally, the direct and indirect effects toward the poverty reduction are considered as another methodology to explore the effects of foreign aid. The assumption is that the effect of foreign aid on poverty reduction is divided into direct and indirect effects through an increase in income. Mosley et al. (2004) and Alvi and Senbeta (2012) extend this methodology.

9.2.3 Effect on Fiscal and Exchange Rates

One of the conditions that ensures the effect of foreign aid is its efficient utilization. However, if the recipient country increases wasteful expenditure when it receives foreign aid, the effect of aid will be offset. Moreover, foreign aid, as a huge capital inflow, may increase the real effective exchange rate, which offsets the effect of the diminishing manufacturing industry. This subsection addresses the following two aspects:

First, fungibility offsets the effect of foreign aid because of the increase in government consumption expenditure of a recipient country. This implies that the recipient country uses foreign aid as a substitute for governmental investment. Nurkse (1953) shows an example of fungibility by describing how a recipient country constructed the opera house by saved money when the donor country provided the power plant. From the theoretical perspective, this study develops Fiscal Response Model (FRMs), and Franco-Rodriguez et al. (1998) complete it. The difficulty with the FRMs model is that the shock that affects fiscal conditions must be known in advance. Thus, it is better to estimate the relationship between fiscal data and foreign aid and check the background; this relationship changes since this approach does not need information regarding the effect in advance. Morrissey et al. (2007) describes this approach in detail. A relationship between foreign aid and government consumption expenditure is observed in African countries (Aiyar and Ruthbah 2008; Martins 2010). Osei et al. (2005) show an analysis using Ghanaian data.

Second, the Dutch disease effect occurs because of capital inflows. Originally, it was observed in the Netherlands in the 1960s and extended the oil exports found in the Northern Sea, weakening the manufacturing industry due to the appreciation of the national currency. Since foreign aid is one of the sources of the capital inflow, the analysis flamework is applicable. Fielding and Gibson (2013) show the Dutch disease effect using data from African countries during 1970–2000. In contrast, Fielding (2010) shows that the Dutch disease effect is not observed in Southern Pacific Island countries, regardless of aid inflow, which affects the exchange rate.

9.3 History of the Economic Growth and Aid to Thailand

9.3.1 Economic Growth in Thailand

Thailand has experienced relatively stable economic growth for more than half a century. In the 1960s, Thailand welcomed the foreign direct investment and foreign trade. During the late 1960s, an unstable situation occurred at the beginning of the Vietnam War. During the 1970s, foreign trade was restricted. The Vietnam War ended in 1975, and the country became unified as a communist country. Furthermore, Lao PDR, a former kingdom, abolished the kingdom and became communist in 1975. Reflecting on these unstable political situations in surrounding countries, foreign trade and foreign direct investment in Thailand were restricted during the 1970s. In this circumstance, Thailand faced a financial crisis at the beginning of the 1980s.

In 1980, the prime minister, Mr. Prem, changed the economic policy to encourage foreign trade and to welcome the foreign direct investment. In 1985, owing the Plaza Agreement, Japanese yen appreciation occurred, and many Japanese companies were established in Thailand. This augmented the economic growth in Thailand in the late 1980s and beginning of the 1990s. Thailand experienced a bubble economy after 1993 and financial crisis in 1997. This effect diminished around 2004, mainly because of the increase in exports using a depreciated currency. The effect of the 2008 global financial crisis was relatively short time and recovery was quick, as the government and firms had saved foreign currency as reserves during the 2000s.

During COVID-19 (2020–2023), the Thai economy was hit because inbound sightseeing dominated approximately 20% of GDP was almost diminished. Additionally, Thailand is facing aging and declining birth rate.

9.3.2 Aid to Thailand

Aid from Japan to Thailand, which started in 1967, is divided into five stages (Institute for International Cooperation, JICA 2003; Sakurai 2021c). The first stage (1967–1976) as a startup included compensation for World War II. The second stage (1977–1989) involved strategic extension. As shown in the previous subsection, in the early 1970s, Japanese products were rejected by Thai people. Furthermore, the United States asked to increase foreign aid to Southeast Asian countries owing to the substitution of aid from the U.S. Fukuda Doctrine in 1977, which included doubling the ODA budget. Meanwhile, the Eastern Sea Board planned to use the natural gas found in the Gulf of Thailand and construct a deep-sea port in the eastern area of Bangkok. During this time, huge infrastructure was constructed in Bangkok and Eastern area of Thailand. The third stage (1989–1996) was the conversion of values. The Cold War ended at that time, and the Cambodian War ended in the Southeast. The Slogan was "peaceful peninsula" or "from the war to the peace Indo-China."

The new types of aid toward the new ages were preferred during this time. The fourth stage (1997–2000) was the financial crisis. During this period, aid was used to diminish the adverse effects of the financial crisis. After the panic caused by the 1997 financial crisis settled down, the Thai government provided aid to surrounding countries such as Laos, Cambodia, and Myanmar, which is the fifth stage (2001–) called "Thailand as a donor country."

The aid amount is estimated by the dummy variable in each stage every year in Sakurai (2021c), inferring that the budget of aid to Thailand is decided at each stage.

9.3.3 National Economic and Social Development Plan in Thailand

Thai government established the National Economic and Development Board (NEDB) in 1951 asked by the World Bank. It was changed to the National Economic and Social Development Board (NESDB) and made a 5-year economic and social development plan in every 5 years. Although not all economic and social policies are successful, many policies have achieved the purpose. Regarding the foreign aid to Thailand, the fifth Economic and Social Development Plan describes the Eastern Sea Board, including foreign aid. Other economic and social development plans show the nationwide distribution of income, including foreign aid.

9.4 Research Results

9.4.1 Relationship Between Foreign Aid and Economic Growth

Previous studies and experiences in Thailand indicate a relationship between foreign aid to Thailand and economic growth. Based on this hypothesis, Sakurai (2021a) explores the relationship between aid and economic growth in Thailand using a third-generation model and finds a positive relationship in the following ways:

First, using the whole country data of Thailand. The estimation period is from 1971 to 2013 using Thai governmental data. Foreign aid is accumulated considering capital accumulation, which mostly constitutes social infrastructure. Using the Cobb–Douglas function, foreign aid is estimated to be positively effective. By contrast, public expenditure is not estimated effectively partly because it is used in rural areas.

Second, constructing the area panel data. As the Thai government does not make capital stock statistics in each province, capital stock data in this research is divided into four areas: north, northeast, central, and south. Although the central area is divided since the 1980s owing to development, the four areas are defined by their natural characteristics. Foreign aid comprises yen loans from Japan and is divided by the evaluation report. Panel data are obtained for 1985–2014. This estimation is partly effective, and the results can be observed more carefully.

A similar methodology was used to examine the effect of foreign aid on economic growth in Vietnam. The estimation is conducted in two ways: for the entire country from 1994 to 2017 and for the effect of yen loans from Japan in 34 of 63 provinces from 2001 to 2016 (Sakurai 2020). The results indicate that neither method has any relationship with foreign aid and economic growth, partly because foreign aid in Vietnam was concentrated in a shorter time period compared with Thailand.

These estimates show that foreign aid in Thailand contributes to its economic growth to a certain extent.

9.4.2 Source of Extending the Economic Growth

Vanguard Effect

As the relationship between foreign aid and economic growth in Thailand is established, the transition mechanism from foreign aid to economic growth is demonstrated as the next step. In Thailand's case, increased foreign direct investment from the late 1980s enhanced foreign aid, augmenting the national income, which is known as "vanguard effect."

Sakurai (2023b) estimates the vanguard effect in Thailand using the following two methods: First, analyzing the relationship between foreign aid and investment from 1975 to 2020 and adding to trade, savings, and growth. The estimated results show that OLS is positively effective, whereas VAR model is ineffective. These results indicate that foreign aid has a positive relationship with investment in the long term. Second, estimating the relationship between foreign aid and foreign direct investment using the VAR model and Granger causality from 1970 to 2020, which is positively estimated to be effective. These results show that foreign aid in Thailand is related to foreign direct investment.

In contrast, Sakurai (2023a) estimates the relationship between the total factor productivity and foreign aid in Thailand directly and shows that that introducing only foreign aid does not contribute to the productivity.

Sakurai (2023a, b) asserts that foreign aid in Thailand induces foreign direct investment, as foreign aid itself does not directly promote economic growth.

Foreign Aid and Sectoral Growth

If the vanguard effect of foreign aid exists, the contribution of foreign aid is weighted mainly by the manufacturing industry. Following Selaya and Thiele (2010), Sakurai (2024a) examines the effect of foreign aid on sectoral growth in Thailand for 1960–2021 to show the effect of foreign aid in Thailand. This estimation method considers the relationship between foreign aid and the industrial GDP. The results show that foreign aid and secondary industry and foreign aid and tertiary industry are positively estimated, whereas foreign aid and primary industry are ineffectively estimated. This finding is consistent with those of the previous studies.

Foreign Aid and Poverty Reduction
Poverty reduction is caused mainly by increased income owing to foreign direct investment. Thus, foreign aid does not necessarily have a direct effect on poverty reduction. Instead, foreign aid to Thailand has an indirect effect of inviting foreign direct investment to reduce poverty. Sakurai (2024b) estimates the poverty ratio and foreign direct investment for 1961–2022 and finds it insignificantly estimated.

The abovementioned results infer that foreign aid in Thailand encourages private companies to locate and that improved productivity through these companies is related to income growth. Specifically, foreign aid does not improve productivity or national income discretely.

9.4.3 Effect Toward the Fiscal and Exchange Rates

Fungibility
An aid provided by the donor country is meaningless if the recipient country uses it inefficiently. In the case of foreign aid, the government consumption expenditure increases as a substitute for investment. This is called fungibility and has been observed in African countries.

Sakurai (2021b) estimates fungibility using three methods. First, the relationship between foreign aid and fiscal conditions, including domestic borrowing, government revenue, and government expenditure, using the VAR model and Granger causality tests during 1961–2014. The results show that an increase in foreign aid decreases domestic borrowing. Second, government expenditure in the fiscal condition is divided into consumption and capital expenditures and estimated using the VAR model and Granger causality tests. The results show that increasing foreign aid causes a decrease in domestic borrowing. Finally, no effect is observed during the 1960s–1970s.

These estimations indicate that foreign aid reduces domestic borrowings of Thai government, although this result changes when limited to the 1960s–1970s. Moreover, previous literature shows that foreign aid is effective for domestic borrowing relatively, whereas its effect on government expenditure is more difficult to observe because expenditure is affected by the political situation. In addition, the relationship between foreign aid and government revenue makes it difficult to understand the relationship between both theoretical and empirical approach. These results indicate that foreign aid to Thailand affects the Thai government's fiscal conditions, mainly by reducing domestic borrowing, and fungibility does not occur in Thailand, especially after the 1980s.

Dutch Disease Effect

As foreign aid is one of the capital inflows between donor and recipient countries, the inflow causes local currency appreciation, affecting the recipient country's exports.

Sakurai (2017) estimates the relationship between foreign aid inflow, real effective exchange rate, and manufacturing GDP ratio for 1972–2014 using the VAR model, Granger causality test, and impulse response test. The results show that aid inflow does not result in the appreciation of the local currency (Thai baht). Rather, the strengthened manufacturing sector caused Thai Baht appreciation. In this regard, the Dutch disease effect of aid inflow does not occur; rather, normal appreciation occurs through strengthened manufacturing sector.

Sakurai (2022) shows that foreign aid to Vietnam does not cause the Dutch disease effect. Following Fielding (2010) in the research of the southern and small islands, it is an effective way to prevent local currency appreciation.

9.5 Conclusion

This chapter focuses on the effect of foreign aid in Thailand from the following three perspectives: the relationship between foreign aid and economic growth, mechanism of this relationship, and effect on fiscal and exchange rates.

The results are as follows: First, foreign aid contributes to Thailand's economic growth to a certain extent. Second, the mechanism contributing to economic growth is mainly the development and extension of the secondary and tertiary industries, including foreign direct investment. Finally, foreign aid improves fiscal conditions by decreasing domestic borrowings without causing the Dutch disease effect.

In conclusion, foreign aid to Thailand is well organized. Foreign aid, together with the foreign direct investment, contributes to macroeconomic growth in the industrial sector. National income improves by increasing the number of employees in the secondary and tertiary industrial sectors. The inflow of foreign aid improves the fiscal deficit without causing currency appreciation. Japan and Thailand share a strong relationship. Nearly 7000 Japanese companies are located in Thailand, and approximately 70,000 Japanese people live there.

The results in this chapter imply the following three points: First, the possibility of extending similar methods to other countries. Although similar approach has been ineffective in Vietnam, partly owing to short-term construction of facilities, it is positively estimated in the near future through efficient use under economic expansion. Second, as this approach has remained effective even after the COVID-19 period, it is expedient to continue this research topic. Finally, it concerns foreign aid and investment from China in the twenty-first century owing to economic growth. After the COVID-19 period, this movement is reflected in increases in income and trade.

The remaining research topics are summarized as follows: First, after the COVID-19 pandemic, this relationship has changed considering business sentiments among Japanese companies. Sakurai (2024c) denotes a decrease in business companies partly explained by the GDP in Thailand in the short term, and the trend shown by the dummy variable decreases during the COVID-19 period. Recovering and establishing a new relationship between Thailand and Japan is required. Second, becoming high- income countries including enough social welfare system is desired. Thailand is classified as an upper middle-income country by the World Bank. Although it looks technologies owned by their own from given by others for becoming the developed countries, the research is still under discussion.

Acknowledgments This work was supported by JSPS KAKENHI Grant Numbers JP19K20886 and JP24K16375.

References

Addison T, Morrissey O, Tarp F (2017) The macroeconomics of aid: overview. J Dev Stud 53(7):987–997

Aiyar S, Ruthbah U (2008) Where did all the aid go? An empirical analysis of absorption and spending. IMF Working Paper WP/08/34.

Alvi A, Senbeta A (2012) Does foreign aid reduce poverty? J Int Dev 24(8):955–976

Arndt C, Jones S, Tarp F (2010) Aid, growth, and development: have we come full circle? UNU-WIDER Working Paper No. 2010/96.

Arndt C, Jones S, Tarp F (2016) What is the aggregate economic rate of return to foreign aid? World Bank Econ Rev 30(3):446–474

Aschauer DA (1989) Is public expenditure productive? J Monetary Econ 23(2):177–200

Besley T, Burgess R (2003) Halving global poverty. J Econ Perspect 17(3):3–22

Borensztein EJ, De Gregorio J, Lee J-W (1998) How does foreign direct investment affect economic growth? J Int Econ 45:115–135

Burnside C, Dollar D (2000) Aid, policies and growth. Am Econ Rev 90(4):847–868

Collier P, Dollar D (2002) Aid allocation and poverty reduction. Eur Econ Rev 46(8):1475–1500

Dollar D, Kraay A (2002) Growth is good for the poor. J Econ Growth 7:195–225

Easterly W, Levine R, Roodman D (2004) Aid, policies, and growth: comment. Am Econ Rev 94(3):774–780

Fielding D (2010) Aid and Dutch disease in the South Pacific and in other small Island states. J Dev Stud 46(5):918–940

Fielding D, Gibson F (2013) Aid and Dutch disease in sub-Saharan Africa. J Afr Econ 22(1):1–21

Franco-Rodriguez S, Morrissey O, McGillivray M (1998) Aid and the public sector in Pakistan: evidence with endogenous aid. World Dev 26(7):1241–1250

Institute for International Cooperation, JICA (2003) Country study for Japan's official development assistance to the Kingdom of Thailand–From "Development Assistance" to a "New Cooperation" (in Japanese)

Iwamoto Y (1990) An evaluation of public investment policy in postwar. Japanese Econ Rev 41(3):250–261. (in Japanese)

Hansen H, Tarp F (2000) Aid effectiveness disputed. J Int Dev 12(3):375–398

Hsiao FST, Hsiao MCW (2006) FDI, exports, and GDP in East and Southeast Asia—panel data versus time series causality analysis. World Dev 69:31–43

JBIC (2000) Eastern seaboard development plan impact evaluation. JICA Evaluation Reports

Kimura H, Todo Y (2010) Foreign aid a vanguard of foreign direct investment? A gravity-equation approach World Dev 38(4):482–497

Martins MG (2010) Fiscal dynamics in Ethiopia: the cointegrated VAR model with quarterly data. CREDIT Research Paper 10/05

Mitsui K, Inoue J (1997) The productivity effect of social capital. Japanese Economy 25(3):3–29

Miyagawa T, Kawasaki K, Edamura K (2013) Reexamination of the productivity of public capital. Econ Rev 64(3):240–255. (in Japanese)

Morrissey O, M'Amanja D, Lloyd T (2007) Aid and government in Kenya: a time series analysis. In: Lahiri S (ed) Theory and practice of foreign aid. Elsevier, Amsterdam, pp 313–332

Mosley P (1987) Overseas aid: its defense and reform. Wheatsheaf Books, Brighton

Mosley P, Hudson J, Verschoor A (2004) Aid, poverty reduction and the 'new conditionality'. Econ J 114(496):F217–F243

Nowak-Lehmann F, Dreher A, Herzer D, Klasen S, Martinez-Zarzoso I (2012) Does foreign aid really raise per capita income? A time series perspective. Canadian J Econ 45(1):288–313

Nowak-Lehmann F, Gross E (2021) Aid effectiveness: when aid spurs investment. Appl Econ Anal 29(87):189–207

Nurkse R (1953) Problems of capital formation in underdeveloped countries. Basil Blackwell, Oxford

Osei R, Morrissey O, Lloyd T (2005) The fiscal effects of aid in Ghana. J Int Dev 17(8):1037–1054

Sakurai H (2017) Foreign aid and Dutch disease in Thailand. Bull Appl Econ 4(2):57–64

Sakurai H (2020) Foreign aid loans and economic growth in Vietnam. Bull Appl Econ 7(1):83–94

Sakurai H (2021a) Foreign aid loans and economic growth in Thailand. In: Effects of foreign aid: evidence from Thailand, New Frontiers in Regional Science: Asian Perspectives, vol 50. Springer, Singapore

Sakurai H (2021b) Fiscal effects of foreign aid in Thailand. In: Effects of foreign aid: evidence from Thailand, New Frontiers in Regional Science: Asian Perspectives, vol 50. Springer, Singapore

Sakurai H (2021c) Foreign aid, poverty reduction, and economic growth in Thailand. In: Effects of foreign aid: evidence from Thailand, New Frontiers in Regional Science: Asian Perspectives, vol 50. Springer, Singapore

Sakurai H (2022) Foreign aid and Dutch disease: the case in Vietnam. Bull Appl Econ 9(2):159–168

Sakurai H (2023a) Foreign aid and productivity in Thailand. Bull Appl Econ 10(1):145–155

Sakurai H (2023b) Vanguard effect of foreign aid in Thailand. Bull Appl Econ 10(1):157–168

Sakurai H (2024a) Aid and sectoral growth in Thailand. Bull Appl Econ 11(1):41–49

Sakurai H (2024b) Foreign aid and direct effect of poverty reduction in Thailand. Bull Appl Econ 11(1):71–84

Sakurai H (2024c) Is Thailand attractive to Japanese companies? Economies 12(5):122

Selaya P, Thiele R (2010) Aid and sectoral growth: evidence from panel data. J Dev Stud 46(10):1749–1766

Yoshino N, Nakano H (1994) Allocation of public Investment in the Metropolitan Area. In: Hatta T (ed) Economic analysis of the concentration in Tokyo. Nihon Keizai Shimbun sha, Japan. (in Japanese)

Yoshino N, Nakajima T, Nakahigashi M (1999) Productivity effect of public capital. In: Yoshino N, Nakajima T (eds) Economic effect of public investment. Nippon Hyoron sha, Japan. (in Japanese)

The manufacturer's authorised representative in the EU is Springer Nature Customer Service Centre GmbH, Europaplatz 3, 69115 Heidelberg, Germany. If you have any concerns regarding our products, please contact ProductSafety@springernature.com

Printed and bound by CPI Group (UK) Ltd, Croydon, CR0 4YY
01/10/2026
02225944-0016